BIO ROOSEVELT

Roosevelt, Eleanor,
1884-1962.
Eleanor and Harry : the
correspondence of
c2002.

ELEANOR AND HARRY

The Correspondence of Eleanor Roosevelt and
Harry S. Truman

Edited and with Commentary by

STEVE NEAL

Foreword by Gloria Steinem

A LISA DREW BOOK

SCRIBNER

NEW YORK LONDON TORONTO SYDNEY SINGAPORE

A LISA DREW BOOK/SCRIBNER
1230 Avenue of the Americas
New York, NY 10020

SCRIBNER and design are trademarks of Macmillan Library Reference USA, Inc.,
used under license by Simon & Schuster, the publisher of this work.

A LISA DREW BOOK is a trademark of Simon & Schuster, Inc.

Set in Aldus
Designed by Colin Joh

Manufactured in the United States of America

1   3   5   7   9   10   8   6   4   2

Library of Congress Cataloging-in-Publication Data
Roosevelt, Eleanor, 1884–1962.
Eleanor and Harry: the correspondence of Eleanor Roosevelt and Harry S.
Truman/[edited by] Steve Neal.
p. cm.
"A Lisa Drew book."
Includes bibliographical references (p. 273) and index.
1. Roosevelt, Eleanor, 1884–1962—Correspondence.
2. Presidents' spouses—United States—Correspondence.
3. Truman, Harry S., 1884–1972—Correspondence.
4. Presidents—United States—Correspondence.
5. United States—Politics and government—1945–1953.
I. Truman, Harry S., 1884–1972. II. Neal, Steve [date]
III. Title.
E807.1.R48 A4 2002
973.918'0922—dc21   2002070792
ISBN 0-7432-0243-0

For information regarding special discounts for bulk purchases, please contact
Simon & Schuster Special Sales at 1-800-456-6798 or
business@simonandschuster.com

For Susan, Erin, and Shannon

And in memory of
Gwendolyn Brooks

Acknowledgments

I am grateful to Eleanor Roosevelt and Harry S. Truman for preserving their correspondence, donating their papers to the American people, and for making the past come alive for future generations. From the moment that I started reading this correspondence at the Truman Library, I wanted to share it with a larger readership.

Robert H. Ferrell, the dean of Truman scholars, encouraged me to undertake this project and generously provided me with transcribed copies of handwritten Truman-Roosevelt correspondence that is often difficult to decipher. I am grateful for his friendship, wry wit, and thoughtfulness. Without his help and wise counsel, I would not have taken on this project. His *Dear Bess: The Letters from Harry to Bess Truman* is the inspiration for this volume.

On several occasions, at the Library of Congress, I met the late Joseph Lash, Mrs. Roosevelt's longtime friend and biographer. He not only made generous comments about my 1984 biography of Wendell L. Willkie but also suggested another book idea. Lash was as engaging in person as in his prose.

Special thanks to the archivists at the Franklin D. Roosevelt and Harry S. Truman presidential libraries. Elizabeth Safly, reference librarian at the Truman Library, and archivists Dennis Bilger and Randy Sowell were particularly helpful.

My editor, Lisa Drew, shares my enthusiasm for the subjects of this book. This book is our fourth collaboration. I am also indebted to her assistants Jake Klisivitch and Erin Curler.

Thanks also to Gerard McCauley, who represented me for twenty-four years and made this book become a reality.

I would like to express my gratitude to Michael Cooke, editor of the *Chicago Sun-Times*, John Cruickshank, vice president for editorial operations, and Steve Huntley, editor of the editorial page, for their encouragement.

Most important, thanks to my wife, Susan, and our daughters, Erin and Shannon. In the first year of our marriage, Susan accompanied me to Hyde Park and assisted me in research at the FDR Library. She also edited the first draft of this volume. After a visit to the FDR Memorial in Washington, Shannon got interested in Eleanor's public career. Erin, who attends Northwestern University, helped with research and also spent many hours transferring the manuscript to discs. I am grateful for my family's love, understanding, and constant support.

Contents

Foreword

by Gloria Steinem

This book brings together many pleasures.

First, there is the discovery of Eleanor Roosevelt in her own words: clear, plainspoken, observant of human nature, passionate about peace and fairness, stubborn, unconventional, and able to be useful anywhere, from lobbying for children's needs in Washington to dealing with chiefs of state in Europe. No one was more shy or hesitant about public life, yet no one grew to be more outspoken and effective in using it. This arc of change makes her a person with whom almost every American can identify, especially women, who understand her journey from helpmate to autonomy, and men or women who stand outside the mainstream of society.

Then, there is getting to know Harry Truman, one of the few politicians who could match Eleanor for plainspokenness and honesty, yet was much more limited than she in his experience of the world and his ability to empathize with those different from himself. He, too, grew to meet the demands of the position he inherited after Franklin Roosevelt's death. Indeed, there were many ways in which their experiences as president and presidential widow were parallel. Both wanted to complete an unfinished program begun by a leader they admired, yet also to meet new challenges and find ways to express their own unique views and abilities. The resulting Truman is all here in these pages, from his understanding that he needed the women's vote to his lack of comfort with women in power, from his courting of Eleanor because of her appeal to African-Americans to his failure to understand the urgency of ending colonialism in Africa.

Readers will also benefit from the letter form itself. It may be the best of populist writing, spontaneous enough to be honest and revealing, yet intended to be read by at least one other person, unlike a diary, and so designed to be understood. Unlike history or journalism, these letters don't pretend that historic events happen outside the context of birthdays and personal sadness, families, and friendships. Unlike novels, they don't try to force life into a beginning, middle, and end. Perhaps the discovery of this correspondence between two very different but mutually interested people is well-timed and will encourage us to appreciate letters as an art form that technology interrupted with the telephone and is now restoring with the Internet. It may remind us to save worthwhile e-mail, rather than treat it as if it were written on the wind.

Finally, there is the pleasure and reward of the text that Steve Neal has woven around these letters. Informed and readable, his additions tell us just what we need to know about context and references, personal relationships and historical facts. It's like having a wise guide at your elbow, one who always seems to know what your level of knowledge is and what you're wondering about, what irony or insincerity or teaching opportunity should not be passed by. We're lucky to have his rare combination of historian, good writer, political analyst, and expert on this exact period in America. Indeed, Eleanor and Harry are lucky to have as a commentator someone who is so devoted to making the past understandable on its own terms, not exerting his own authority at its expense.

All these elements are combined to give us lessons that are useful now and will remain useful in the future. The importance of having honest and wide-ranging friends to anyone isolated by power is underlined by the ombudswoman role Eleanor Roosevelt played. She informed and lobbied Harry Truman on such diverse realities as hate crimes against Japanese Americans, the demobilizing of U.S. soldiers after World War II, food for hungry Europeans, and the plight of North Africa under French colonial rule. The degree to which modern struggles have long precedents is evident in such Truman Era realities as resistance to civil rights, diversity in political appointments, and females in the White House press corps. Indeed, the last was so great that as first lady, Eleanor Roosevelt encouraged the hiring of more women journalists by allowing *only* women to report on her weekly press conferences—a tactic that was still considered outrageous when modern feminists unwittingly reinvented it decades later.

In this time of declining voting rates, it is also crucial to see the personal nature of such decisions as Truman's use of the atomic bomb or his refusal to let the Nazi army keep its weapons and turn them against the Soviets. Each move was within presidential power and has had deep and long impact. So will many decisions being made right now by political leaders we elected or allowed to be elected. Thanks to this book, readers may find it harder to divorce ourselves from the humanity of political leaders, or from our responsibility for putting them there.

Eleanor and Harry—even the title makes you want to pick up this book. That's a symbol of its value in drawing us into history. Instead of forbidding giants striding through a depersonalized past, we see contemporaries talking about the dailiness of decisions. Since we know from hindsight that these two people helped to shape our world, we also understand that history is made by Eleanors and Harrys—and that we could be one of them. Steve Neal has paid us the ultimate honor of creating a book that empowers its readers.

Introduction

Harry Truman designated Eleanor Roosevelt the "First Lady of the World." From 1946 through 1953, she would be the most influential and highest-ranking woman in the Truman administration as a member of the U.S. delegation to the United Nations General Assembly.

When they first met in 1935, she greeted him at a White House reception. As the wife of President Franklin D. Roosevelt, Eleanor was a driving force in the social activism of the New Deal. Truman, elected to the Senate from Missouri in 1934, supported the Roosevelt agenda. But he felt unappreciated. "If I remember correctly when I flew home to introduce her," he wrote of Mrs. Roosevelt in 1939, "she didn't even say thank you."

In correspondence with family members, Truman made disparaging references to Mrs. Roosevelt's political activity. The Missouri senator would not have disagreed with a 1942 Gallup Poll that reported many Americans felt that "she is too much in the public eye" and "she ought to stay at home, where a wife belongs." The most frequent criticism of Mrs. Roosevelt, according to the poll, was that "she is always getting her nose into the government's business" and "she talks too much." The same poll indicated that an equal number of people approved that "she has a personality of her own and doesn't allow herself just to sit at home and do nothing."

In the summer of 1944, she made a futile effort to persuade her husband that Vice President Henry A. Wallace deserved renomination. It bothered her that the professional politicians were leading the movement to dump Wallace. When the Chicago convention nominated Truman, Mrs. Roosevelt wrote Wallace: "I had hoped by some miracle you could win out, but it looks to me as though the bosses had functioned pretty smoothly. I am told that Senator Truman is a good man, and I hope so for the sake of the country."

On the Thursday afternoon of April 12, 1945, Mrs. Roosevelt summoned Truman to the White House. "Harry," she said in a somber tone, "the president is dead."

Even though Truman knew that FDR had been in ill health, he did not know how to react. "Is there anything I can do for you?" he asked.

"Is there anything we can do for you?" Mrs. Roosevelt answered. "For you are the one in trouble now."

This marked the beginning of an extraordinary friendship. Soon afterward, Truman presented her with the desk at which Franklin D. Roosevelt had worked in the Oval Office. In the months ahead, Mrs. Roosevelt maintained a warm and sympathetic correspondence with her husband's successor. She would not hesitate to offer advice on foreign and domestic policies, nominations for senior positions in the administration, and political strategy. "I can't tell you how much I appreciate your letters," Truman replied. Though she could sometimes be condescending, he treated her with deference and respect. Truman once confided to his budget director that Mrs. Roosevelt, while a great lady, could also be aggravating.

Truman, who was born on May 8, 1884, was six months older than Mrs. Roosevelt, born on October 11, 1884. But they grew up in different worlds. He was the grandson of Missouri pioneers and spent much of his youth on the farm. Truman reflected the values and work ethic of rural America. Eleanor, born in New York City, was a member of the aristocracy. On her mother's side, she was descended from Philip Livingston, one of the nation's founding fathers and signer of the Declaration of Independence. Her father, Elliott Roosevelt, was the younger brother of President Theodore Roosevelt. While Truman went to public schools in Independence, Eleanor attended finishing school in London. At the age of eighteen she made a formal debut in New York society. After graduating from high school, Truman worked as a railroad timekeeper and then as a bank clerk.

Each of them had known adversity. As an eight-year-old Eleanor lost her mother. Eleanor's father, an alcoholic, died two years later. She would be raised by her maternal grandmother. Truman's life would be disrupted by his father's financial setbacks. When his parents needed him, he gave up a promising banking career to work on the family farm.

Their marriages were studies in opposites. Eleanor married her cousin

Franklin Delano Roosevelt on March 17, 1905. From the start, she worried that Franklin was too attractive and charming to be content with her. Their marriage produced a half dozen children, one of whom died in infancy. In the fall of 1918, she made the painful discovery that her husband was in love with a younger woman, her own social secretary, Lucy Mercer. Eleanor offered to grant Franklin a divorce, but he declined out of concern that a scandal could end his public career and also because his mother threatened to cut off his income. Eleanor and Franklin, who became partners in politics and the nation's most renowned power couple, never again lived as husband and wife. She later burned Franklin's letters from their courtship. When Eleanor agreed to remain in the marriage, Franklin promised that he would never see Lucy again. But when he died in April of 1945, she was at his side.

From their first meeting when he was six years old, until the end of his life, Truman was totally devoted to Bess Wallace. When they were married in June of 1919, he was thirty-five years old and she was thirty-four. After more than thirty years of marriage, he wrote Bess: "You are still on the pedestal where I placed you that day in Sunday School in 1890." Shortly after the 1944 Democratic National Convention, Truman wrote his wife about a White House luncheon with President Roosevelt. "The President told me," Truman wrote, "that Mrs. R. was a very timid woman and wouldn't go to political meetings or make any speeches when he first ran for governor of N.Y. Then, he said, 'Now she talks all the time.' "

In looking back on her marriage, Mrs. Roosevelt wrote: "He might have been happier with a wife who was completely uncritical. That I was never able to be, and he had to find it in some other people. Nevertheless, I think I sometimes acted as a spur, even though spurring was not always wanted or welcome. I was one of those who served his purposes."

Truman hoped that Mrs. Roosevelt could find a similar role in his administration. In the fall of 1945, he confided to Secretary of State James F. Byrnes that she was among two people that he "had to have" on his political team. The other was Henry A. Wallace, then serving as secretary of commerce. The president said that he needed Wallace because of his close ties to organized labor and Mrs. Roosevelt because of her popularity among African-Americans. Within a year, Truman forced

Wallace to quit the cabinet after Wallace publicly questioned U.S. policy toward the Soviet Union. Byrnes, a former Senate colleague for whom Truman had great admiration, was also eased out for having the effrontery to make foreign policy pronouncements without consulting the president of the United States.

Following her husband's death, Mrs. Roosevelt made it known that she would have greater freedom to speak out on public issues. "Because I was the wife of the President certain restrictions were imposed upon me," she wrote in "My Day," her syndicated newspaper column. "Now I am on my own and I hope to write as a newspaperwoman." As the most admired woman in America, she felt a responsibility to speak out against injustice. "Of one thing I am sure: Young or old, in order to be useful we must stand up for the things we feel are right," she wrote in the first month of the Truman presidency, "and we must work for those things wherever we find ourselves. It does very little good to believe something unless you tell your friends and associates of your beliefs."

She wrote with this same passion and conviction in her letters to Truman. They discuss the beginning of the Cold War, the rebuilding of postwar Europe, the creation of the state of Israel, the Chinese civil war, and the start of the modern civil rights movement. Truman explains his motives in making the commitment to Greece and Turkey that would become known as the Truman Doctrine. She reports to Truman about her travels abroad, her work at the United Nations, and the evolution of the Universal Declaration of Human Rights, which Truman regarded as her greatest accomplishment. Mrs. Roosevelt urges him to appoint more women to senior positions in the federal government. In response to her criticism, he tries to defend his misguided loyalty program. Mrs. Roosevelt laments that the loyalty boards were a gross violation of civil liberties. On more than one occasion, she offers to resign from the United Nations delegation. Truman, who valued her advice and foreign policy contributions, would not allow her to quit.

This correspondence is without parallel in American history, and it is doubtful there will ever be anything like it again. When there is a changing of the guard, there have always been tensions between a new chief executive and his predecessor's family. It is difficult to imagine Lyndon B. Johnson and Jacqueline Bouvier Kennedy, Theodore Roosevelt and Ida

McKinley, or George Herbert Walker Bush and Nancy Reagan as pen pals, even though these chief executives had been vice presidents to these first ladies' husbands. But Eleanor Roosevelt and Harry Truman formed a bond in 1945 that would deepen over the years as they shared their most personal thoughts, hopes, disappointments, and, finally, their vision of the postwar world. Two other notable Americans might have maintained a similar correspondence. Thomas Jefferson and Abigail Adams had been friends for years until Jefferson ousted her husband, John, from the presidency in 1800. For the first three and a half years of Jefferson's presidency, Abigail had no contact with her husband's successor. But when Jefferson's daughter Mary Jefferson Eppes died in 1804 at the age of twenty-five, Abigail wrote him that she had wept at the news. Though Jefferson responded with warmth and sought a rapprochement, John and Abigail were not ready to forget past differences. It would be another eight years before they resumed their correspondence with Jefferson. Truman and Mrs. Roosevelt, who sometimes clashed over issues and personalities, often discussed their differences in this intimate and often lively correspondence.

Mrs. Roosevelt, who had early doubts that Truman would be an effective president, thought he served the nation well. She "learned that he had a remarkable understanding of the office and duties of the President. He was a student of the Constitution and it was important to our nation that he was a jealous guardian of the ideas of the Founding Fathers. I felt that he had to make more than his share of big decisions as President and that he made very few mistakes in times of crisis."

This collection of 254 letters is a documentary history of the Truman era. But more than that, this book is the story of a friendship.

CHAPTER 1

1945

In the first announcement of his presidency, Harry S. Truman vowed to continue the policies of Franklin D. Roosevelt. "The world may be sure that we will prosecute the war on both fronts, east and west, with all the vigor we possess to a successful conclusion," he declared. On the same night that he was sworn in by Chief Justice Harlan Fiske Stone, the new president made it known that the organizational meeting of the United Nations would go forward as scheduled.

There was speculation that President Truman might appoint Eleanor Roosevelt as a special delegate to the San Francisco conference, which would begin on April 25, 1945. But she was not ready to resume her public career less than two weeks after her husband's death. "It was almost as though I had erected someone a little outside of myself who was the president's wife," she wrote in *This I Remember*. "I was lost somewhere deep down inside myself."

She had been the most active first lady in the history of the American presidency. Eleanor Roosevelt became the first presidential wife to travel by airplane across the Atlantic, visit soldiers in the Pacific, and travel abroad without her husband. At the White House, she established another precedent in holding weekly press conferences. Her policy was that only women reporters could attend these sessions. On leaving the White House, she expected to have a lower profile. When a reporter attempted to interview her on a New York sidewalk, Mrs. Roosevelt quietly declined: "The story is over."

Following FDR's death, Truman ordered flags to be flown at half-mast for thirty days. "All of us have lost a great leader, a farsighted statesman, and a real friend of democracy," he said in a radio address to U.S. servicemen. "We have lost a hard-hitting chief and an old friend of the services.

Our hearts are heavy. However the cause which claimed Roosevelt, also claimed us. He never faltered—nor will we."

While seeking to carry on the Roosevelt legacy, Truman wanted his own team. In the first hundred days of his administration, Truman got rid of two-thirds of the Roosevelt cabinet. Eleanor, who did not always agree with her husband's selections, gave Truman mixed reviews on his appointments. She had never been close to Labor Secretary Frances Perkins, named by FDR in 1933 as the first woman member of a presidential cabinet. But when Perkins got eased out, Eleanor regarded it as a setback for women. "If we look back over Miss Perkins' whole record we will find that she accomplished a great deal," Mrs. Roosevelt wrote in her column. "A woman will always have to be better than a man in any job she undertakes. There is no woman in the cabinet today, but there will be again in the future. When there is, I hope she will get more support from the women of her own political party than has been the case in the past."

Eleanor liked Truman but doubted whether he was up to the job. "His family is gone, the house is bare & stiff & he's the loneliest man I ever saw," she reported to a friend after a White House luncheon in June of 1945. "He's not accustomed to night work or reading & contemplation and he doesn't like it. He's not at ease & no one else is. I am so sorry for him & he tries so hard." Truman knew so little about foreign policy, Eleanor told another friend, that she almost felt like crying. "I was appalled at how little he knew."

Yet the American people sensed that he knew what he was doing. The early months of the Truman presidency marked the end of World War II and the beginning of the atomic age. At the end of the year, *Fortune* reported that three-fourths of the public rated his performance as good to excellent on foreign policy, and two-thirds of the people felt that he was effective in dealing with Congress.

Truman took nothing for granted and did not presume that those numbers would hold. He was genuinely interested in Mrs. Roosevelt's opinions and welcomed her letters. As the historian William Leuchtenburg has noted: "Truman understood that if he was to win acceptance as FDR's heir, he needed to please one person beyond all others: Eleanor Roosevelt."

April 16, 1945

My dear Mr. President:

There have been many thousands of letters, telegrams and cards sent to me and my children which have brought great comfort and consolation to all of us. This outpouring of affectionate thought has touched us all deeply and we wish it were possible to thank each and every one individually.

My children and I feel, in view of the fact that we are faced with the paper shortage and are asked not to use paper when it can be avoided, that all we can do is to express our appreciation collectively. We would therefore consider it a great favor if you would be kind enough to express our gratitude for us.

Sincerely,

Eleanor Roosevelt

The next morning, Truman held the first news conference of his presidency and read this letter to more than three hundred reporters. When Mrs. Roosevelt moved to Hyde Park, the president sent along a stenographer to help manage her correspondence. Soon afterward, Truman was embarrassed when a senior aide, Eddie McKim, ordered White House secretaries to quit answering Eleanor's condolence letters. "Mrs. Roosevelt is no longer riding the gravy train," McKim said in issuing the order. When this unfortunate comment showed up in print, Truman fired McKim.

The White House
April 20, 1945

Dear Mr. President,

As you see by the paper accompanying this little donkey, he has long been in my husband's possession and was on his desk. He looks a bit obstinate and Franklin said he needed a reminder sometimes that his decisions had to be final and taken with a sense that God would give guidance to a humble beast. Once having decided something, the obstinate little donkey kept his sense of humor and determination going against great pressure.

I cannot leave this house without thanking you and Mrs. Truman again for your kindness and consideration.

My best wishes for you and our country and may God bless and guide you.

Sincerely yours,

———————

April 25, 1945

Dear Mrs. Truman:

As you know, the President's wife is always asked to be Honorary President of the Girl Scouts. I have found that this does not take very much time.

I have been asked to act as Honorary Vice-President, and also that I send you a line about their letter asking you to serve. I have agreed to serve as Honorary Vice-Chairman with the understanding that I can do no active work for them for some time.

My sons and I have been working hard trying to straighten out various details, but it is still difficult to believe that my husband is not off on a trip.

My very best wishes to you,

Very sincerely yours,

———————

April 28, 1945

Dear Mrs. Roosevelt:

I am sorry that I have been so long in thanking you for the little donkey which you sent me for my desk.

He certainly is in a typical mulish attitude and, as the President used to say, when I have a hard decision to make I will look at him, think of you and the President, and then try to make the best decision.

Sincerely yours,

Mrs. Roosevelt moved out of the White House on the morning of April 23. When she gave Bess and Margaret Truman a private tour, they were startled to find it in poor structural condition. The floors and ceilings *sagged, plaster was cracking everywhere, carpets were threadbare and dusty, and some of the drapes were rotting. Congress had approved $50,000 in expenditures for housekeeping and maintenance. But Mrs. Roosevelt may have thought it wasteful to spend taxpayer funds during the war for her family's comfort. For nearly half of his presidency, Truman would live in Blair House, the guest house of the president, which is on Pennsylvania Avenue across from the White House, while the executive mansion was being renovated.*

New York
May 8, 1945

Dear Mr. President,

I listened to your Proclamation this morning and I was deeply moved. I am so happy that this Day has come and the war in Europe is over. It will in a small way lighten your burdens for which we are all grateful.

My congratulations to you on your Proclamation and on your birthday, and my best wishes that your future birthdays will be happier ones.

Very sincerely yours,

Don't bother to answer please! My warm regards to Mrs. Truman.

In his address to the American people, Truman declared: "Our victory is but half-won. The West is free, but the East is still in bondage to the treacherous tyranny of the Japanese. When the last Japanese division has surrendered unconditionally, then only will our fighting be done." Mrs. Roosevelt observed in her column, "I can almost hear my husband's voice make that announcement, for I heard him repeat it so often." But she could not celebrate because men were still dying in the Pacific war. "Some of my own sons," she wrote, "with millions of others, are still in danger."

May 10, 1945

Dear Mrs. Roosevelt:

Your note of the 8th is most highly appreciated. The whole family were touched by your thoughtfulness.

I noticed in your good column today you expressed some surprise at the Russian attitude on the close of the European War.

I think that I should explain the situation to you. On Wednesday, April 25, our minister to Sweden sent a message to me saying that Himmler wanted to surrender to General Eisenhower all their troops facing the western front and that the Germans would continue to fight the Russians. Before our state department could get the message deciphered the prime minister called me from London and read the message to me. That was the great mystery of the trip to the Pentagon building.

The matter was discussed with our staff and the offer was very promptly refused. The Russians were notified of our joint action. Prince Bernadotte of Sweden informed our minister that Hitler had had a brain blowup of some sort and would be dead in twenty-four hours—so Himmler had informed him. The p.m. and I decided that when the Gestapo butcher said a man would be dead in twenty-four hours he usually made good on the promise.

Negotiations went on for two more days—we always insisting on complete, unconditional surrender on all fronts. The German idea, of course, was to split the three great powers and perhaps make things easier for themselves. Our headquarters kept me informed all the time by almost hourly messages. We were nearly at an agreement and the famous Connally statement came out and completely upset the apple cart. Himmler was displaced by Admiral Doenitz and a new start was made.

Germans delayed and delayed, trying all the time to quit only on the western front. They finally offered Norway, Denmark, Holland, and the French ports they still held, but wanted to keep resisting the Russians. Our commanding general finally told them that he would turn loose all we had and drive them into the Russians. They finally signed at Rheims the terms of unconditional surrender effective at 12:01 midnight of May 8-9.

In the meantime Churchill, Stalin, and I had agreed on a simultaneous release at 9:00 a.m., Washington time, 3:00 p.m., London, and 4:00 p.m., Moscow time. Then the Associated Press broke faith with General Eisenhower. The Germans kept fighting the Russians and Stalin informed me that he had grave doubts of the Germans carrying out terms. There was fighting on the eastern front right up to the last hour.

In the meantime Churchill was trying to force me to break faith with the Russians and release on the seventh, noon, Washington time, 6:00 p.m., London, 7:00 p.m., Moscow. I wired Stalin and he said the Germans were still firing. I refused Churchill's request and informed Stalin of conditions here and in England and that unless I heard from him to the contrary I would release at 9:00 a.m., May 8. I didn't hear so the release was made, but fighting was still in progress against the Russians. The Germans were finally informed that if they didn't cease firing as agreed they would not be treated as fighting men but as traitors and would be hanged as caught. They then ceased firing and Stalin made his announcement the ninth.

He had sent me a message stating the situation at 1:00 a.m., May 8, and asking postponement until May 9. I did not get the message until 10:00 a.m., May 8, too late, of course, to do anything.

I have been trying very carefully to keep all my engagements with the Russians because they are touchy and suspicious of us. The difficulties with Churchill are very nearly as exasperating as they are with the Russians. But patience I think must be our watchword if we are to have world peace. To have it we must have the wholehearted support of Russia, Great Britain, and the United States.

I hope this won't bore you too much, but I thought you'd like to know the facts. Please keep it confidential until it can be officially released.

Please accept my thanks again for your good message.

Most sincerely,

Until the last possible moment, Churchill kept pressing Truman to make the announcement without the Russians. "He finally had to stick to the agreement—but he was mad as a wet hen," the president wrote in a letter to his mother and sister. When Mrs. Roosevelt noted in her col-

umn that the Russians had delayed their announcement, Truman
wanted her to know that he had played straight with Stalin.

Hyde Park
May 14, 1945

Dear Mr. President:

I was very much touched to have you take the trouble to write to me that long letter in longhand about the Russian situation. Please, if you write again, do have it typed because I feel guilty to take any of your time.

I am typing this because I know my husband always preferred to have things typed so he could read them more quickly and my handwriting is anything but legible.

Your experience with Mr. Churchill is not at all surprising. He is suspicious of the Russians and they know it. If you will remember, he said some pretty rough things about them years ago and they do not forget.

Of course, we will have to be patient, and any lasting peace will have to have the three Great Powers behind it. I think, however, if you can get on a personal basis with Mr. Churchill, you will find it easier. If you talk to him about books and let him quote to you from his marvelous memory everything on earth from Barbara Fritche to the Nonsense Rhymes and Greek tragedy, you will find him easier to deal with on political subjects. He is a gentleman to whom the personal element means a great deal.

Mr. Churchill does not have the same kind of sense of humor that the Russians have. In some ways the Russians are more like us. They enjoy a practical joke, roughhouse play, and they will joke about things which Mr. Churchill thinks are sacred. He takes them dead seriously and argues about them when what he ought to do is laugh. That was where Franklin usually won out because if you know where to laugh and when to look upon things as too absurd to take seriously, the other person is ashamed to carry through even if he was serious about it.

You are quite right in believing that the Russians will watch with great care to see how we keep our commitments.

A rumor has reached me that that message from Mr. Stalin to you was really received in plenty of time to have changed that hour but it was held back from you. Those little things were done to my husband now and then. I tell you of this rumor simply because while you may have known about it and decided that it was wise just not to receive it in time, you told me in your letter that you did not receive it and I have known of things which just did not reach my husband in time. That is one of the things which your military and naval aides ought to watch very carefully.

Sometime when you have time, since my son, Elliott, is in Washington now and then, you might like to let him tell you about what he learned of the Russians when he was there. He was in Russia quite a good deal and helped establish our air force there and he has an old friend who is the only American who has flown with the Russians from the very beginning. Elliott gets on well with them and understands the peculiar combination that can look upon human life rather cheaply at times and yet strive for an ideal of future well-being for the people and make the people believe in it. He has an understanding of their enjoyment of drama and music and the arts in general and he realizes what few people seem to understand—namely that when you telescope into a few years of development in civilization which has taken hundreds of years for the people around you to achieve, the development is very uneven.

I will, of course, keep confidential anything which comes to me in any letter from you and I will never mention it, and I would not use a private letter in any public way at any time.

I would not presume to write you this letter only you did say you would like me to give you some little personal impressions of these people, gathered from my husband's contacts, before you went to meet them and as I realize that may happen soon, I thought perhaps you would like this letter now.

If you or any of your family ever feel like getting away from formality and spending a few days with me in this very simple cottage I should love to have you and I am quite accustomed to the necessary secret service protection.

With much gratitude for the trouble which you took, and with my kind regards to Mrs. Truman and your daughter, believe me,

Very cordially yours,

Surprised that Truman had reacted to her column by writing her a detailed letter, Mrs. Roosevelt responded in kind with this thoughtful message. This exchange marked a turning point in their correspondence. She now realized that Truman took her views seriously and that her syndicated column was an invaluable public forum.

May 18, 1945

Dear Mrs. Roosevelt,

You don't know how very, very much I appreciated your letter of the fourteenth, in reply to my longhand letter explaining the situation with Russia. It gave me a lift and also a lot of information which will be very helpful to me.

I had a very pleasant visit with Elliott and Anna and they also gave me some vital information, of which I can make very good use, I am sure.

Whenever I can be of service in any way, please feel free to call on me.

Sincerely yours,

An Army Air Corps pilot in World War II, Mrs. Roosevelt's son Elliott flew more than three hundred combat missions, was twice wounded, and rose to the rank of brigadier general. Anna, the eldest child and only daughter of Eleanor and Franklin, had accompanied her father to the Yalta conference and served as an aide during the final months of his presidency.

May 26, 1945

Dear Mrs. Truman:

Many thanks for your check for the food which you bought from the supply we had in the White House. I very much appreciate your doing this.

I hope you are comfortably settled by now and that all is going well. I am still trying to sort out and divide possessions for my children and with two of them in the Pacific, it is a little difficult to decide what they may want. A house that has been lived in as long as the house here, certainly gathers and keeps a great many things which are now difficult to dispose of.

With many thanks again and my warm good wishes, I am,

Very cordially yours,
Eleanor Roosevelt

May 31, 1945

Dear Mrs. Roosevelt:

Indeed I feel very much indebted to you for letting us have all that food. It was a great help. I have thought of you so often, realizing how much you must have to do in sorting out your many belongings and in the great accumulation which followed you from here. Even moving from an apartment seemed to bring to light any number of possessions, and I am appalled to think of what you must have faced after living for twelve years in the one place.

If you plan to be in Washington any time I hope you will let me know so I may see you again. It is something that I always look forward to. Thank you for your note and I hope that even your capable hands are not being overwhelmed with work.

Sincerely yours,
Bess W. Truman

June 3, 1945

Dear Mr. President:

I am enclosing a copy of a letter which I have just sent to Mr. Hannegan, as I have been doing a lot of thinking along these lines since I have been back in New York State.

. . . I have no idea whether you agree with me or not, but all I can do is to send you the results of my observations and my conversations with people in the last few weeks.

I should also like to bring to your attention, in case you missed it, a broadcast which came from overseas in Germany the morning of June 2nd, shortly after midnight. I listened because I know Bill Chaplin, the AP reporter who was one of the speakers. I know he is an honest and reliable reporter. This was the last apparently of three reports from Germany but it was the first I heard and it horrified me. I think it would be worth your while to get it and read it. It came over WEAF in New York City. If such conditions actually exist in Germany I think the people of this country have a right to feel outraged and I gather from letters I received from boys now in Germany that these conditions are not exaggerated by this reporter. I am quite sure that both the Secretary of War and General Marshall as well as yourself should read these broadcasts.

Please do not bother to answer this letter. I simply felt that I had an obligation to write to you.

Very cordially yours,

June 3, 1945

Dear Mr. Hannegan:

I have been thinking a good deal about the political situation as I view it from New York State. I know that my husband felt very strongly that we have to carry the congressional election in 1946 in order to win in 1948. If Governor Dewey is not defeated the chances are that we will be defeated in 1948, so what happens to him is vitally important.

I notice a number of things. Governor Dewey certainly learned from the last campaign that he could not ignore the colored vote and, at the expense of some of his most conservative support, he is now playing up very strongly to the minority groups in this state and also to the liberals.

On the other hand, the impression is spreading that the Democratic Party as far as President Truman is concerned, is doing a good job from the liberal point of view in most of the things which he has done, but that in Congress, particularly in the Senate, we are still going to have a strong fight by the conservative southern Democratic senators on our hands. If they filibuster on the FEPC and on the Poll Tax, I think we will have a big group of people feeling that there is a chance even though there is a conservative moneyed power group in the Republican Party, that the Republican Party may be more liberal from the point of view of racial and religious questions. We may lose a certain number of people to that party who would ordinarily be Democrats, but who want to serve notice that there is one issue on which they will vote with the party which they consider is doing the right thing on that issue.

You may find others who will feel that neither party with the conservative element can be trusted and that both parties are controlled by these elements, and the time has come to form a third party. That third party, of course, will not win, but on the other hand it will defeat the Democratic Party because we know the Democratic Party can not win unless it has the liberal vote and some liberal Republican elements voting with it.

I know that you feel very strongly, and I know that Mr. Fitzpatrick in New York feels very strongly that we must build up the Democratic Party organization throughout the country. I am entirely in agreement with this because we have to have people to put on campaigns and to do the work not only of the campaigns but the in-between campaign work. However, the day when an organization such as Tammany in New York and Pendergast in Kansas City could really swing elections has gone by. The people want to know what the things are for which the party stands, and they want to be convinced that those things are going to be put through. Mr. Kelly in Chicago has a good organization, but if Mr. Kelly had not played fair with a great many people he would not hold his organization. That holds good of practically all of your Democratic Party groups today. So while these organizations are vitally important to the party, I think you have to add something which has often been neglected, namely, a program which meets the needs and wins the approval of the rank and file of the voters.

At the present time, that would include many things concerning veterans, social security, education, and above all, the sense that we are moving forward in our foreign policy to a peaceful world and in our economic policy to a realization of responsibility for economic situations throughout the world which would affect our own in the long run.

I know, of course, it is rather presumptuous of me to talk to you about the general political situation which you and the others must have considered already, probably in much more detail and with far better powers of observation than I can possibly bring to it at the present time.

There is one phase of the whole picture with which I think I am more familiar and more closely connected than many of the people whom you know well, namely, the situation of the women who are not the regular party workers, but who are the women you have to have with you to win in campaigns. Many of them are feeling that while Miss Perkins was not particularly popular during the last few years as Secretary of Labor, still she was a woman in the Cabinet. There will be no woman in the Cabinet and there has been no suggestion so far of any woman or women in comparably important positions. Most of the women whom you have to have with you to win elections, do not expect positions, but they like to feel that some women are in the policy making positions and I think that they must feel that this is not just for a brief time but permanently.

I know many men are made a little uncomfortable by having women in these positions, but I think the time has come to face the fact that you have to win as many women's votes as you do men's votes and that the Democratic Party probably has more strength among women if it stands as the liberal party and the party of human rights than it has among the men.

From the point of view of doing something for our biggest minority group—the colored people—I think you will have to make some good appointments to commissions where you choose a man because he is a good man and has ability, and it just happens he is colored which you forget about in the work which he does.

I think the administration will have to try to get the FEPC and the Poll Tax vote out on the floor of the Senate and not allow it to be killed by a filibuster. If you can get a vote on these two issues, it is one step forward and the men who vote against them are known and their position is out in the open. A fight can be made on them on their record in voting. If these two issues are killed without a record vote and then there is discrimination in employment and the economic situation becomes unfair to racial and religious groups, I think we will be in danger of creating a lack of unity in the nation as a whole which will affect the Democratic Party more than it will affect the Republican Party.

I will be interested to know what you think of these points because, of course, I am interested in the success of the Democratic Party, and I am equally interested in the progress of our nation which transcends party lines.

Very sincerely yours,

Robert E. Hannegan (1903–1949), Democratic national chairman from 1944 until 1947, played a critical role in the removal of Wallace and selection of Truman for the vice presidency. In May 1945, Truman appointed him postmaster general, which then had cabinet rank. By sending the president a copy of this letter, Mrs. Roosevelt signaled that she would remain politically active. Now that the war was ending, she favored a return to the social activism of the New Deal.

June 5, 1945

Dear Mr. President:

I have never thanked you for your kind thought in sending the wreath up to my husband's grave on Memorial Day. The little ceremony was dignified & moving & I was glad that I could be there.

You have been very kind & I am very grateful.

Sincerely yours,

July 2, 1945

Dear Mr. President:

It has been suggested to me by the United Feature Syndicate for which I write a column, that they would be glad to have me go to Russia.

. . . I haven't spoken to the syndicate about going at any immediate time because I wanted first to make sure that it would meet with your approval to have me go to Russia, either now or in the spring.

I would want to go as a correspondent in the usual way, but I realize that being my husband's widow, there would have to be a little more of the formal paying of respects and possibly even some entertainment. I would do my best to keep this down to a minimum, but I naturally do not want to be rude or to offend the Russian government and the Russian people. I would primarily be gathering information on the situation and interests of women and children from every angle and I would hope that the whole trip could be undertaken and finished in the space of four to six weeks.

Please be entirely frank in your own feelings in the matter because it is far more important that you not be hampered or bothered by anything anyone else does, and I know that your path at the present time must be anything but smooth.

With all good wishes to you in the fight for the quick ratification of the Charter, believe me.

Very cordially yours,

_____

August 8, 1945

To the President:

Welcome home. Much interested in your great achievements.

Eleanor Roosevelt

_____

August 9, 1945

Dear Mrs. Roosevelt:

I certainly did appreciate very much your message of last night. We seem to have had a reasonably successful conference. I am hoping to make a report on it tonight over the radio.

It was kind and thoughtful of you to remember me.

With very best wishes from Mrs. Truman and myself, I am

Sincerely yours,

The Potsdam Conference, which opened on July 17, 1945, and concluded on August 2, marked Truman's debut on the world stage. Stalin arrived late and Churchill left early when British voters chose new leadership. The allies agreed to Truman's proposal for delegating peace treaties to a Council of Foreign Ministers. The American president also succeeded in his effort to bring the Soviets into the war against Japan. The summit would have been held earlier, but Truman held out for a later date until

*the atomic bomb could be tested. During the conference, the president
learned that he had the weapon that would end the war.*

New York
August 15, 1945

Dear Mr. President,

I greatly appreciate your calling me last night. It is a weight off one's
heart to have the war over. For you, however, I appreciate only too well
what the new problems are. I feel that our safety lies in attacking [illegi-
ble] these problems as he [FDR] did the war problems. The government
must keep control till we are on an even keel from the economic standpoint. You will have pressures from every side. I am sure your own wisdom and experience and faith in God will guide you aright.

My best wishes to Mrs. Truman. These are great days in which we
live. God bless you both.

Sincerely yours,

*Mrs. Roosevelt supported Truman's decision to drop the atomic bomb,
which ended the war, noting that it was fortunate that the allies developed this weapon before the Germans. "The new atomic discovery has
changed the whole aspect of the world in which we live," she wrote in
her column. "It has been primarily thought of in the light of its destruc-
tive power. Now we have to think of it in terms of how it may serve
mankind in the days of peace."*

*Following the Japanese surrender, Truman designated Sunday, August
19, as a day of prayer to honor "the memory of those who have given
their lives to make possible our victory."*

August 18, 1945

Deeply regret will not be able to attend service. Tomorrow my
thoughts will be with you all at that time.

Eleanor Roosevelt

August 20, 1945

Dear Mrs. Roosevelt:

We were sorry you could not be with us yesterday.

We had a very nice service and it would have been complete and perfect if you had been there.

Sincerely yours,

September 1, 1945

Dear Mrs. Roosevelt:

I have just returned to the White House study from the executive office. The first thing I always do is to look at the Scripps-Howard News and read the editorial page and your column. Today you've really "hit the jackpot"—if I may say that to the First Lady.

I am asking one of my good Senatorial friends to put it in the Congressional Record on Tuesday for the sake of history. I only turned the reports loose because I was very reliably informed that the sabotage press had paid a very large price for them in order to release them on V.J. Day. It is my opinion that they'll be a nine days cause for conversation and be forgotten in victory.

I see red every time this same press starts a ghoulish attack on the President (I never think of anyone as the President but Mr. Roosevelt).

My very best regards and greatest respect I am

Sincerely,

New York
September 7, 1945

Dear Mr. President:

I am glad you liked my column and very much flattered that you read it.

May I say how much I admire your courage as shown in your message? You may be defeated, but you have stated your position clearly and I am sure Congress must uphold you if you make one or two clear talks to the people. . . .

Cordially yours,

On September 6, Truman sought to fulfill FDR's agenda with a twenty-one-point agenda for postwar recovery, including legislation for full employment, unemployment compensation, affordable housing, public works funding for the construction of airports and highways, an increase in the minimum wage, and establishing a Fair Employment Practice Committee on a permanent basis. Truman quoted Franklin D. Roosevelt's statement endorsing an economic bill of rights: "In our day these economic truths have become accepted as self-evident. We have accepted, so to speak, a second bill of rights under which a new basis of security and prosperity can be established for all—regardless of station, race, or creed." Among these rights, Truman noted, were the right to a useful and remunerative job, the right to a living wage, the right of every family to a decent home, adequate medical care, and a good education. "All of these rights spell security," Truman said, quoting FDR. "... America's own rightful place in the world depends in large part upon how fully these and similar rights have been carried into practice for our citizens. For unless there is security here at home there cannot be lasting peace in the world."

September 10, 1945

Dear Mr. President:

I am enclosing a copy of a letter which I have written to Speaker Rayburn. I know you are aware that my husband was interested and thought this picture would be a valuable addition to the Capitol and historically worthwhile for the future.

This is just to let you know what I had written to the Speaker.

Very cordially yours,

As a memorial to her husband, Mrs. Roosevelt suggested that Congress commission a painting of the late president with wartime allies Churchill and Stalin. Truman replied that he would be glad to endorse this proposal to Rayburn.

Hyde Park
September 11, 1945

Dear Mr. President:

The Rogers estate, which joins ours at Hyde Park, was, as you know, leased by the War Department for the military police school. Now that the military police are no longer here, there is great interest in the village in having all or some of the property owned by the government, selected as the permanent headquarters of the United Nations.

I have told those who came to me that a decision of this kind would have to be made by a majority of the nations and that our government could make no such decision alone.

The idea seems to me good, however and I wondered if our house and the Vanderbilt mansion couldn't all be used at times of meeting and make a very acceptable center?

You will get the local petition eventually, but I thought I'd pass the idea along now.

Very cordially yours,

September 14, 1945

Dear Mrs. Roosevelt:

Appreciated your note of the eleventh regarding the site for the headquarters. Of course, your suggestion is an excellent one but I don't know what the program will be with regard to the location of the headquarters.

Mr. Stettinius asked me when he left here what attitude he should take if the members decided to make the headquarters in the United States and I told him to accept the nomination if they offered it to us.

Sometime when you are in Washington I will be glad to discuss the whole thing with you.

Sincerely yours,

It would have been a fitting tribute to FDR if the United Nations had adopted Hyde Park as its home. But larger American cities were actively campaigning to become the world's county seat. Boston, Chicago, Philadelphia, and Atlantic City were among the contenders. In December of 1945, the United Nations' site-selection panel met in London and recommended that the international organization be located some-where east of the Mississippi. In 1946, New York City was chosen as the permanent site for the United Nations.

October 2, 1945

My dear Mrs. Roosevelt:

Thanks very much for sending me the Six-Point Program for Africa and the Peace Settlement. I am most happy to have it.

It looks as if the foreign ministers meeting in London is stymied. The attitude of Russia and the Russian insistence that we recognize the governments of Rumania and Bulgaria, which we can't do, was the cause.

We will have to take another approach to the matter, I believe.

I do appreciate very much your sending me the African suggestion.

Sincerely yours,

Mrs. Roosevelt had sent a one-page policy statement from the New York–based Council of African Affairs. It called for a specific timetable for ending imperial rule in Africa and urged the United Nations to take an active role in making nations out of colonies. The council said that a British proposal for regional coloniul cooperation would allow "the perpetuation of colonial imperialism." Neither Truman nor his foreign-policy team gave priority to African affairs. In contrast with his predecessor, who favored a breakup of the colonial empires, Truman accepted the status quo and established full diplomatic relations with South Africa's pro-apartheid government headed by General Jan Smuts.

October 10, 1945

To Eleanor Roosevelt:

Mrs. Truman and I want you to know that we shall be thinking of you on your birthday. We hope the day will bring you great happiness because you have made countless lives happier through your understanding sympathy and acts of kindness. We both send you our love.

Harry S. Truman

October 14, 1945

Dear Mr. President:

So many thanks to you and Mrs. Truman for your warm & thoughtful telegram.

I look forward to seeing you both on the 27th. Sometime will you both plan to come up here for a day or a weekend that we know you are coming? It's getting cold now but will be lovely if you like autumn weather but the spring or summer may appeal to you more.

With sincerest thanks,

Cordially yours,

October 17, 1945

My dear Mrs. Roosevelt:

Thanks a lot for your cordial invitation to Hyde Park.

I am sincerely hoping that Mrs. Truman and I will be able to accept that invitation sometime in the not too far distant future.

We are looking forward to a pleasant visit with you on the twenty-seventh of October.

Sincerely yours,

November 1, 1945

Dear Mrs. Roosevelt:

It has just been called to my attention that your son Franklin had not been invited to the ceremonies aboard the *USS Franklin D. Roosevelt.*

I am deeply regretful at this oversight on the part of the navy officials in charge of the ceremony. I am glad that he finally was able to be present. He should, however, have been seated next to you on the platform.

I am sure, from long experience, you know how difficult it is to keep all of these things straight.

With kindest regards,

Very cordially,

November 4, 1945

Dear Mr. President:

It was more than kind of you to write to me. Franklin, Junior, had wonderful seats and neither of us could have expected more at the ceremonies aboard the USS *Franklin D. Roosevelt*. The officers couldn't have been more courteous before, as well as at the ceremonies.

Franklin, Junior, told me you thought I was upset, but I assure you I was not. Such occasions always seem formal to me and I behave accordingly, I imagine!

Please never worry about such little things as far as I am concerned.

With every good wish I am,

Very sincerely yours,

Franklin Jr., who looked a great deal like his father, served in the navy during World War II and received the Purple Heart, Silver Star, and Navy Cross for his combat service. He entered the navy as an ensign in 1944, and was discharged as lieutenant commander.

"One of the pleasant duties in the exacting life of a president is to award honors to our fighting men for courage and valor in war," Truman said at the New York Navy Yard. "In the commissioning of this ship, the American people are honoring a stalwart hero of this war who gave his life in the service of his country. His name is engraved on this great carrier, as it is in the hearts of men and women of goodwill the world over—Franklin D. Roosevelt."

November 1, 1945

My dear Mr. President:

I am very anxious that the Administration do all it possibly can in providing full employment. It seems to me if a group of people, such as those who worked for instance for special legislation in the past, might be framed within Mr. Snyder's office, they might do some very good work both for the people and with Congress to uphold your program.

I know that Mr. Allen works on legislation but I feel that no one man can possibly do all the work that needs to be done.

Very sincerely yours,

John W. Snyder (1895–1985), a St. Louis banker and one of Truman's closest friends and advisers, faced the challenge as director of reconversion of leading the nation from a wartime to a peacetime economy. George E. Allen (1896–1973), a lawyer and businessman, had been secretary of the Democratic National Committee since 1943. In this role, he advised President Roosevelt to choose Truman for the vice presidency. After Truman moved up to the presidency, Allen became one of his more influential advisers. He was the new president's chief lobbyist on Capitol Hill. Truman also assigned him to make recommendations on phasing out wartime agencies.

November 6, 1945

Dear Mrs. Roosevelt:

Thank you for your letter of November first. I am very hopeful that we can get the Congress to pass the major parts of the program announced in my message to the Congress of September sixth 1945. I am particularly hopeful that the Full Employment legislation will be passed, and am bending every effort to that end. You probably read my public statement about it in the Wage-Price policy speech of October thirtieth 1945. I am doing all I can privately to get the bill out of committee.

I have a small group of people working on different parts of the program both in Mr. Snyder's office and out of it. As you probably learned long ago, it is not easy to get the right kind of people with the correct social point of view who have influence with those congressmen who are blocking the program.

I wonder whether there is anyone in particular that you have in mind. I am most anxious to get the program adopted, and would be very thankful to you for any further suggestions you can make. I certainly hope you will continue to write me your views frankly from time to time.

With kind regards,

*The Employment Act of 1946, which Truman signed into law, made
it the policy of the federal government "to pursue all practicable means
. . . to promote maximum employment, production, and purchasing
power."*

November 20, 1945

Dear Mr. President:

I hope you will forgive my writing you this letter, but, I like a great
many other citizens have been deeply concerned about the situation as
it seems to be developing both at home and abroad. I have a deep sense
that we have an obligation first of all, to solve our own problems at
home, because our failure must of necessity, take away hope from the
other nations of the world who have so much more to contend with than
we have.

It seems to me, therefore, that we must go to work.

The suggestion that was made the other day that a survey of our
resources be made on which we base not only our national economy, but
what we lend to other nations, would seem to me sound, if the person
making the investigation had sufficient standing to be accepted by management and labor as well.

In situations of this kind, my husband sometimes turned to Mr.
Bernard Baruch, because of his wealth of experience and his standing with
the industrialists of the country. At the same time, I think that even the
young labor leaders, like Walter Reuther and James Carey, believe in his
integrity. If it could be possible to get the Detroit situation started up by
giving both management and labor something so they would at least
agree to work until, let us say, next October on condition that Mr. Baruch
was asked to gather a staff of experts, I feel he would consult with both
sides as he always has in the past.

If there was a limit for the time of the report, I think labor would not
feel that it was being taken for a ride.

When it comes to lending money, it seems to me that we should lend
to other nations equally. If we lend only to Great Britain, we enter into
an economic alliance against other nations, and our hope for the future

lies in joint cooperation. If we could only lend in small amounts at present, until we get into production we cannot sell to any of these countries in great quantities and there is no value in their having the money unless they can use it, it would be helpful. They would also profit by this type of survey and we would be making no promises we could not carry out.

If you talk to Mr. Baruch, I think you must do so only if you yourself, feel confidence in him, because once you accept him you will find, as my husband did, that many of those around you will at once cast doubts upon whatever he does, but that would be true even if the job were given to the Angel Gabriel.

I think Mr. Baruch has proved in the past his ability to see things on a large scale, and where financial matters are concerned, he certainly knows the world picture which is what we need at the present time.

I am very much distressed that Great Britain has made us take a share in another investigation of the few Jews remaining in Europe. If they are not to be allowed to enter Palestine, then certainly they could have been apportioned among the different United Nations and we would not have to continue to have on our consciences the deaths of at least fifty of those poor creatures daily.

The question between Palestine and the Arabs, of course, has always been complicated by oil deposits, and I suppose it always will. I do not happen to be a Zionist, and I know what a difference there is among such Jews as consider themselves nationals of other countries and not a separate nationality.

Great Britain is always anxious to have someone pull her chestnuts out of the fire, and though I am very fond of the British individually and like a great many of them I object very much to being used by them.

Lastly, I am deeply troubled by China. Unless we can stop the civil war there by moral pressure and not by the use of military force, and insist that Generalissimo Chiang give wider representation to all Chinese people, which will allow the middle of the road Democratic League to grow, I am very much afraid that continued war there may lead us to general war again.

Being a strong nation and having the greatest physical, mental and spiritual strength today, gives us a tremendous responsibility. We cannot use our strength to coerce, but if we are big enough, I think we can lead, but it will require great vision and understanding on our part. The first and foremost thing, it seems to me, is the setting of our own house in order, and so I have made the suggestions contained in the first part of this letter. I shall understand, however, if with the broader knowledge which is yours, you decide against it, but I would not have a quiet conscience unless I wrote you what I feel in these difficult times.

With every good wish, I am,

Very cordially yours,

November 26, 1945

Dear Mrs. Roosevelt:

Thanks very much for your letter of the twentieth, to which I have given much thought.

I have particularly had under consideration for some time the suggestion about a study of our national resources with a view to what we can afford to do. I think that is a very good suggestion, and expect to take some action on it.

I doubt very much whether that kind of study, however, would have much to do with the immediate situation in Detroit, although it is barely possible that it might influence the ultimate conclusion in a great many labor situations.

With respect to our foreign loans, I am sure that you have a deep appreciation of the reasons for our policy. We feel that it is necessary not only for the welfare of Great Britain but for our own welfare and for the welfare of the entire world that the British economy be not allowed to disintegrate. Equally important is the necessity of reestablishing world trade by helping the British expand their own trade instead of taking refuge in a tightened sterling bloc.

What we hope to do for Great Britain we also hope to do eventually for Russia and our other Allies, for it will be impossible to continue a stable world economy if a large part of the world has a disordered economy which would result in bitter trade rivalries and impassable barriers.

I'm very hopeful that we really shall be able to work out something in

Palestine which will be of lasting benefit. At the same time we expect to continue to do what we can to get as many Jews as possible into Palestine as quickly as possible, pending any final settlement.

In China, as you know, a definite commitment was made by the three major powers to support the Central Government in disarming and removing the Japanese troops now in China. I know you realize how important to the future peace in the Far East and throughout the world is this objective. All of us want to see a Chinese government eventually installed and maintained by free elections—one which will include all democratic elements. I do not see how we can do that unless we first help clear the land of the Japanese aggressors.

All of these things take a great deal of time as you know from personal experience. I am sure that it was the late President's experience, as it is mine, that we are very apt to meet criticism in the press and often in the Congress from those who are unfamiliar with the facts and to whom the facts cannot be disclosed. He often talked to me about how difficult that part of the Presidency was. However, I feel proud that our objectives are the same as those which actuated your late husband. Indeed I have no other aim than to carry them out.

I want you to know how much I appreciate your writing to me from time to time, and hope you will continue to do so.

With kindest regards,

Very sincerely,

———

New York
December 13, 1945

Dear Mr. President:

The United Feature Syndicate for whom I write my daily column has asked me again if I still plan to go to Russia in the spring, as they would have to start the machinery if I am to go.

I am very much interested in going unless something unforeseen happens, and I would like to go about the middle of March for about four or five weeks. This, however, may conflict with the other interest about which you telephoned me in reference to the United Nations Organization. I would feel that was the more important.

Could you tell me if there might be a conflict and whether I should keep my time fairly flexible for the spring? I would not want to make any definite commitments with regard to Russia and then have to give up the trip, as I think it might have a bad reaction.

I do not like to bother you with all of this, but I shall appreciate your advice.

Looking forward to seeing you and Mrs. Truman on January 7th, I am,

Very cordially yours,

December 17, 1945

Dear Mrs. Roosevelt:

Replying to yours about your proposed trip to Russia. I think you can go ahead with your arrangements for the trip in March, if you like, without interfering with the meetings of the United Nations Organization. The first meeting will be sometime in January and should not last over thirty days. It will be an organization meeting and will decide on the location in the United States, etc.

The next meeting will not come until the latter part of April which will give plenty of time for your trip. Hope you have a happy and pleasant one. I was highly pleased when you accepted the UNO appointment. I shall send the names down as soon as the House acts.

Hope you have a lovely Christmas.

Most sincerely,

December 18, 1945

Dear Mr. President:

I am enclosing a copy of a letter which has come to me, on which I have removed the name and address of the writer. He is an employee in close contact with these people and I thought the facts he gives should be brought to your attention.

Very sincerely yours,

December 21, 1945

My dear Mrs. Roosevelt:

I read your letter about the treatment of American-Japanese in the West with a lot of interest and have forwarded the letter to the Attorney General with a memorandum asking him to find a solution for it.

This disgraceful conduct almost makes you believe that a lot of our Americans have a streak of Nazi in them.

Sincerely yours,

On December 21, Truman wrote Attorney General Tom Clark: "I am enclosing you a letter which I have just received from Mrs. Roosevelt. I have read it and it certainly makes me feel ashamed. . . . Isn't there some way we can shame these people into doing the right thing by these loyal American-Japanese? I'll listen to any suggestion you may have to make on the subject." Clark ordered an immediate investigation of the hate crimes against Japanese reported in Mrs. Roosevelt's letter. On the attorney general's recommendation, Truman directed the Justice Department to launch a national investigation of violence and discrimination against Japanese Americans.

December 21, 1945

My dear Mrs. Roosevelt:

I am pleased to inform you that I have appointed you one of the representatives of the United States to the first part of the first session of the General Assembly of the United Nations to be held in London early in January 1946. A complete list of this government's delegation is enclosed herewith.

The United States representation at the first meeting of the General Assembly will be headed by the Secretary of State as senior representative or in his absence by the honorable Edward R. Stettinius, Jr.

In so far as the General Assembly will deal with matters covered by the report of the Preparatory Commission, the [actions of the United States on some issues] will be guided by my special instructions. I am, however, authorizing the senior representative after consulting with the other representatives to agree to modifications of the preparatory commission's recommendations which in his opinion may be wise and necessary.

In so far as matters may arise which are not covered by the report of the preparatory commission, I shall transmit through the senior representative any further instructions as to the position which should be taken by the representatives of the United States. I have instructed the senior representative to act as the principal spokesman for the United States in the General Assembly.

You, as a representative of the United States will bear the grave responsibility of demonstrating the wholehearted support which this government is pledged to give to the United Nations Organization, to that end that the organization can become the means of preserving the international peace and of creating conditions of mutual trust and economic and social well-being among all peoples of the world. I am confident that you will do your best to assist these purposes in the first meeting of the General Assembly.

Sincerely yours,

Several weeks earlier, Mrs. Roosevelt had demurred when Truman asked whether she would consider serving as one of the five American delegates. "Oh, no! It would be impossible. How could I be a delegate to help organize the United Nations when I have no background or experience in international meetings?" she said. At the president's urging, she agreed to think about it. "I knew that I believed the United Nations to be the one hope for a peaceful world," she later wrote. "I knew that my husband had placed great importance on the establishment of this world organization. So I felt a great sense of responsibility." Truman announced that Secretary of State James F. Byrnes would be heading a U.S. delegation that included UN Ambassador Edward Stettinius, Senators Tom Connally and Arthur Vandenberg, and Mrs. Roosevelt. The Wall Street lawyer and veteran diplomat John Foster Dulles was among five alternates nominated by Truman.

CHAPTER 2

1946

When Truman nominated Mrs. Roosevelt as a member of the U.S. delegation to the United Nations, she understood the symbolic importance of her appointment. "I knew that as the only woman I had better be better than anybody else," she recalled. "So I read every paper and they were very dull sometimes because State Department papers can be very dull. And I used to almost go to sleep over them. But I did read them all. I knew that if I in any way failed that it would not just be my failure. It would be the failure of all women and there would never be another woman on the delegation."

Senator Tom Connally of Texas, chairman of the Foreign Relations Committee, who was also a member of the U.S. delegation to the London conference, took a chauvinistic view about the participation of women in the United Nations. During the winter meeting, he told fellow delegates that he opposed granting membership to the World Federation of Trade Unions on the UN Economic and Social Council. If the trade federation gained admission, he solemnly warned, "all sorts of other groups, including women's organizations, would have to be taken in."

"Would you like to have a woman in here dictating to us what to do?" Connally asked. The other male members of the U.S. delegation had similar viewpoints.

By the spring of 1946, Mrs. Roosevelt had gained recognition as one of the more valuable members of the General Assembly. When the Nuclear Commission on Human Rights was established, she became its chairman. In this role she would have the responsibility for drafting an international bill of rights.

Eleanor did not approve of the anti-Soviet direction of U.S. foreign policy and blamed former British prime minister Winston Churchill. "It looks to me as tho' the President was running in Churchill's company too much," Mrs. Roosevelt wrote a friend, "and I am a bit nervous. FDR could cope with Churchill but he might fool someone not cognizant of world affairs." She became even more worried after Churchill, with Truman at his side, went to Fulton, Missouri, in March and called for an Anglo-American alliance to resist Soviet aggression. Mrs. Roosevelt said that the world should not be split "into armed camps."

Yet the more she dealt with the Soviet Union, the more frustrated she became. "No amount of argument ever changes what your Russian delegate says or how he votes," she wrote after the first session of the 1946 General Assembly. "It is the most exasperating thing in the world."

Truman appointed Mrs. Roosevelt's friend Bernard Baruch as U.S. representative to the United Nations Atomic Energy Commission in March of 1946. By the end of the year, Baruch proposed a plan for international control of atomic energy. "An armament race in an atomic world is unthinkable," Eleanor wrote in her column. The United Nations commission approved the Baruch plan, which was vetoed by the Soviets in the Security Council. In the wake of this veto, Mrs. Roosevelt had few illusions about Stalin and Foreign Minister V. M. Molotov.

Elliott Roosevelt's *As He Saw It*, which was published in the fall of 1946, accused Truman of squandering his father's legacy and blamed the United States and Great Britain for the collapse of their wartime alliance with the Soviet Union. "Somewhere, at some point in the months since Franklin Roosevelt's death, his brave beginning has been prejudiced," Elliott wrote. ". . . The peace is fast being lost." Mrs. Roosevelt, who wrote the book's foreword, disagreed with her son's instant analysis of the Cold War. "Naturally every human being reports the things which he sees and hears and lives through from his own point of view," she wrote. "Each personality leaves an impression on any situation and that is one reason why accounts of the same facts are often so varied. I am quite sure that many of the people who heard many of the conversations recorded herein, interpreted them differently, according to their own thoughts and beliefs." Her sons Franklin Jr. and James were appalled that Elliott had written a pro-Soviet apologia and disavowed his book. But when her cousins Joseph and Stewart Alsop wrote a column noting that Elliott's book had put him at odds with other members of his family, Mrs. Roosevelt defended her son.

In her correspondence with Truman, she never mentioned the controversial book. The president, though, had not heard the last from Mrs. Roosevelt's politically ambitious sons.

London
January 12, 1946

Dear Mr. President:

I want to thank you very much for the opportunity you have given me in being part of this delegation. It is a great privilege and my only fear is that I shall not be able to make enough of a contribution. I do feel, however, that you were very wise in thinking that anyone connected with my husband could, perhaps, by their presence here keep the level of his ideals. Just being here, perhaps, is a good reminder, which I think is what you had in mind.

I feel that the meeting is starting off with good feeling though there was a little difference of opinion over the election of the president of the Assembly.

I am sending a little note to General Eisenhower about a group of men who came to see me, representing soldiers of this area. They were very well behaved and, I thought, very logical. They said that the men with points below 45 realized that they had to stay here and were entirely reconciled; those with more than 60 had gone home; but those in between were very anxious to have a definite policy announced. A great many of them feel that more men are kept in the area than are really needed for the work and that this is done by officers who find their jobs not too unpleasant and like to have a good number of men under them. One boy said he would give anything to do one good day's work. I have had that said to me by a number of men, and written me by a number of them; and of course their living conditions are not pleasant as the officers'. I think, however, if it is possible for the War Department to give them some kind of a definite answer as to the plans made for bringing them home, it would make a great difference. One boy told me he had been six years in the army; he had volunteered for a year, here, after being in the Pacific, but he had been here a great deal longer than that and was now anxious to get home. They do feel that there is some injustice in the way people are sent home and that I know is difficult to eliminate in any great big undertaking. But certainly a clear and definite policy could now be formulated, and therefore in my note to General Eisenhower I am giving him the same information I am giving you in this letter. They are good boys but if they don't have enough to do they will get into trouble. That is the nature of boys, I am afraid in any situation.

With thanks and best wishes, I am,

Gratefully yours,

In London, more than five hundred American soldiers had protested the army's demobilization policy. Under this system, individuals rather than whole units were discharged on the basis of points for combat, overseas duty, military decorations, and parenthood.

February 2, 1946

Dear Mrs. Roosevelt:

I appreciate very much your good letter of January twelfth, which just now reached me.

I think you are doing a wonderful job with the United Nations. I really believe it has gotten off to a good start and, I am sure, its future is now assured.

Regarding your suggestion to General Eisenhower, since your letter was written he has enunciated a definite policy on the return and discharge of the remaining armed forces. Secretary Patterson has just returned from a tour around the world and expects to go on the radio with an explanation of the program. I think that will clear the matter up completely. Of course, it is a most difficult matter to discharge five and one-half million men in five months and not have some injustices.

All together the army and navy have discharged seven and one-half million soldiers and sailors since May first—a record unequaled in the history of the world. It has been done in a fairly orderly manner and with every effort possible for justice to the soldier and sailor. There was no way in the world to make a fair discharge system except on the point system. In World War I the army was demobilized by divisions. Two-year men and three-month men were discharged at the same time—that program could not be followed in this demobilization.

Another very great difficulty has been the demobilizing of experienced officers and noncommissioned officers, leaving us with an army of four million, at least half of it untrained, with practically new officers and noncommissioned officers.

We are now preparing to send home all the men in the Philippines, all those in Near East, all those in India, and all those in Great Britain by the first of July this year, provided we can dispose of surplus property in those areas. The occupation forces of Germany and Japan will each require about a quarter of a million men, and we will require at least a quarter of million at home to maintain and service those abroad.

I hope by June 30, 1947, to have the whole program completed.

One of the difficulties with which I have been faced has been the fact that the wars both ended suddenly, far in advance of the anticipated date, and while some preliminary work had been done on demobilization and occupation, we were still unprepared to meet the situation.

Considering everything, I think both the army and navy have done a remarkable job. One of the most difficult things always in demobilization of an army is to find competent and efficient leaders. As you know, from your long experience, that is true also in civil government. We are bound to make a lot of mistakes—it is customary also for the privates to throw bricks at their officers but you can't run an army without placing authority over it in somebody. I think our top leaders have been excellent—most of our division commanders have been good men but, in the service of supply, we have had difficulty because that end of the army has to be run more like a business than a military organization.

I am hoping though, by the thirtieth of June this year, we will have eliminated most of the trouble and injustices that were bound to take place on the point system discharge.

I am always happy to hear from you and appreciate your interest in what is taking place.

Sincerely yours,

February 18, 1946

Dear Mr. President:

I was told on my return that you had sent a beautiful wreath to be placed on my husband's grave on his birthday. I cannot tell you how deeply touched I am by your kind thought.

With my sincere thanks, I am,

Very sincerely yours,

———————

New York
March 1, 1946

Dear Mr. President:

As you requested, I am putting down a few of the things which I talked to you about on Wednesday.

I hope you can find the time to read this horribly long screed, and I make my profuse apologies for taking up so much of your very valuable time.

It was a pleasure to see you.

Very cordially yours,

———————

Memo for the president:

First—the economic situation in Europe.

I feel very strongly that it can not be handled piecemeal. For the safety of the world, we have decided to change the center of European economy from Germany. Much of coal and heavy industry emanated from Germany in the past. Now, as far as possible, Germany will be an agricultural nation. Unfortunately in giving Poland some of Germany's best land, we have complicated the industrial situation somewhat because she will have to have not only enough industry to meet her own internal needs, but enough industry to keep her people on a reasonable living basis which will mean a revival, at least, of the old toy industry and other light industries. When we made this situation, we also made the decision that Europe had to have in Great Britain, France, Holland, and other countries, the things which Germany had once provided.

Owing to the fact that this Second World War has done more than destroy material things, bad as that situation is in all these countries, a much greater responsibility is going to devolve on us not only materially but for leadership.

Great Britain is better off than the rest of Europe, but even in Great Britain our help in the provision of goods is going to be necessary. In Europe it will not only be the provision of goods without which loans would be merely a farce, since you can not start a factory with money alone—you have to have machinery. We will also have to provide skilled administrators and skilled technicians. This will be necessary because Germany in overrunning Europe wiped out one group of administrative officials, those who ran the towns and villages and cities, and those who ran the factories and business, etc. The Germans put in people whom they felt they could trust and they were usually efficient in large part. When we came and reconquered Europe we had to liquidate this second group and now there is no one left to take the leadership.

The young people returning from concentration camps and forced labor camps will nearly all of them spend some time in sanitariums, but they will not only have to rebuild their bodies. The suffering they have been through will have left a mark on their personalities.

I happen to remember the effect of unemployment and poverty in some of our mining areas in the depth of the Depression. It took several years for people to regain self-confidence and initiative, and that was not comparable to what these people in Europe have been through. That takes a large group out of the leadership area.

Amongst the resistance groups, you have young people who have missed out on five or six years of education which they must either now try to get or they must get something else which will make it possible for them to earn a living. Even more serious is the handicap that the virtues of life in the resistance during the invasion period have now become far from virtues in a peaceful civilization. Lying, cheating, stealing and even killing was what they had to do. Now these are criminal offenses!

The whole social structure of Europe is crumbling and we might as well face the fact that leadership must come from us or it will inevitably come from Russia. The economic problem is not one we can handle with a loan to Great Britain, a loan to France, a loan to Russia. It must be looked on as a whole. When we make the loans we must be prepared to send goods. This will mean very careful allocation over here so that our people will obtain only essentials and everything else, during the next couple of years, will go where it is needed even more.

The economic problem is tied up with the problem of food. You can not rehabilitate people and expect them to work unless they are getting an adequate diet. At present that is not possible anywhere in Europe and the Far East and shortly we are going to have a real famine in India, and Burma, I am told.

We are going to have to learn to stretch as we have never stretched before as far as food is concerned. I think we should begin an intensive campaign over the radio and in the newspapers to tell our people how to do this and to awaken in them a realization of the consequences, not per- haps this year or next, but five years hence if these people in Europe and Asia starve to death, or are not able to rehabilitate themselves and there- fore are not able to buy some of our goods when our own savings have been spent. Even more serious is the threat of epidemics to world health, since starvation saps resistance to disease and there are no real bound- aries today which will protect us if epidemics get started.

Second—Russia.

I do not feel that there is any mystery about Russia as Senator Van- denberg in his speech indicated. I liked his speech as a whole very much, but these unanswered questions I think may lead to the flaming of uncertainty in this country which I think is one of the things we do not wish to do.

In a great country like the USSR where her soldiers for the first time have discovered what other people have in the way of consumer goods, it must be realized that in one way or another, all people being human beings, they are going to demand the satisfying of the normal desires of people for better living. For that reason I think that intelligent people at the head of their government are anxious to establish economic condi- tions which will allow them to import and export without difficulty. Hence the agitation in Iran, the Dardanelles, etc. They are going to ask for political control to safeguard economic agreements but it is security in the economic situation that they seek. They must have it to secure political security at home but I do not think the political controls abroad are their first considerations.

Along the European border of the USSR, however, she is chiefly concerned with her military security. That is why she will try to control the governments of the nations in all those areas and why she dreads seeing Germany built up as an industrial power against her. She will liquidate or allow governments under her control to liquidate any of the displaced people now outside her borders if they show signs of dissatisfaction or unrest against her control in these countries. She has not enough real security and stability to live with an opposition at home and this is difficult for us to understand. We have had no political refugees in our country since the days of the Civil War. The opposition is always in our midst and frequent changes occur, but we do it through the ballot and peacefully. They do it through revolution and the use of force. This is largely a question of maturity and, of course, trust in the people themselves and not such great dependence on the absolute control on the head of the government.

It will take some time for Russia to achieve this, but there is no reason why we should not explain this to her. It will have to be stressed for her that the vast majority of displaced people in Europe today who long to go back to the countries of their origin, must be able to go back in safety and have enough freedom within their countries to feel that they control their national government internally, and their association with the Soviets is exclusively a real protection for the future.

This holds good for what we call the Balts who are people from Estonia, Latvia, Lithuania, and also for many Ukranians outside of Ukraine today.

Poland has several factions and people are going back, if they are not shot by one faction are afraid of being shot by the other. I suppose this holds good and will hold good for some of the other countries. Czechoslovakia seems to have worked out under Dr. Benes, a fairly satisfactory kind of government for everyone concerned. She does not, however, seem to feel free to differ with the Soviets judging by the way Masaryk voted and that is because the Soviets haven't really been strong enough to explain that they are willing to have people do what they think is right and they will not attribute to them any less fundamental agreement amongst themselves.

I think we should get a very much better understanding of the displaced persons situation but perhaps that can wait until the committee on refugees makes its report to the UNO [United Nations Organization]. It might be well to prepare our people for the report, however, and also to make clear why certain things have to be said to Russia.

Third—Mr. Winant.

If Mr. John G. Winant could be made our permanent member on the Economic and Security Council, I think he could make the most valuable contribution of anyone I know because of his long association with the Europeans on the ILO [International Labor Organization in Geneva], and as ambassador to London. He is really liked and trusted. I know that there are some stories circulated about him, but I am quite sure that he is fundamentally a loyal and honest person. I should like you to give him a chance to tell his side of any stories if they should be brought up as a reason for not appointing him.

Fourth—Food.

I wonder if in your food production program, we could not enlist the cooperation of South America and possibly increase their production by allocating to them some agricultural machinery?

Fifth—Mr. David Gray.

Mr. David Gray, our minister to Ireland, asked me to give you his regards and to tell you we were going on leading the fight to have the Irish turn over the German diplomatic people to the courts as has been requested. Ireland is a curious country and even the Catholic Church situation is different from anywhere else in the world. I hope if Mr. Gray does get permission to return for a time this spring that you will allow him an opportunity to tell you about their very peculiar politics.

Now I must say something to you which I hate to say because I think you have so many troubles and I am conscious of them.

I know that in naming Mr. Pauley you were doing what Mr. Hannegan quite naturally asked you to do. I remember very well the pressure under which my own husband was placed and his agreement to name Mr. Pauley as Assistant Secretary of the Navy, and then we had a long discussion about it because I was very much opposed to having Mr. Pauley in any position where oil could be involved. Franklin assured me that if he put Mr. Pauley in as Assistant Secretary of the Navy, he would have nothing to do with oil because Mr. Forrestal would be over him and he would never be a secretary.

I have seen in the papers both that Franklin had agreed to appointing him as Assistant Secretary and that he was to succeed Mr. Forrestal. I have been thanking my lucky stars that nobody asked me how I felt on this, as I would hate to have to say that I was opposed to his appointment, but I feel it only honest to tell you how very strong my opposition is. I know Mr. Pauley did a remarkable job in raising money for the Democratic National Committee, but he was in a position to do that job legitimately, and I am not sure that it was always done with the strictest of ethical considerations in the forefront.

Any President frequently suffers from his friends as much as from his enemies, and it is the sense of loyalty and gratitude which often gets men in public life into the greatest of trouble. In this case, I think you would be bringing on yourself unnecessary anxiety and trouble if Mr. Pauley should by chance get through. He may not want an ambassadorship, but that would be considerably safer if he was not sent to a country that dealt with oil.

Mrs. Roosevelt favored a plan developed by former treasury secretary Henry Morgenthau Jr. that would have destroyed Germany's industrial capacity and reduced it to a pastoral and agricultural state. "Such a program could starve Germany to death," Truman wrote in his memoirs. "That would have been an act of revenge, and too many peace treaties had been based on that spirit." Mrs. Roosevelt thought Germany deserved harsh treatment. "Anyone who looks at the German people knows that they have suffered less than any people in Europe," she wrote in her column. "What are we doing? Are we planning to make them strong again so we can have another war?"

Truman agreed with Mrs. Roosevelt's recommendation that the

United States had a vital interest in rebuilding war-torn Europe. The Marshall Plan would be the culmination of this effort. As for the European food crisis, Truman named former president Herbert Hoover as chairman of the Famine Emergency Committee. In this task, Hoover did a great deal of good.

Mrs. Roosevelt, who valued the Soviet Union's role in the Allied victory, was more optimistic than Truman about future dealings with the Kremlin.

Winant, a liberal Republican and former three-term New Hampshire governor, served as ambassador to the Court of St. James from 1941 until 1946. In this position he did much to help consolidate the wartime alliance between Roosevelt and Churchill. FDR gave serious thought to naming Winant as his running mate in 1944, which would have meant that he rather than Truman would have assumed the presidency. Winant, who had served in the thirties as assistant director of the International Labor Organization, an agency of the League of Nations, had hoped to become the first secretary-general of the United Nations. Norway's Trygve Lie, though, gained this distinction. The "stories" to which Mrs. Roosevelt referred were that Winant had passed some bad checks while serving as ambassador. Even so, he remained popular with the British. Truman named him in 1946 as U.S. representative to the United Nations Economic and Social Council.

Edwin W. Pauley, a self-made millionaire and oil tycoon, had served as FDR's wartime envoy to the Allies on Lend-Lease tanker exchanges. One of the Democratic Party's top fund-raisers, Pauley had promoted Truman for the vice presidency. In January of 1946, Truman repaid the favor by nominating him for undersecretary of the navy. Before his death, Roosevelt had discussed Pauley for this slot and asked for Truman's help in winning Senate confirmation. So Mrs. Roosevelt's opposition jolted Truman. Another FDR stalwart, Interior Secretary Harold Ickes, quit the cabinet over the Pauley nomination.

March 11, 1946

My dear Mrs. Roosevelt:

I appreciated very much your note of the sixth regarding chairman-ship for the food drive.

I have asked the Secretary of Agriculture, the Secretary of Commerce, and Mr. Herbert Hoover to act as a committee for implementing the food drive. I have forwarded a copy of your note to Mr. Anderson, who is the chairman.

Thank you so much for your interest in this program,

Sincerely yours,

In the 1940s, Henry J. Kaiser became known as the nation's "Miracle Man" and "Number One Industrial Hero" for building a steel industry on the West Coast and developing a new automobile company. A White House favorite during the Roosevelt years, Kaiser made the list of FDR's potential running mates in 1944. The plainspoken Truman did not hold Kaiser in similar esteem and privately referred to him as a "piss-cutter."

New York
March 14, 1946

Dear Mr. President:

I know you are planning to attend the ceremonies at Hyde Park on April 12th, and I should like to know if there is any way in which I could make your trip more comfortable. How many will be in your party? I understand it may not be possible for Mrs. Truman to accompany you.

In view of the fact that Mr. Ickes had so much to do with the house and grounds in the beginning, I wonder if it would cause you the slight-est embarrassment if I were to ask Mr. and Mrs. Ickes to attend the cere-monies? I consider them my personal friends and would like to ask them to be present if it is agreeable to you.

Very cordially yours,

March 7, 1!

Dear Mrs. Roosevelt:

Thanks a lot for all your trouble in sending me the memorandum
your visit to London. I read it with a lot of interest and it will be helpf
to me.

I am sorry about the Pauley matter but I merely thought I was carry
ing out the Program. Personally I think very highly of Pauley and
think he is an honest man.

I sincerely hope we can get this United Nations program imple-
mented so it will work, and I know we can do it if we make up our minds
to do it. Your suggestion on the financing and rehabilitation of Europe is
most interesting. It certainly was a pleasure to me to have an opportunity to discuss the situation with you the other day.

Sincerely yours,

*Soon afterward, Pauley asked to have his nomination withdrawn. A dis-
appointed Truman thought his friend had been wronged. The president
accused Pauley's critics of waging a campaign of vilification and base-
less charges.*

New York
March 6, 1946

Dear Mr. President:

I have just been over the plans which are ready to continue the United
Nations Relief and Rehabilitation Administration clothing drive which
was conducted by Mr. Kaiser and turned into the United Nations food
collection drive.

I think they have a broader setup and probably can do the best work of
any group in this country. They must however have a chairman and I am
wondering if Mr. Kaiser will again be chairman or if you are thinking of
someone else? The sooner they get started the better.

I am deluged with letters from people wanting to do something to
help and this will give these people an outlet as soon as it is regularly
started.

Very sincerely yours,

March 19, 1946

Dear Mrs. Roosevelt:

I am expecting to attend the ceremony at Hyde Park and to make a short address. I will have my military and naval aides, Mr. Ross, and possibly some members of the Roosevelt Memorial Foundation, if they are able to come.

Of course, I'll be most happy to have you invite Mr. and Mrs. Ickes. I never had any quarrel with Mr. Ickes—the quarrel was all on his side. He raised all the fuss and caused all the trouble himself and I regretted it but, under the circumstances, there was nothing for me to do but let him quit. As you know, he had been trying diligently to quit ever since April twelfth but I always had great admiration for him and thought he was a good public servant. Apparently his idea was to take himself out in a blaze of glory at the expense of the administration, which he was supposed to support. I regretted that very much.

I am looking forward to a most pleasant visit with you on the twelfth.

Sincerely yours,

Truman regarded Ickes as a schemer and faker. During the Pauley controversy, Ickes went before the Senate Naval Affairs Committee and testified that Pauley had told Democratic leaders in 1944 that he could raise $300,000 for their campaign war chest if they would drop federal claims to offshore oil lands. Instead of calling this to public attention at the time, Ickes waited for two years until Pauley faced Senate confirmation. Ickes was seeking to transfer control of the oil reserves from the navy to the Interior Department. Truman thought that Ickes was overreaching. Before Ickes testified on the Pauley nomination, Truman advised him to be truthful but if possible to give Pauley the benefit of the doubt. Ickes told senators that Pauley had dubious ethics and implied that Truman had sought to muzzle him. When Truman stood by his nominee, Ickes announced that he would quit "rather than commit perjury for the sake of the party." Truman gladly accepted the resignation and gave Ickes three days to move out of the Interior Department.

Despite this bad blood, Truman recognized that Ickes had been close to the Roosevelts and could not object to his presence at Hyde Park.

When Ickes did not attend, the columnist Drew Pearson erroneously reported that Truman had kept him from coming.

————————

March 13, 1946

Deeply appreciate your telegram asking me to serve as member Famine Emergency Council. But regret I belong to no organizations and am going to West Coast for two weeks so cannot serve in organization work. Will talk and write on subject and do all I can that way.

Eleanor Roosevelt

————————

March 19, 1946

Dear Mrs. Roosevelt:

I wish to thank you sincerely for your telegram of March thirteenth, telling of your readiness to help in the work of the National Famine Emergency Council.

I note particularly your readiness to talk and write on the subject and do all you can in a personal way. That is exactly what I had hoped for. In that way you can do a great deal of good. I do not feel that the inability to serve in organization work which you mentioned will be a handicap, and since the Council plans no general meetings, your trip to the West Coast will not interfere.

Again I wish to thank you for your prompt and wholehearted expression of cooperation.

Very sincerely yours,

————————

April 27, 1946

Dear Mr. President:

I am sending you this report and I shall appreciate it if you will return it to me after you have read it. The author was one of the economic advisers in Europe and has had a long experience in Europe in the past.

Mr. Baruch tells me that what he has to say is undoubtedly true. I have always known that a certain group in Great Britain will try to bolster Germany's economy as they are really afraid of a strong Russia because that group in Great Britain is more afraid of economic change than anything else. I am also afraid that Mr. Murphy, our representative in Germany, has always played with this group and this line of thought. From my point of view it threatens not only the peace of Europe but of the world. Therefore I have the temerity to send this report and to ask you to read it through.

I am also enclosing a newspaper clipping about your telegram to Abraham Flaxer of the New York SCMWA. What you say in your telegram is of course, absolutely right but, I wish you had been able to say it in some other way. I doubt whether Mr. Schwellenbach is familiar enough with labor leaders to know who among them are the Communists and who are not or surely he would have told you. In the Department of Labor there are people who know and there should be some one among your executive assistants who are close enough to labor to know.

There are many of the labor leaders who are accused of being Communists and then deny it, and then of course, there is always a question, but Abraham Flaxer never denied it, so it would seem to me to have been unwise to have sent a telegram to him when the same end could have been achieved in some other way.

As you know, I want friendly relationships with Russia but I certainly do not want red baiting accusing people of being Communists, or accusing them for other reasons, using the Communist claim, but this whole business in the labor movement is one that should be carefully watched and handled and there should be somebody to watch it for you.

Very cordially yours,

May 1, 1946

Dear Mrs. Roosevelt:

I am indebted to you for making it possible for me to read that report, which in compliance with your request, I am returning herewith. The facts developed in the report should give us pause. They give force to the warning in Macbeth that "we have scotch'd the snake, not killed it."

I have brought the document to the attention of Mr. Snyder, director, War Mobilization and Reconversion, and desire to assure you that its ominous disclosures will not be overlooked.

Very sincerely yours,

Mrs. Roosevelt believed that the struggle over Germany was a threat to the stability of postwar Europe and world peace. Robert D. Murphy (1894–1978), who had been among FDR's more versatile diplomatic troubleshooters, served as political adviser to General Lucius Clay, military governor of occupied Germany.

Federal judge Lewis B. Schwellenbach (1874–1948), one of Truman's former Senate colleagues, was chosen by the president to succeed Frances Perkins as labor secretary. Like Mrs. Roosevelt he sought to reduce the influence of communism in the labor movement. But she disagreed with his later effort to outlaw the Communist Party.

New York
May 27, 1946

Dear Mr. President:

I was immensely impressed by your speech before the Congress, and I realize what very great burdens these last few weeks have put upon you. My admiration is great for the way in which you have acted in the public interest and ignored the political considerations.

You will forgive me, I hope, if I say that I hope you realize that there must not be any slip, because of the difficulties of our peacetime situation, into a military way of thinking, which is not natural to us as people. I have seen my husband receive much advice from his military advisers and succumb to it every now and then, but the people as a whole do not like it even in wartime, and in peacetime military domination goes against the grain. I hope now that your anxiety is somewhat lessened, you will not insist upon a peacetime draft into the army of strikers. That seems to me a dangerous precedent.

I am also a little bit troubled over the reorganization of the Labor Department which will divide some of the functions of the Children's Bureau. Many of us who worked for the establishment of the Children's

Bureau are deeply concerned that in this reorganization it should at least become more efficient and not less efficient.

I know the various arguments because in previous plans for reorganization, Mr. Smith of the Budget Bureau, my husband and various others, discussed these questions at length. I think it is logical to move it under Social Security and I hope that it will remain with Miss Lenroot who has shown her capacity and ability to run it successfully, intact enough so that the main operations go on and perhaps only such things as deal directly with labor are taken away. I hope you have talked the whole thing over with Miss Lenroot and with some of the other people in her department who have worked for a long while on these questions.

The Children's Bureau is close to the hearts of many of the women in organized groups throughout the nation and they will be deeply interested in the outcome of whatever you do.

Politically you are going to need the women if you decide to run in 1948 and if you decide not to run, whoever is nominated will go down to defeat unless the great mass of women, both Republican and Democrat, backs him in the next campaign.

With my congratulations on your courage and all good wishes, I am,

Very cordially yours,

In the first six months of the postwar era, more than 2 million American workers went on strike. A railroad strike threatened to paralyze the nation's transportation system. Truman ordered the government to take control of the railroads and asked Congress for authority to draft striking workers. As he appeared before a joint congressional session, Truman learned that a settlement had been achieved. Mrs. Roosevelt thought the president had overreacted. Organized labor would retaliate by sitting out the 1946 midterm elections.

June 10, 1946

Dear Mrs. Roosevelt:

I hope you will pardon my delay in answering your letter of May twenty-seventh, but as you can well imagine I have been quite busy.

It is very heartening to get your kind expressions with reference to some of the recent events in Washington. I have tried to carry out what I think is the best interests of the nation as a whole. I am sure that I have succeeded in wiping from my own mind any thought of the political considerations involved.

The dangers to our whole economic system stemming from the stagnation of the railroads were so great that there was no room for any politics. I am afraid, however, that in some quarters the old criterion of politics was still quite important.

As you know, the Senate has removed from the bill the provision for drafting strikers against the government. I assure you that it was not easy for me to recommend such legislation. I tried to hedge it around with as many safeguards as possible. Among those safeguards was a limitation of its provisions to a handful of national industries in which a stoppage of work would affect our entire economy. There was also the limitation that its provisions could be made applicable only to those industries which already had been taken over by the government. I am afraid that the Senate has taken all of the teeth out of the proposed emergency legislation.

It is difficult to understand how the Congress can expect the President adequately to cope with emergencies such as faced this country ten days ago when the railroads were stalled, when the coal mines were in great danger of being closed down, and when a general shipping strike was imminent.

I am glad that you approve of moving the Children's Bureau over to the Federal Security Agency. I, too, have been much impressed by the work of the Children's Bureau. I certainly do not think its activities should be curtailed in any way. I expect to talk to Miss Lenroot about the situation.

I welcome your advice and suggestions, and hope you will continue to write to me.

With kindest personal regards,

Sincerely yours,

Hyde Park
June 1, 1946

Dear Mr. President:

I read in the papers this morning that Mr. Stettinius' resignation has really come in and that you and Secretary Byrnes hope he will reconsider.

I am wondering just what his reasons are, but in any case I feel there is no one who has had his long experience, nor been as devoted to the ideal of the United Nations, and if it is possible for you and Secretary Byrnes to get him to continue, I think it will keep a great many of us from feeling that the cause is a lost cause.

I cannot help feeling that we need to be firm but we haven't always been firm in the right way in our foreign policy because one can only be successfully firm, if the people one is firm with, particularly the Russians, have complete confidence in one's integrity and I am not sure that our attitude on questions like Spain and the Argentine and even in Germany itself, has been conducive to creating a feeling that we would always keep our word and that we would always talk things out absolutely sincerely before we took action. We are bound to differ, of course, because we have fundamental differences, but I think these should be made clear. If at the top there was a complete sense of confidence and security and the policies at the top were really carried on at every level things might go better.

Very cordially yours,

June 4, 1946

Dear Mrs. Roosevelt:

I appreciated very much your good letter of the first and nobody was more surprised than I when I received the letter from Stettinius that he wanted to quit as representative of the United Nations Security Council. I urged him to stay but he was very anxious to quit, saying that he felt his job with the United Nations had been completed. I don't think it has but there is no way I can force a man to stay on the job if he doesn't want to stay.

I am truly sorry that you are not pleased with the attitude of the

United States toward Spain, Argentine, and Germany. Certainly we are trying to be consistent in these matters and are making every effort possible to get the United Nations on its feet as an active organization. I think that is the most important thing we have ahead of us. Naturally we expected to have difficulty with the Russians, French, and British but none of the difficulties are insurmountable and I have every reason to believe that most of them will work out in a satisfactory manner. The conditions with which we are faced are not new as the result of the conflict—they are only greater in magnitude than they have been in the past because they are world-wide.

I do appreciate most sincerely your interest and your kindness in writing me. I'll be glad to hear from you on any subject at any time.

Sincerely yours,

Truman did not share Mrs. Roosevelt's high opinion of the former chairman of United States Steel. During the Roosevelt years, Stettinius had served as chairman of the War Resources Board, administrator of the Lend-Lease program, and undersecretary of state. In November 1944, FDR named him to replace the ailing Cordell Hull as secretary of state. Truman believed that Stettinius had been promoted beyond his abilities, and one of Truman's first decisions as president was to make a change at the State Department. Mrs. Roosevelt was disappointed by Truman's choice of James F. Byrnes, a former senator from South Carolina and former Supreme Court justice, who had also been FDR's deputy president. As a consolation prize, Stettinius got named as the nation's first permanent representative to the United Nations and hoped to remain a player in the shaping of U.S. foreign policy. When his advice was ignored, he became frustrated and resigned in June of 1946. Three years later he died of a heart attack at the age of forty-nine.

June 16, 1946

Dear Mr. President:

I have just been sent a copy of the report of the Survey Committee on Displaced Persons sponsored by the American Council of Voluntary Agencies for Foreign Service, Inc. The chairman of the council is Mr.

Joseph P. Chamberlain, whom you will know by reputation, as well as you will probably know Mr. Earl G. Harrison, chairman of the Committee on Displaced Persons.

It is too long a report for you to be bothered to read it. I had it briefed, however, and I think you might be interested in just glancing over the notes which were made for me and so I send them to you.

It seems to me that our refugee committee under the United Nations is going to advocate something very similar, but whether they do or not, it is perfectly obvious that we are going to have a combination or strengthening of some groups to finish up this job on displaced persons and, the sooner it is done, the better the whole situation will be in Europe and for that matter in the Far East.

I hope some of the congressional group will read this report because it is such a big job that we will need to think out very carefully how it can be accomplished in collaboration with other nations.

Very cordially yours,

———————

June 20, 1946

Dear Mrs. Roosevelt:

I appreciate very much your letter of the sixteenth in regard to the displaced persons situation. We are working on that problem as hard as we can—it is a difficult one to solve.

I was very happy and pleased at your sending me the digest of the report of the Survey Committee. It is most interesting.

Sincerely yours,

Joseph P. Chamberlain (1873–1951), a longtime advocate in behalf of Jewish refugees from Western Europe, helped thousands of displaced persons emigrate to the United States. Chamberlain, a professor of law at Columbia University, founded voluntary organizations to promote human rights, raised funds, and lobbied the government. Earl Harrison, dean of the University of Pennsylvania law school, was appointed by Truman in 1945 as chairman of a task force to investigate the condition of European refugees. Harrison reported that six hundred thousand refugees desperately needed help.

Hyde Park
June 30, 1946

Dear Mr. President:

I have just received an item from *Newsweek*, which states that you have told your advisors to be on the lookout for women qualified to take over several top jobs in the administration.

This item was sent to a friend of mine, who forwarded it to me, by the chairman of the Women's Congressional Committee, in Washington. This group represents a rather large number of women's organizations and I think among them there are several people who have been afraid that in the reorganization of the government, women were being eliminated from important jobs and functions, such as the Children's Bureau, which has been of particular interest to women, and in being integrated with other groups, were passing out of control of the women who had headed them and might be completely changed in their aims. This item will, I think, encourage them.

I used to have to remind the gentlemen of the party rather frequently that we Democrats did not win unless we had the liberals, labor, and women, largely with us. Among our best workers in all campaigns, are the women. They will do the dull detail work and fill the uninteresting speaking engagements which none of the men are willing to undertake. I hope you will impress this fact on those who are now organizing for the congressional campaigns and in preparation for 1948.

With every good wish I am,

Very cordially yours,

July 8, 1946

Dear Mrs. Roosevelt:

I appreciated very much yours of June thirtieth regarding the item in *Newsweek*.

I am hoping we can find some key positions for some of our able Democratic women.

I have been particularly interested in getting Mrs. Perkins placed but I haven't yet had a place I thought was equal to her ability, which I could offer her, and there are several others who ought to be in the Administration setup. I hope we can work it out.

Sincerely yours,

Truman often said that he put women "on a pedestal" and he was certainly devoted to his wife, Bess, and daughter, Margaret. He also greatly admired Mrs. Roosevelt. But he did not share her commitment to the political empowerment of women. Less than three months into his presidency, Truman eased out Perkins as labor secretary because, he privately acknowledged, he wanted only men in his cabinet. Though his predecessor and successor would each name a woman to their cabinet, Truman never did. In September of 1945, he appointed Perkins to the Civil Service Commission and she served for nearly eight years. In the first three years of Truman's administration, he named only three women to positions requiring Senate confirmation, compared with thirteen by FDR at a similar point. But partly because of Mrs. Roosevelt's influence, Truman improved on this record. By the end of his eight-year presidency, he had nominated eighteen women for offices requiring Senate confirmation, one more than FDR had named in twelve years. This included Eugenie Anderson as the first woman ambassador in American history. When Truman was asked to consider making history by nominating Frances Allen, then a federal judge, for the Supreme Court, he demurred. Truman confided to an aide, "The justices don't want a woman [on the high court]. They said they couldn't sit around with their robes off, and their feet up, and discuss their problems."

July 18, 1946

Dear Mrs. Roosevelt:

As one of the representatives of the United States to the first part of the first session of the General Assembly of the United Nations, you made a contribution of great importance to the successful establishment of the United Nations as a functioning organization and to the leadership exercised by the United States in its affairs. I take pleasure in informing you that I have reappointed you to serve as a representative of the United States to the second part of this first session, which is now scheduled to convene in New York in September 1946. A complete list of the persons I am now appointing to this government's delegation is enclosed.

I have asked the Honorable Warren R. Austin to act as senior representative and in that capacity, he will be the principal spokesman for the United States in the General Assembly. It is understood, of course, that the Secretary of State may himself attend part of the session and that while he is there he will be senior representative of the United States.

In accordance with the United Nations Participation Act of 1945, I shall transmit through the senior representative such instructions as may be necessary with respect to the casting of the vote of the United States in the General Assembly and its committees or other agencies. As to many matters which may come up, these instructions will vest considerable discretion in the senior representative to determine the position of the United States after consultation with the other representatives.

I have complete confidence that you will effectively discharge in the best interests of the United States and of the United Nations the most important responsibilities which this appointment will place upon you.

Very sincerely yours,

Hyde Park
July 22, 1946

Dear Mr. President:

The enclosed paragraph came in a letter from one of our boys who had been stationed for some time in China.

I thought it might interest you in view of the radio comment which I heard this morning on the statement by Mme. Sun Yat-sen. I have long believed that of all the Soong sisters, she is the most truly democratic and devoted to the well-being of her people. I would give considerable thought to what she says.

Very sincerely yours,

July 23, 1946

Dear Mr. President:

I received your letter about my appointment to serve on the second part of the first session of the General Assembly of the United Nations.

I will of course do the best I can to be a satisfactory representative and I am deeply honored by your appointment and this evident trust in me.

Very sincerely yours,

Adlai E. Stevenson of Illinois (1900–1965) and Representative Helen Gahagan Douglas of California (1900–1980), who were among Mrs. Roosevelt's favorite public officials, were named by Truman as alternate delegates to this session of the General Assembly.

———————

July 26, 1946

Dear Mrs. Roosevelt:

I appreciated your note of the twenty-second enclosing paragraph on the free interchange of students.

Nothing would please me better than to see that happen but it is going to take a lot of understanding and good will to make it work.

I also appreciate very much your statement about Mme. Sun Yat-sen.

It was a pleasure to reappoint you as a delegate on the second part of the First Session of General Assembly of the United Nations.

Sincerely yours,

Charles Jones Soong, founding father of a modern Chinese dynasty, converted to Christianity, moved to the United States in his youth, studied for the ministry at Vanderbilt, and returned to China as a missionary. He later made a fortune publishing Bibles and encouraged his children to seek positions of power and prominence. The eldest daughter married a wealthy banker who later became premier of China. Middle daughter Ch'ing-ling married Sun Yat-sen, founder of modern China and first president of the Chinese Republic. Soong's youngest daughter, Meiling, attended Wellesley and later became Madame Chiang Kai-

shek, the wife of China's leader. Her brother, T. V. Soong, was the long-time finance minister of Chiang's regime. By the summer of 1946, it was apparent that Chiang's Nationalist government was in trouble. Earlier in the year, Truman's administration had provided more than $1.5 billion in military aid and pipeline equipment to the Nationalists. General George C. Marshall, Truman's special envoy to China, sought to negotiate an end to the civil war. But neither Chiang nor his rival, Mao Tse-tung, gave Marshall much help.

September 27, 1946

Dear Mr. President:

I have just received a report from China which was sent to me by a friend in whom I have implicit confidence and she in turn vouches for the reliability of the person sending this information.

I thought you ought to see it.

Very cordially yours,

October 1, 1946

Dear Mrs. Roosevelt:

Thanks for your note of September twenty-seventh enclosing me a quotation on China, which I am glad to have.

It is a most difficult matter to find out really what the truth is in regard to this situation.

The great blow was the looting of the industrial plants of Manchuria and I have serious doubts about an industrial recovery in that part of the world in less than a generation. Of course, if they don't get their civil strife settled there never will be a recovery.

I still have faith in General Marshall.

Sincerely yours,

Mrs. Roosevelt had passed on another report about the corruption of Chiang Kai-shek's Nationalist regime. Like her husband, Truman wanted to extend Chiang's tenure as China's leader. But the Chinese economy was on the verge of collapse and the future of the Kuomintang was questionable at best. General Marshall, called out of retirement by Truman, sought to negotiate an end to the Chinese civil war.

———————

October 12, 1946

Dear Mr. President:

The birthday message from you and Mrs. Truman brought me a great deal of pleasure. It is always heart-warming to be remembered on one's birthday.

I am deeply appreciative of your kind thought and hope that I shall have the pleasure of seeing you and Mrs. Truman before too long.

Very cordially yours,

———————

New York
November 8, 1946

Dear Mr. President:

I know the election must have been a disappointment to you, as it was to me. I had expected some losses but not quite such sweeping ones.

However, I am not at all sure that you will not get as much out of a straight-out Republican Congress, which now has to take the responsibility for whatever happens, as you got out of the type of opposition which the coalition of reactionary Democrats and Republicans created.

With my very best wishes to you and my warm regards to Mrs. Truman and Margaret, I am,

Very cordially yours,

———————

November 14, 1946

Dear Mrs. Roosevelt:

I certainly appreciated your note on the election.

You are exactly right about the congressional situation—it couldn't be much worse than it was last winter. In fact, I think we will be in a position to get more things done for the welfare of the country, or at least to make a record of things recommended for the welfare of the country, than we would have been had we been responsible for a Congress which was not loyal to the party.

Mrs. Truman and Margaret want to be remembered.

Sincerely yours,

"Had enough?" was the GOP's slogan in the 1946 midterm elections, and the American voter answered in the affirmative. For the first time in sixteen years, the Republicans won both houses of Congress and a majority of the nation's governorships. The party holding the White House traditionally loses seats in the midterm elections. But the Democrats suffered even bigger losses because many voters were weary of labor troubles, inflation, food shortages, and black markets. Among the new faces of 1946 were freshmen congressmen John F. Kennedy of Massachusetts and Richard M. Nixon of California. "The New Deal as a driving force," the Chicago-Sun *asserted, "is dead within the Truman administration." But as luck would have it, Truman would turn this setback into an advantage by running against the "good-for-nothing, do-nothing Eightieth Congress" in his 1948 campaign.*

November 8, 1946

Dear Mr. President:

Things seem to be moving rather slowly in the United Nations. When I accepted membership on your Committee for Higher Education, I had thought that this Assembly meeting would not take place in September and it did not occur to me that there might be any conflict in the meetings of the Assembly and your Committee on Education.

To my regret, I am now worried for fear we will not be through in time for me to attend the meeting scheduled for December tenth and eleventh. I missed one meeting this summer and was unable to attend a subcommittee meeting.

I am writing you now so that there will be ample time for you to appoint someone who is free. I do not know whether you know Miss Charl Williams of the National Education Association. She was one of our first, if not the first, vice chairmen of the Democratic National Committee, and has been in educational work all of her life. She might be a useful member of the committee. However I am not making any specific recommendations.

I am very sorry indeed to have to withdraw from the Committee because it is something in which I am very much interested. I have just heard that I am to serve on the Human Rights Commission again and that the first meeting in 1947 will be in January.

Very cordially yours,

November 14, 1946

Dear Mrs. Roosevelt:

Replying to yours of the eighth regarding your position on the Education Committee, I sincerely hope that things will not interfere so you can't go through with that program.

I don't want to be selfish and appear to work you to death but it seems to me that for its first start you would be an ideal person to set the American policy.

Of course, if this interference with Assembly meetings becomes increasingly apparent, I'll be glad to consider your recommendation of Miss Williams. I hope, however, it will not be necessary for you to leave the Committee on Education.

Sincerely yours,

November 15, 1946

Dear Mr. President:

Many thanks for your letter in answer to mine about the Committee on Higher Education. Every day it seems to me less likely that we will be free in early December and today I was told that Mr. Spaak was setting the closing date for December fourteenth, which is after the date of your committee meeting in Washington.

I do not know that the members of the committee would like having Miss Williams as she represents more the point of view of the public school group, than does Mr. Brown, the secretary. I think it might be good leavening for them to have someone with that point of view.

I am sorry that I can not be more than one person, but I just do not see how I can be of service to you when I quite evidently will not be able to attend the next meeting on the ninth and tenth of December.

Very cordially yours,

In the summer of 1946, Mrs. Roosevelt was among thirty people named by Truman to the National Commission on Higher Education. George F. Zook, president of the American Council on Education, was the panel's chairman. Roosevelt refers in this letter to Paul-Henri Spaak of Belgium, the first president of the United Nations General Assembly.

New York
December 2, 1946

Dear Mr. President:

I am enclosing a letter and release which I received. I have been asked to write you about the conscientious objectors.

I think it might be wise to release these men who are still in prison.

Very sincerely yours,

December 6, 1946

Dear Mrs. Roosevelt:

I appreciate very much your note enclosing a letter from the Committee for Amnesty for all conscientious objectors. This matter is being worked out in the Justice Department on the basis of individual cases.

I don't think there should be a general release or pardon to those conscientious objectors who shirked their duty as citizens of the United States and profited by the actual risk of the men who were willing to fight.

Some of the conscientious objectors are honestly objectors—a great many just didn't want to fight and I know what I am talking about because I had experience with them in the first World War. We are trying our best to arrange matters so there will be no injustice done to any honest conscientious objector but the malingerers should have all that is coming to them.

Sincerely yours,

P.S. The most sincere conscientious objector I ever have met was one on whom I placed a Congressional Medal of Honor, not long ago. He served in the Medical Corps of the Navy and carried wounded marines and sailors to safety on Okinawa under fire. He was a real conscientious objector who believed the welfare of his country came first. I shall never forget what he said to me when I fastened the medal around his neck. He said he could do the Lord's work under fire as well as anywhere else.

Mrs. Roosevelt enclosed a letter from the Committee for Amnesty in New York, which was chaired by the labor and peace activist A. J. Muste. From 1940 through 1953, he had major influence as executive director of the Fellowship of Reconciliation, a group that advocated resolving labor disputes and social conflicts through nonviolence. Muste, who had been a Protestant minister, became disillusioned with the organized church when most denominations supported America's participation in two world wars. Truman had little sympathy for Muste's amnesty campaign. This is the first of two references that Truman makes in this volume to Private Desmond T. Doss of Lynchburg, Virginia, whose acts of valor on Okinawa earned him the nation's highest military honor. No other conscientious objector had ever received the Congressional Medal of Honor.

December 19, 1946

Dear Mr. President:

I expect to be in Washington to keep a few engagements from the second to the fifth of January and I should appreciate it very much if I could have the opportunity of talking with you.

Would any time in the afternoon of the third be convenient for you? I am lunching with a group in the State Department that day.

With my best wishes to you and Mrs. Truman and Margaret for a Merry Christmas and a Happy New Year, I am,

Very cordially yours,

December 23, 1946

Dear Mrs. Roosevelt:

I'll be happy to see you any time that is convenient to you on the third. Three o'clock on the afternoon of the third will be entirely satisfactory to me if that will meet with your plans. I shall be most happy to see you.

I sincerely hope that you have the happiest sort of a Christmas and a successful and prosperous New Year.

Sincerely yours,

CHAPTER 3

1947

In January of 1947, General George C. Marshall (1880–1959) succeeded Byrnes as secretary of state. As the chief of staff during World War II, he played a major role in planning Allied strategy on a global scale. Churchill paid tribute to him as "the true organizer of victory." Working with Truman, General Marshall developed a program to rebuild war-torn Europe. Mrs. Roosevelt welcomed this change at the State Department and hailed the Marshall Plan.

On January 27, the first session of the Human Rights Commission convened at Lake Success, Long Island. Eleanor was unanimously chosen as the chairman of the eighteen-nation panel. Under the direction of John Humphrey, a Canadian specialist in international law, the commission began preparing the Universal Declaration of Human Rights. "The work in this period was an intense education for me in many ways, including constitutional law," Mrs. Roosevelt later wrote, "and I would not have been able to do much but for the able advisers who worked with me."

Though grateful that Truman backed her efforts at the United Nations, Mrs. Roosevelt did not hesitate to publicly dissent when she thought the administration was wrong. She disagreed with the Truman Doctrine, the president's pledge of military and economic aid to Greece and Turkey. It would have been better, she argued, if Truman had made his case to the United Nations instead of going it alone. "Feeling as I do that our hope for peace lies in the United Nations," she wrote in her column, "I naturally grieve to see this country do anything which harms the strength of the UN."

During her husband's administration, Mrs. Roosevelt had become an outspoken champion of civil rights. But FDR, whose political coalition included the segregationist South, had given little priority to the struggle for racial equality. Early in the Truman presidency, Mrs. Roosevelt challenged American political leaders to do better: "If we really believe in Democracy we must face the fact that equality of opportunity is basic to any kind of Democracy. Equality of opportunity means that all of our people, not just white people, but all of our people must have decent homes, a decent standard of health and educational opportunities to develop their abilities as far as they are able."

Truman, who had been greatly disturbed by mob violence against black veterans, proved to be as bold in the field of civil rights as his predecessor had been timid. In June of 1947, with Mrs. Roosevelt at his side, he became the first president to address the National Association for the Advancement of Colored People. "It is my deep conviction that we have reached a turning point in the long history of our country's efforts to guarantee freedom and equality to all our citizens," he said. "Recent events in the United States and abroad have made us realize that it is more important today than ever before to insure that all Americans enjoy these rights. When I say all Americans, I mean all Americans."

As much as she admired Truman's civil rights leadership, Eleanor viewed his loyalty program as repressive. She was disappointed that her old friend Henry A. Wallace had allowed himself to be used by the Communist Party. Mrs. Roosevelt was the keynote speaker at the founding meeting of the Americans for Democratic Action, which was established as a liberal alternative to Wallace's Progressive Citizens of America.

Late in the year, Mrs. Roosevelt wrote Truman: "It happens that I have given up any activities with the Progressive Citizens of America because I am convinced that there are people in the top levels of that organization that still are clearly connected with the Communist Party in this country or are too chicken-hearted and afraid of being called redbaiters. Therefore, they serve the purposes of the party."

But she then noted the absurdity of guilt by association: "I remember when my husband and I heard about a list the FBI had of organizations that were considered subversive and anyone who had contributed to these organizations was automatically considered to be questionable. My husband told me I could ask to see it and we spent an evening going through it and believe it or not, my husband's mother was one of the first people named because she had contributed to a Chinese relief organization and both Secretary Stimson and Secretary Knox were listed as having contributed to several organizations. . . . Forgive me for writing a long letter again but I have been troubled by what looks like a real chance that some of the methods of the Russians might be coming our way."

January 7, 1947

Dear Mr. President:

I have enclosed an appeal I recently received from a group of interned illegal Jewish homeless immigrants on Ellis Island and wonder if anything can be done to prevent their deportation?

With every good wish, I am,

Yours very sincerely,

———————

January 16, 1947

My dear Mrs. Roosevelt:

This is in reply to your letter of January seventh in which you enclosed a letter of appeal sent to you by a group of Jewish stowaways who are now detained on Ellis Island.

I have taken this matter up with the Attorney General and he has carefully gone into the problem with the Immigration and Naturalization Service. These boys are a part of a large group of stowaways who arrived in this country during 1946. Under the immigration law, of course, they are required to be returned, at the expense of the steamship company, to the ports of their embarkation.

The Attorney General advised me that because of the increase in the number of stowaways since the end of the war he initiated a survey to ascertain if there was any basis for relief. I am also advised that a Special Committee of the 79th Congress appointed from the House Committee on Immigration and Naturalization conducted an investigation of this situation at the Port of New York where the problem is most acute, and thereafter submitted a bill to the Committee for strengthening the existing immigration law pertaining to the exclusion of stowaways. In view of this it is the Attorney General's opinion that since lawful immigration is so urgently needed by so many displaced persons, the greatest good for the greatest number can only be accommodated by lending all the facilities of our Government to lawful immigration and following a policy of strict exclusion of the illegal or stowaway immigrants.

As you know, in my recent message to the Congress I emphasized the duty of the United States to accept its portion of the world's burden as to displaced persons and urged the Congress to consider appropriate legislation to enable a greater number of displaced persons to lawfully immigrate to the United States. I believe such a measure is of paramount importance and, as much as I am sympathetic with the plight of these particular stowaways, I am, nevertheless, of the opinion that their individual cases must give way to the larger problem of the many thousands of homeless people in Europe who seek to come to the United States as legal immigrants.

I am always grateful to you for your vigilant interest in matters of this kind. I am returning herewith the enclosure with your letter.

Very sincerely yours,

January 20, 1947

Dear Mr. President:

I appreciate your answering my letter about the Jewish stowaways and I can fully understand the situation.

With many thanks and best wishes,

Very sincerely,

Truman said in his 1947 State of the Union message that the United States should liberalize immigration law to provide for the admission of World War II refugees: "I urge the Congress to turn its attention to this world problem, in an effort to find ways whereby we can fulfill our responsibilities to these thousands of homeless and suffering refugees of all faiths."

January 8, 1947

Dear Mr. President:

You will remember that I told you how sorry I was that John Winant resigned from the Economic and Social Council.

I have heard from people here Herbert Lehman might be interested in taking that work. I know that Mr. Byrnes hoped that it would be Mr. La Follette. I am just passing along the suggestion of Herbert Lehman because he seems to me far better fitted than anyone else, if he is willing to consider it.

I am not, of course, asking for any favor, I am simply passing on the information in case it is helpful to you. Mr. Lehman's contacts and knowledge of people and countries in the whole world would be helpful to a new member of the Economic and Social Council.

Very cordially yours,

January 13, 1947

My dear Mrs. Roosevelt:

I appreciated very much your note of the eighth in regard to Mr. Lehman.

I think very highly of Governor Lehman and I wish I had known of his interest before I had made some commitments on Winant's successor. As it is, I'm tied up in such a way that I can't offer him a job at present.

I turned your letter regarding the Jewish matter over to the Attorney General and he is getting me the facts on it.

Sincerely yours,

Herbert H. Lehman (1878–1963), governor of New York from 1933 until 1943, later served as the first director general of the United Nations Relief and Rehabilitation Administration. A wealthy investment banker, he refused to accept a salary for his public service. He would become Eleanor's closest ally in New York reform politics.

February 1, 1947

Dear Mr. President:

I have no idea whether the British people who are planning the memorial to my husband will ask you to send some one to represent you when the statue will be unveiled in April 1948. I have been invited and unless something unforeseen happens I plan to attend.

If you should be asked to send some one, I wonder if you would be willing to consider sending my husband's old friend and early law partner, Major Henry S. Hooker. He is most anxious to go because of the early connection and many years of friendship. I agreed to send you this note on the chance that a request would be made. I have tried not to ask you for favors but this is one request that I did not feel able to refuse.

Very cordially yours,

————————

February 5, 1947

My dear Mrs. Roosevelt:

In reply to your letter of February first, of course I would be most happy to designate Major Henry S. Hooker to represent the President of the United States at the unveiling of the proposed monument to Mr. Roosevelt in Grosvenor Square.

I hope you are enjoying this cold wave we are having.

Sincerely yours,

————————

February 6, 1947

Dear Mrs. Roosevelt:

This is to acknowledge your telegram of February fourth. Pardon me for not having made earlier acknowledgment of your second letter of resignation from membership on the President's Commission on Higher Education.

I appreciate how full your schedule is and hesitate to add to your burden of work. I can readily understand how difficult it is for you to attend meetings of the commission.

May I ask you to continue your membership with a very distinct understanding that you will not be expected to attend meetings while your work on the Human Rights Commission continues, nor even later, except on such occasions as are entirely convenient to you. When the usual notifications of meetings of the Commission on Education reach you, Miss Thompson can receive them with this understanding and such notices will not even require an acknowledgment.

Quite frankly, I would like to have the prestige which your name gives to the Education Commission. And I know Dr. Steelman feels the same way about it. I hope you can continue your membership under these conditions.

Very sincerely yours,

February 11, 1947

Dear Mr. President:

I am sorry but I find that it is impossible for me to give adequate time to the work of your Committee on Higher Education, and though you may not realize it, that work is under considerable criticism because there is a feeling, in the National Education Association for instance, that the emphasis is being placed on private education and too little thought given to public education.

Knowing that it is not possible for me to be at the meetings, I would not feel that it is right for me to continue to be a member or have my name connected with it when I could do no work.

I suggested that Miss Charl Williams might take my place because she has been for a long time in the NEA and was the first vice chairman of the Democratic National Committee.

It is because I feel this work is so important that I think someone who can give it adequate attention and thought should be named.

With very deep regret, I am

Very cordially yours,

February 12, 1947

Dear Mrs. Roosevelt:

In the light of your letter of February eleventh I feel that I have no recourse but to accept your resignation as a member of the Commission on Higher Education. I do this with deep regret but with heartfelt appreciation of the valuable counsel which you have given to the work.

I shall immediately look into the situation which you bring to my attention and I am sure that we can find a way to change anything that needs to be changed.

Gratefully and sincerely,

When Truman refused to accept Mrs. Roosevelt's resignation from this panel in the fall of 1946, his approval rating had plunged to the lowest point of his first term. By the winter of 1947, his numbers were improving. Even so, he was most reluctant to lose the benefit of Mrs. Roosevelt's popularity.

February 27, 1947

Dear Mr. President:

This is just a note to tell you how much I appreciate your support of the International Refugee Organization budget.

I feel it is so important that we redeem our pledges, I am always grateful for your support.

Very sincerely yours,

April 17, 1947

Dear Mr. President:

I have carried on a lengthy correspondence with Secretary Acheson and I have seen a State Department representative sent by Secretary Acheson to explain the Greek-Turkish situation to me.

I went to see Averell Harriman the other day to try to get some enlightenment from him. I know that his appointment was very favorably received. Harry Hopkins thought highly of him but that was largely because he knew he could count on Averell to carry out directions. I have known him since he was a little boy. I like him very much personally but I came away from talking to him, feeling that there was not sufficient realization of the domestic situation we are facing and its tie-up with the foreign situation.

Our domestic and foreign policies are so closely tied together and the various moves made of late are so politically oriented, I feel some very clear-sighted thinking is needed.

Between the Pepper Bill and the Vandenberg Amendment to the Administration Bill, I hope that you might find some middle course. For that reason I am enclosing a copy of a wire which has come to me that expresses anxiety and makes some suggestions similar to those which have been made from other people. I am not sending it because it came from Aubrey Williams, but because it is comprehensive enough to be a good sample of a considerable amount of thinking which seems to be going on throughout the country.

I do not believe that the Democratic party can win by going the Republican party one better in conservatism on the home front. Nor do I believe that taking over Mr. Churchill's policies in the Near East, in the name of democracy, is the way to really create a barrier to communism or promote democracy.

I do not think your advisers have looked far enough ahead. Admiral Leahy as always, will think of this country as moving on its own power.

Both in Commerce and in Agriculture, we have not been far-sighted enough to see that:

1. The safeguarding of food supplies for the world, even though it might mean keeping a little more than we need on hand, was a wise policy.

2. The getting of businessmen to work in Europe and Russia is the only way we can really hope to rehabilitate Europe and establish democracy.

Mr. Acheson is rather more sympathetic to the British point of view than I would be and what with Mr. Lewis Douglas, who will certainly be sympathetic to Mr. Churchill's point of view, I am afraid we are apt to lose sight of the fact that if we do not wish to fight Russia, we must be both honest and firm with her. She must understand us, but she must also trust us.

Please give my kind regards to Mrs. Truman and to Margaret. I hope the latter is feeling encouraged about her work. So many people have spoken to me favorably after hearing her on the radio.

Very cordially yours,

———————

May 7, 1947

Dear Mrs. Roosevelt:

It was thoughtful of you to write me, as you did in your letter of April 17 . . . telling me of your concern over recent world developments and giving me guidance. The Greek-Turkish matter which you mentioned has, I think, caused me more worry and soul-searching than any matter in these past two years. I felt the grave responsibility of the decision and the drawbacks to any course of action suggested. But it has also brought me, when the decision was made and as the issues have developed here and abroad, a growing feeling of certainty in the rightness of our step.

Your own concern and the concern of the sender of the wire you enclosed seem to be mainly, first, that we should not try to stop communism by throwing our economic weight in at points which are of strategic importance but deficient in democracy, and, second, that we must outsell communism by offering something better, that is, a constructive and affirmative program which will be recognized as such by the entire world and which can be effected without resort to the totalitarian methods of the communist police state.

On the first half of this I would argue that if the Greek-Turkish land bridge between the continents is one point at which our democratic forces can stop the advance of communism that has flowed steadily through the Baltic countries, Poland, Yugoslavia, Rumania, Bulgaria, to some extent Hungary, then this is the place to do it, regardless of whether or not the terrain is good.

The necessity at this point for formulating and carrying out a detailed operation to improve the situation is urged by Mr. Williams in his wire to you. While the details may differ considerably from those outlined by him, I am determined that the instructions to our mission will be worthy of the "support of all democratic nations" and will give no basis for the fear that it may be solely a "futile attempt to stop communism without offering anything better than the strengthening of autocracy and dictatorship." A great deal of study is being carried on in anticipation of the successful passage of the legislation. The FAO Report and the report of the Porter Mission will be considered and used along with the exceptional knowledge of our two ambassadors.

In answer to the second part of your concern, I would not disagree that we must have a democratic, constructive and affirmative program of wide scope. But I would argue with deep conviction that we have led in evolving, have helped to build, and have made clear to all who will understand, the most comprehensive machinery for a constructive world peace based on free institutions and ways of life that has ever been proposed and adopted by a body of nations. And I would urge that in evaluating the step we are about to take, we should keep clearly in mind all the effort this country has engaged in sincerity to make possible a peace economically, ideologically, and politically sound.

I know that I do not need to catalogue for you the international organizations to which I refer. Besides this machinery for peace, we have tried to eliminate the sources of war and, by our proposal for a four-power pact for the disarmament of Germany we have tried to remove from Europe what may be the greatest basic cause of friction: the fear of German aggression or the use of German territory for purposes of aggression.

To what seems to me nearly the limit, we have made concessions to Russia that she might trust and not fear us. These include: agreement at Teheran to support Tito's partisans in Yugoslavia; agreement at Yalta to give the Kurile Islands and southern Sakhalin to Russia, to recognize the independence of Outer Mongolia and Soviet interests in Darien, Port Arthur and the Chinese Eastern Railway; also at Yalta, agreement on the Curzon line as the western border of the Soviet Union, and to the admission of Byelorussia and the Ukraine to the United Nations; at Potsdam, agreement to the annexation by Russia of the northern portion of East Prussia, to the recognition of Soviet claims for preferential reparations from western Germany, to the necessity for modifications of the provisions of the Montreaux Convention. In the peace treaty negotiations we have made concessions partly in regard to reparations from Italy and in our efforts to meet the Yugoslav and Soviet points of view on boundaries and administration of Venezia, Givlia and Trieste.

In addition, we have contributed to the defense of Russia during the war in lend-lease eleven and a quarter-billion dollars and provided them with military aid and technological information. Since the war we have contributed to Russian relief through UNRRA two hundred and fifty million dollars and sold them on thirty-year credit, goods totaling another one-quarter billion dollars.

We have also protested, so far in vain, against what seemed to us violation of democratic procedures pledged at the Yalta Conference, in Poland, Rumania, Bulgaria and Yugoslavia.

To relieve suffering and to take the first steps toward material rehabilitation we have appropriated nearly four and one-quarter billion dollars and have asked for three hundred fifty million dollars more in post-UNRRA relief. Let us think, therefore, of Greek and Turkish aid against the background of these positive measures.

The results of our efforts thus far disappoint and dishearten many in this and other countries. I think we must place the blame not only on the obstructive tactics of elements opposed to our ideas of a democratic peace, but, also, to a certain extent, on our own reticence in stating the democratic purposes we have in mind.

So it seems to me, as it did to sixty-seven senators who voted for the Bill that we must take our stand at this strategic point in a determined effort not to let the advance of communism continue to overtake countries who choose to maintain a free way of life, who have requested our aid, and who do not wish to submit to subjugation by an armed minority or by outside pressure.

I have emphasized what seems to me to be the inescapable fact that this country has gone to great lengths to develop and carry out a constructive policy in world affairs. I have not discussed specifically the point you make that our domestic policy has a great influence on the manner in which we carry out our foreign policy. I am in complete agreement with you that what happens within this country is perhaps the most decisive factor in the future of world peace and economic well-being. We simply must not fall into political division, economic recession, or social stagnation. There must be social progress at home. I shall continue to point out to the country what seem to me the measures most suited to accomplish this progress. I shall continue to take every action within my own power to see that the United States has a progressive domestic policy that will deserve the confidence of the world and will serve as a sound foundation for our international policy. I shall at all times be grateful for any suggestions and criticisms which you may care to send me.

Nor does it seem to me that we can overlook the fact that as much as the world needs a progressive America, the American way of life cannot survive unless other peoples who want to adopt that pattern of life throughout the world can do so without fear and in the hope of success. If this is to be possible we cannot allow the forces of disintegration to go unchallenged.

I certainly appreciate your kind personal message to Mrs. Truman which I was glad to convey to her and your expression regarding Margaret's singing is especially gratifying. She will be greatly pleased.

It was necessary to check the facts before I could answer. It took some time—hence the delay. I regret that it took so long.

HST

In early 1947, the British government advised Truman that it could no longer provide economic and military aid to Greece, where pro-Soviet insurgents were gaining strength. The American president responded with what would become known as the Truman Doctrine: "I believe that it must be the policy of the United States to support free peoples who are resisting subjugation by armed minorities or by outside pressures." Mrs. Roosevelt feared that the United States was assuming Britain's old imperialist role in the Mediterranean.

The telegram that Mrs. Roosevelt enclosed was from the New Deal activist Aubrey Williams (1890–1965), who disapproved of the right-wing Greek government and Truman's blank check to anticommunist forces.

Eleanor believed that Churchill manipulated Truman. "FDR could cope with Churchill," she wrote a friend in 1946, "but he might fool someone not cognizant of world affairs."

W. Averell Harriman (1891–1986), FDR's wartime envoy to Churchill and Stalin, had replaced Wallace as secretary of commerce. Harriman encouraged Truman to take a hard line against the Soviets.

Lewis Douglas (1894–1974), who succeeded Harriman as ambassador to Britain, and Under Secretary of State Dean Acheson (1893–1971) were staunchly protective of the Anglo-American alliance.

Hyde Park
May 13, 1947

Dear Mr. President:

I can not tell you how much I appreciate your kindness in wanting to give me the Rand portrait of my husband.

Our youngest son, John, has no portrait of his father and is delighted at the prospect of receiving this one, and I am so grateful to you for making it possible.

I read that you had flown out to see your mother, and I do hope that you are not having real anxiety about her.

With my warm good wishes to Mrs. Truman and Margaret, I am,

Very cordially yours,

May 15, 1947

My dear Mrs. Roosevelt:

I am very happy indeed that you are pleased with the arrangement made for the Rand portrait.

I found my mother in not such good health as I had expected to find her but when a person is 94½, you really can't expect them to come through a broken bone in the best of health.

Sincerely yours,

I am sure you had a perfect mother's day. Our baby was away preparing to sing.

Ellen Emmet Rand (1875–1941), one of the more renowned portrait artists in the first half of the twentieth century, was a cousin of the novelist Henry James. She painted the official portraits of three secretaries of state and twice painted FDR. One of these portraits belonged to FDR's mother and hung in the living room of the family's Hyde Park mansion. The other Roosevelt likeness, which FDR designated as his official portrait, was prominently displayed in the White House. But Truman replaced it with Frank Salisbury's Roosevelt and sent the Rand portrait to Hyde Park. Mrs. Roosevelt gave it to her youngest son. It is now displayed in the FDR Library.

New York
May 16, 1947

Dear Mr. President:

Because of the various things I have heard, I am sending you this note.

I know that it was my husband's wish and intention that all of his papers should eventually be in the library at Hyde Park. He particularly did not want them left in the Archives in Washington or in the Library of Congress because he felt that concentration in one place was very unwise. He also felt that they would be more available to historians in the library at Hyde Park and I am sure they will be.

I hope you will not mind my telling you this, but I feel so strongly that in this one particular I would like to see his wishes carried out, that I am expressing what I have heard my husband say over and over again.

Very cordially yours,

May 31, 1947

My dear Mrs. Roosevelt:

I appreciated very much your letter of the sixteenth and, as you know, my only effort has been to carry out what I thought were the wishes of the late President.

You perhaps are not familiar with the facts—Brewster, Ferguson, and a few of the Republican chairmen in the House are extremely anxious to conduct a fishing expedition through the private files of President Roosevelt and that I am trying to prevent with all the power that I have. There are certain confidential communications which passed between him and some of the heads of states which should not be published at this time. This is particularly true of the correspondence between him and Mr. Stalin. I don't see how he continued as patiently as he did with developments as they were then progressing, but he didn't let his personal feelings enter into his international commitments and the country is certainly lucky that that was the case.

It is my intention, as soon as the Republican Congress has exhausted its investigative program, to have all the papers of the late President placed in the Library at Hyde Park where he wanted them. There are some of his papers which are necessary to keep here in the White House until the treaties are signed. Hardly a week goes by that I do not find it necessary to read some of these communications to find out just exactly what our commitments are. He never had an opportunity to tell me everything that had taken place. I imagine I have read a mile of documents since I have been in this office and I still have to read more of them when conditions come up which are affected by these agreements.

I have carried out every commitment that the late President made to the letter, and expect to continue to carry them out. Our friends the Russians have failed to carry out a single commitment they made either with him or with me, but we still are trying to get a peaceful settlement for both the European and Asiatic situation.

Sometime when you are down this way I can talk with you more frankly than I can write.

Sincerely yours,

Franklin D. Roosevelt, in establishing the first presidential library, donated his papers to the American people and deeded sixteen acres of his family's estate at Hyde Park for the construction of a library and museum. Congress accepted his offer and approved legislation making the library a federal agency. Until FDR's initiative, presidents had traditionally given their papers to the Library of Congress.

Senators Ralph Owen Brewster of Maine and Homer Ferguson of Maine, staunch Republican partisans, were eager to discredit FDR. As members of the Joint Congressional Committee of Inquiry, established in 1946 to investigate the attack on Pearl Harbor, Brewster and Ferguson alleged in a minority report that Roosevelt was to blame for this disaster. When the GOP took control of the Senate in 1947, Brewster became chairman of the War Investigating Committee.

June 7, 1947

Dear Mr. President:

I was deeply distressed when I got out to Los Angeles to speak at the dinner for the Southern California State Committee group to find that Mr. Pauley and my son, James, had entirely different points of view on a proposed policy plan which had been drawn up by James and the policy committee for submission to the state committee.

I found that owing to Mr. Pauley's suggestion, this document which was to have been given to people at the Jackson Day dinner, was not to be distributed but that James told them he would have to have it mailed to members of the state committee for future action and when that was done of course it would be in the papers.

Mr. Pauley took the position that he disagreed with certain things in the statement and felt that what was said on foreign policy was an insult to you. I read it through very carefully and it did not seem to me in any way insulting. It voiced simply the questions which are in many people's minds and it seemed to me that it gave to Mr. Gael Sullivan an opportunity, if he wanted to clear up some of these questions, and if he disapproved, to ask the state committee to change the things he thought unwise. He could even have expressed censure of James as state chairman and I think it would have left the feeling better among the people who attended the dinner.

I, of course, had no sense that his presence or absence at the dinner was an insult to me, but I think he did do harm to the position of the Democratic Party in the eyes of one of the largest dinners that they have ever had in Los Angeles.

You know that I have never seen eye-to-eye with Mr. Pauley. He has always fought Mrs. Helen Gahagan Douglas and I have always so believed in the things she has stood for. He did a very good job of raising money for the national committee. He often disagreed with my husband.

As I think back upon the many things which were said about my husband by southern Democrats and others within the party, I cannot see that the language in which this proposed statement is couched, is in any way insulting to you. I think a clever national chairman with a wiser national committeeman could have handled this situation and left the party in better condition instead of in a worse condition.

I understand that Mr. Pauley was much annoyed because in a press conference I said that I felt ways had to be found to get on with Russia. That does not mean we have to appease Russia. I do not believe the Russians want to go to war. Neither do we but I think the ingenuity to find ways to get what we want rests with us.

I thought General Marshall's speech at Harvard was the beginning of a constructive suggestion, but it seems to me something has to happen soon. And some people in the industrial world in this country have got to be brought to the realization that the thing which will strengthen Russia above everything else, is a depression in this country. She is waiting and longing for that and the effect on the rest of the world will be disastrous.

I do not attribute high-mindedness to the Politburo. I think undoubtedly they hope that the peoples of the world will turn to communism. There is only one way of answering that and that is by proving to the peoples of the world that democracy meets their needs better. This is a question of many things, which have to be worked on simultaneously on a world scale.

There is too much to be done in the world to allow for resentments. The real honest questioning such as was contained in the California State Democratic Committee document might have better been met with real answers which many people are confronting and on which they seek wider understanding of government policies.

I hope you will forgive my speaking so frankly, but I have your interests and the interests of the party at heart.

Very sincerely yours,

June 16, 1947

Dear Mrs. Roosevelt:

I deeply regret the combination of circumstances which prompted your letter of June seventh which was placed in my hands upon my return from Canada. I am grateful for the assurance that you had no sense of personal insult because of the incident in Los Angeles. That generous expression is characteristic of you.

It would be impossible for me to believe that there was any intent to accord you anything less than the highest measure of courtesy and respect. Any other course is unthinkable.

I want you to know that I have read your thoughtful letter very carefully. I, too, wish some people in the industrial world could be brought to a realization of the consequences which their course will inevitably bring down upon their own heads as well as the nation.

You have placed the proper emphasis on the paramount issue in our international relations. With what you say on so momentous a program I am in entire accord. If we are to stem the tide of communism, we must, as you say, prove to the peoples of the world that democracy meets their needs better.

As to the controversy, which Mr. Gael Sullivan's actions aroused, I can only hope that peace may be made at the meeting which Mr. Sullivan has called for June twenty-sixth, announcement of which has been made in the papers.

Very sincerely yours,

James Roosevelt (1907–1991), Mrs. Roosevelt's first son, worked in the insurance and motion picture businesses and also did a stint as President Roosevelt's senior aide. During World War II, he served in the Marine Corps and received the Navy Cross and the Silver Star. Following the war, he became chairman of the California Democratic Party. Pauley, who had long been active in state and national politics, regarded the president's son as a carpetbagger and opportunist. Truman agreed with that assessment.

June 19, 1947

Dear Mrs. Roosevelt:

I had intended replying to your note of June fifth before this, but as you know I have been traveling rather steadily all of this month and am just now catching up with my correspondence.

I shall be delighted to see you on Sunday, June twenty-ninth, and suggest you come to the White House at 3 p.m. If it would not interfere with any plans you may have I would very much like to have you drive with me to the ceremonies at the Lincoln Memorial. I believe the ceremonies are scheduled to begin at 4 p.m.

With kindest personal regards,

June 22, 1947

Dear Mr. President:

I am looking forward to seeing you on the 29th, and I shall be happy to drive with you to the ceremonies.

Very cordially yours,

On June 29, 1947, Truman became the first president to address the National Association for the Advancement of Colored People. His speech at the Lincoln Memorial was carried on a national radio broadcast. Mrs. Roosevelt and Oregon senator Wayne L. Morse, who was then a liberal Republican, were also on the program. "Mamma won't like what I say because I end up by quoting old Abe," Truman wrote his sister. "But I believe what I say and I'm hopeful we may implement it." In the same letter, the president indicated that he did not approve of the former first lady's civil rights activism. "Mrs. Roosevelt," he wrote, "has spent her public life stirring up trouble between blacks and whites."

June 30, 1947

My dear Mrs. Roosevelt:

I am enclosing you the articles from the *London Observer*, which appeared in the *Baltimore Sun*. They are most interesting and, I think, constructive in connection with the plan which General Marshall and I are trying to inaugurate in Europe.

Sincerely yours,

Hyde Park
July 6, 1947

Dear Mr. President:

I am enclosing an excerpt from a letter which came to me the other day. I do not know whether it is possible to add any people from the group suggested to this committee which you have named.

If it is possible, it might be a good thing since the group reaches out and all of them are very conscious of their desire for representation.

Very cordially yours,

Thank you for the clipping which I found [illegible] interesting.

Truman had just named a nineteen-member committee to study the impact of foreign aid on the domestic economy. The distinguished panel included former senator Robert M. La Follette Jr., industrialist Paul G. Hoffman, labor leader George Meany, and Robert Gordon Sproul, president of the University of California at Berkeley. But there were no women or members of minority groups. Mrs. Roosevelt wanted more diversity.

———

July 14, 1947

My dear Mrs. Roosevelt:

I appreciated your note of July sixth enclosing an excerpt from a letter which had come to you in regard to the Committee to look into the economic situation of the United States. I have asked the staff to look into the situation and see what can be done about it.

This Congress seems to be doing everything possible to hamstring the country and prevent it from meeting its obligations.

There was an excellent editorial in the *Washington Post* this morning on this situation, which I am enclosing.

Sincerely yours,

The Post *urged the admission of European refugees to overcome the labor shortage. In a special message to Congress on July 7, 1947, Tru-*

*man had called for legislation to make it possible for displaced persons
to enter the United States. Illinois congressman William G. Stratton
had sponsored legislation in April 1947 that would have allowed the
immigration of four hundred thousand displaced persons. Truman privately favored this legislation, which failed to pass. The president reluc-
tantly signed the Displaced Persons Act of 1948, which discriminated
against Jews and Catholics. Truman won approval in 1950 for a more
inclusive immigration policy.*

July 26, 1947

Dear Mr. President:

Mr. Hershel Johnson told me that you were sending my name to the
Senate again as a member of the United States Delegation to the United
Nations General Assembly.

I am very grateful to you for this further opportunity to work with
the United Nations and only hope that we will accomplish something
worthwhile and justify your confidence in us.

I hope the summer is proving a little restful for you and your family.

Very cordially yours,

Hyde Park
August 9, 1947

Dear Mr. President:

I have waited to write you because after sending off our wire I realized
what an avalanche of messages that you would receive. Nevertheless I
want to send my deep sympathy for I know so well how much you will
miss your mother. As long as the older generation is able to [illegible] a
certain protection, when they go [illegible] feeling.

The fact that your mother was ill was a preparation for the final blow
but when you have thought daily about someone their passing is an
added ache. She must have been a wonderful person and her pride in you
must give you happiness.

I hope your trip will bring you some [illegible] and I just wanted you to know that my thoughts were with you and your family in the sad days just passed.

Cordially yours,

P.S. Please do not answer.

August 14, 1947

My dear Mrs. Roosevelt:

You don't know how very much I appreciated your beautiful letter of sympathy dated August ninth.

Of course, just as you say, we always feel somewhat lost after an experience of the sort through which we have just gone, but we have to adjust ourselves according to the situation as we find it.

The sympathy of our friends is one of the things that makes it bearable. I certainly appreciate your writing me as you did.

Sincerely yours,

Martha Ellen Young, the president's mother, died July 26, 1947, at the age of ninety-four. She was a woman of extraordinary vitality and always spoke her mind. "I never thought he would be president, but he'll be a good one," she predicted when her son succeeded Roosevelt. "He's a good man and has a lot of common sense and he'll do the job the best he knows how."

New York
August 21, 1947

THE PRESIDENT
THE WHITE HOUSE:

I understand that the Jews on the ship in a French harbor have until six o'clock tomorrow afternoon to land in France or be returned to concentration camps in Germany. It seems to me since they want to go to Cyprus some pressure might be brought to bear on Great Britain to allow them to do so. Their plight is pitiful and I hope you may feel that you can exert some influence on Great Britain

August 23, 1947

My dear Mrs. Roosevelt:

I read your telegram with regard to the Jews with a lot of interest. This situation is a most embarrassing one all the way around and has been most difficult to approach. I hope it will work out.

I understand that these ships were loaded and started to Palestine with American funds and American backing—they were loaded knowing that they were trying to do an illegal act.

The action of some United States Zionists will eventually prejudice everyone against what they are trying to get done. I fear very much that the Jews are like all underdogs—when they get on top they are just as intolerant and cruel as people were to them when they were underneath. I regret this situation very much because my sympathy has always been on their side.

Sincerely yours,

Eight days after Truman wrote this letter, the United Nations Special Committee on Palestine made the unanimous recommendation that Great Britain terminate its mandate for Palestine. Seven of the eleven member states on the committee voted for splitting Palestine into Jewish and Arab states.

As Truman faced hard decisions in the Mideast, he worried that the zeal of American Zionists could hurt their cause. Long before he became president, he had supported the creation of a Jewish state.

September 3, 1947

Dear Mr. President:

I have just heard from our national committeeman, Mr. Flynn, that the probability is, since Mr. Hannegan is going to resign, that Mr. Anderson may be made national chairman and that his position is going to be opposed to Mr. Anderson.

I thought it only fair that I should tell you that I could never support Mr. Anderson. I consider him a conservative and I consider that the only chance the Democratic Party has for election in 1948, is to be the liberal party. We cannot be more conservative than the Republicans so we cannot succeed as conservatives. If the country is going conservative, it is not going to vote for any Democratic candidate.

It is very important to the world as well as to the United States that the Democratic Party wins in 1948, but I would feel that the kind of party which was built up and guided by Mr. Anderson would be a conservative party and I would withdraw completely from any activity in connection with it.

Very sincerely yours,

September 29, 1947

Dear Mrs. Roosevelt:

Your letter of September third was waiting for me when I returned from Rio de Janeiro. I am glad that you gave me the benefit of your frank opinion about the national chairmanship, even though Mr. Flynn gave you erroneous information.

I sincerely hope that the selection of Senator McGrath, now in process of confirmation, will meet with your approval. Let me assure you once more—if such assurance is needed—that I shall always welcome an expression of your views on every aspect of party policy. I set a high value on your judgment.

When I see you, if you are interested, I can tell you the reasons for Mr. Flynn's pique. He made a recommendation for a judicial appointment which, in all conscience, I could not accept.

With every good wish,

Always sincerely,

Truman had, in fact, offered the party chairmanship to Clinton P. Anderson (1895–1975), secretary of agriculture, on the condition that he would also stay in the cabinet. Though Mrs. Roosevelt had good information about Truman's choice, she distorted Anderson's politics. He was a liberal but not an ideologue. Anderson, who declined the chairmanship, was elected to the Senate from New Mexico in 1948. He kept the seat for twenty-four years.

October 11, 1947

To: Eleanor Roosevelt

May I extending birthday greetings express my heartfelt appreciation of the wonderful work you are doing as the country's representative to the General Assembly of the United Nations. In you democratic institutions, particularly freedom of the press, have an earnest, able, and eloquent defender. You have earned the nation's thanks. Congratulations and happy birthday.

Harry S. Truman

Mrs. Roosevelt replied, "I am deeply appreciative of your approval of my work with the General Assembly at the United Nations. It encourages me to continue to do my best."

October 28, 1947

Dear Mrs. Roosevelt:

I am sorry to learn that the expected continued sessions of the General Assembly make it improbable that you can get to Washington next month as you had planned.

Personally this is a disappointment to me. I know I shall profit whenever I can hear firsthand about the trend of things at Lake Success. Again let me congratulate you on the valiant work you are performing. In you, your country and all our democratic institutions have an able defender.

Thanks for the good wishes regarding the special session. I felt that the growing menace of chaos in Europe and the rising prices at home demanded the attention of the Congress.

I hope you will continue to get a little rest before you go on for more hard work in Geneva.

Very cordially yours,

November 13, 1947

Dear Mr. President:

I have wanted to write you for a long time as I have been getting from all of my friends, Republicans and Democrats alike, such violent reactions to the Loyalty Tests. And now, after the dismissal of the ten people from the State Department, and the article in the *Herald Tribune,* I feel I must write you.

I do not feel that Dr. Meta Glass should be the only woman on the Committee for Review as she is not a strong enough person. I feel more people, not lawyers, should be on and another woman might well be appointed. Perhaps Mrs. Lewis Thompson of Red Bank, New Jersey, who is a strong Republican but also a liberal, might help to interpret the work of this Committee to the public. Certain things need to be interpreted to the public. My own reaction is anything but happy. I feel we have capitulated to our fear of Communism, and instead of fighting to improve Democracy, we are doing what the Soviets would do in trying to repress anything which we are afraid might not command public support, in order to insure acceptance of our own actions.

I am sorry that I cannot see you before I go to Geneva to the Human Rights Commission meetings and since this session of the General Assembly is drawing to an end, I want to thank you for your kindness in appointing me. It has been interesting work and I hope that I have been helpful. When I return from Geneva and the holidays are over, I will try to come to Washington in order to see you again.

With best wishes to Mrs. Truman and Margaret, and congratulations to her on her successes, and wishing you all a Happy Thanksgiving and Christmas season, I am,

Very sincerely yours,

November 26, 1947

Dear Mrs. Roosevelt:

Your letter of November thirteenth was of great personal interest to me, and I have read it with sympathetic reactions to the ideas you express. I can well understand that you may be disturbed by some of the articles and summaries that have been published about the loyalty review of the present incumbents and new employees of the civil service posts.

I have told the Civil Service Commission, the members of the Loyalty Review Board, and the press that I did not wish this inquiry to become a "witch hunt," but rather to establish what I think is the truth, that the overwhelming number of civil servants in the United States are not only faithful and loyal, but devoted patriots. It is, of course, contrary to American tradition to inquire into the political or philosophical views of anyone, and I think that is why all of us feel a certain repugnance to this program, but I became convinced that it was necessary, not because as you say, "we were trying to repress anything we were afraid might not command public support," but because there were certain indications of a small infiltration of seriously disloyal people into certain sensitive parts of the government.

The disclosures of the Canadian government, and in particular the report of the Canadian Civil Service Commission as to the way in which previously quite innocent and simple people had been trapped and led into a situation of securing and revealing information to agents of another government—contrary to all instructions and policies of government service—were sufficient to convince me that we had to make some positive and constructive inquiry into the state of affairs in our own civil service.

The Civil Service Commission, into whose hands I placed most of the development of the programs, is cautious and fully aware of the constitutional rights of human beings that need to be protected. We all must remind ourselves that no one has a constitutional right to work for the government. He has a constitutional right to express himself and his opinions any way he chooses and to associate himself with organizations that are quite opposed to our government, or even attempt to alter the Constitution, but it is not appropriate that he should carry on such activities while working for the government of the United States.

The Loyalty Review Board, which is made up of distinguished persons outside the government, is I think going to prove not only an advantage in distinguishing the true from the false and in uncovering actual disloyalty, but it will also serve to protect the civil liberties of individuals in this new and unusual field. I am very interested in your reaction to the Board, and I do want to tell you of a very great difficulty which we experienced in finding enough of the right kind of people to serve.

There are a good many lawyers on the Board, I agree. The reason for having so many lawyers is that it is hoped that the Board will sit in panels of three on the cases, and that at least one lawyer will be a member of each panel. A legal mind, while it may be narrow in some instances, is, as I think you know, very strong on the right and proper procedures for the handling of witnesses and the establishing of true evidence as against rumor and slander, before making a conclusion of fact that the individual charged with an offense is guilty. I really believe that a sound, conservative legal mind will be of great assistance in establishing a proper method of carrying on this inquiry.

However, there are still several positions to be filled on the Loyalty Review Board, and we are attempting to secure a number of other persons of broad public interests who are not lawyers. I have noted with interest your recommendation of Mrs. Lewis Thompson of Red Bank, New Jersey, and I will send her name to the Civil Service Commission with the suggestion that they look into that possibility.

I am grateful for your letter because I am always glad to have your views.

Thank you very much for your good wishes and your congratulations to Margaret on her success as a singer. I hope that you will come to see me when you return from Geneva.

Very sincerely,

On March 22, 1947, Truman issued Executive Order 9835, which established the loyalty program for the executive branch of the federal government. Five days later, Mrs. Roosevelt wrote in her column: "Any order of this kind carries a certain amount of danger with it, in that it may be possible to misuse its provisions. If a wave of hysteria hits us, there will be very little protection for anyone who even thinks differently from the run-of-the-mill." Her prophecy was remarkably accurate. "One of the defects in the program, which we did not realize at the outset," Truman wrote in his memoirs, "was that once a person had been cleared by a loyalty board, or finally by the Loyalty Review Board, all of the data about that individual remained in the file."

New York
November 25, 1947

Dear Mr. President:

I read your message to Congress and I want to tell you that I thought it very courageous and very good in every way. I am sure you have had many favorable comments.

The old Greek Prime Minister came to see me and asked me to tell you how grateful they are for what has been done for Greece. They hope you will back some form of a middle-of-the-road government and try to draw the two extremes together.

I leave on Friday for the Human Rights Commission meeting in Geneva, and I am sorry not to have had the opportunity of seeing you before I go. I hope I shall be able to get to Washington around the 12th of January, and that you will be free to see me. If I may, I shall ask for an appointment when I know just when I will be in Washington.

With my every good wish to you and Mrs. Truman and Margaret, I am,

Very cordially yours,

On November 17, 1947, Truman addressed a special session of Congress and sought funding for the European Recovery Program, which would become known as the Marshall Plan. "The future of the free nations of Europe hangs in the balance," he declared. "The action which you take will be written large in the history of this Nation and of the world." At the end of the year 2000, the Brookings Institution rated Truman's initiative as the federal government's most important accomplishment of the half century.

The Greek prime minister sent his appreciation to the president for the Truman Doctrine, which provided economic and military aid to help prevent a communist takeover.

Hyde Park
December 23, 1947

Dear Mr. President:

This is just to tell you that I read your committee's report on civil rights and thought it very good.

While I am writing about this, I want to tell you how very courageous I thought your message was on the Marshall Plan. The Republicans are playing into our hands with their voluntary anti-inflation measures but we will have to act immediately to make the best of it. If they do a lot of arguing over the Marshall Plan I think they will find themselves in hot water there too.

Very cordially yours,

Franklin D. Roosevelt Jr. had been named by Truman in December of 1946 as vice chairman of the President's Committee on Civil Rights. In October of 1947, the committee issued a report, "To Secure These Rights," which powerfully documented America's racial divide. It recommended the establishment of a civil rights division in the Justice Department, a permanent Commission on Civil Rights with enforcement power, tough measures against police brutality, and a federal anti-lynching law. The committee also urged the elimination of poll taxes, which were used in the South to prevent blacks from voting. In its boldest recommendation, the panel called for an end to segregation. Mrs. Roosevelt fully endorsed the committee's three dozen recommendations.

December 30, 1947

Dear Mrs. Roosevelt:

I appreciated very much your good letter of December twenty-third and I think our record is fair and clean on the Marshall Plan—also the anti-inflation program.

Of course, I'll be most happy to see you on January thirteenth. I am sure there will be no difficulty about arranging it.

Mrs. Truman and Margaret join me in wishing you a most Happy and Prosperous 1948.

Sincerely yours,

_____

December 27, 1947

Dear Mr. President:

I am deeply appreciative of your Christmas wire and grateful for your very kind words about my work in Geneva. I worked everyone very hard and I was happy to have the work finished so I could be home for Christmas.

Many thanks and every good wish to you for the New Year.

Very cordially yours,

CHAPTER 4

1948

Shortly before the Democratic National Convention opened in Philadelphia, President Truman was asked whether Mrs. Roosevelt would be acceptable to him as a vice-presidential running mate. "Why, of course, of course," he answered with a smile. "What do you expect me to say to that?"

There had been speculation for months about such a possibility. The North Dakota State Democratic Central Committee passed a resolution in 1947 endorsing a Democratic ticket of Truman and Mrs. Roosevelt. "At first I was surprised that anyone should think that I would want to run for office, or that I was fitted to hold office," she wrote in *Look* magazine. "Then I realized that some people felt that I must have learned something from my husband in all the years that he was in public life! They also knew that I had stressed the fact that women should accept responsibility as citizens.

"I heard that I was being offered the nomination for governor or for the United States Senate in my own state, and even for Vice President. And some particularly humorous souls wrote in and suggested that I run as the first woman President of the United States! The simple truth is that I have had my fill of public life of the more or less stereotyped kind." She had no interest in seeking elective office and would defer to her children. James Roosevelt said years later that his mother would not allow her name to be considered for the vice-presidential nomination "because she was afraid of it."

Much to Truman's annoyance, three of Mrs. Roosevelt's sons were leaders of a movement to draft General Dwight D. Eisenhower for the 1948 Democratic presidential nomination. "I rather liked and respected

President Truman and thought he did a good job in a difficult situation following Father's death," James said three decades later. "I just did not think he could be elected, so I looked for someone who could."

The president's renomination was assured only after Eisenhower withdrew his name from consideration on the eve of the convention. When Truman sought to name Supreme Court justice William O. Douglas as his running mate, White House counsel Clark M. Clifford enlisted Mrs. Roosevelt to help persuade the reluctant Douglas. "She said she would be happy to try," Clifford recalled. "But even her efforts produced no movement." After Douglas turned him down, Truman chose Senate Minority Leader Alben Barkley for the vice-presidential nomination.

In the early months of 1948, Mrs. Roosevelt opposed the Truman administration's Middle East arms embargo and urged splitting Palestine into Jewish and Arab states. When Truman switched his position from the partitioning of Palestine and recommended a United Nations trusteeship, Mrs. Roosevelt vehemently opposed this shift and threatened to quit the UN delegation. Though she had urged U.S. recognition of the newly created Jewish state, Eleanor disapproved when Truman did so without advising American representatives at the UN She supported the first UN peacekeeping mission, which was initiated to prevent wars between Israel and its Arab neighbors.

Mrs. Roosevelt spoke in behalf of the Universal Declaration of Human Rights at the 1948 General Assembly in Paris. "It is not a treaty. It is not an international agreement. It is not and does not purport to be a statement of law or of legal obligation," she declared. "It is a declaration of basic human rights and freedoms."

This declaration was among the goals stated in the United Nations Charter adopted at the San Francisco Conference, which pledged "to save succeeding generations from the scourge of war, which twice in our lifetime has brought untold sorrow to mankind . . . to reaffirm faith in fundamental human rights . . . to establish conditions under which justice and respect for the obligations arising from treaties and other sources of international law can be maintained; and to promote social progress and better standards of life in larger freedom."

Mrs. Roosevelt, who was in Paris during the 1948 presidential campaign, gave Truman little chance against Republican Thomas E. Dewey. Following Truman's upset victory, she wrote her longtime friend Joseph Lash: "It is rather nice to be an American when the people so evidently take their democracy seriously & do their own thinking as they did in this election. I did not have enough faith in them! Dewey just wasn't big enough & I think they felt more sincerity if not ability in Truman."

Hyde Park
January 16, 1948

Dear Mr. President:

I happened to see Mrs. Anna Rosenberg last evening and I find she is not doing very much in the public field at present and would like to be useful. I do not think she could give full time, but could give several days a week. She is a wonderful organizer and I thought perhaps you would like to consider her as head of your consumer food group.

She would not be interested unless it is really planned this time to do a truly educational job and an honest one all down the line.

I hope that you are going to make a real fight for every one of the social things that you mentioned in your message. Our party people in Congress should truly back you on those. With a little help from the liberal Republicans we ought to get some of them through.

The great trouble is that Mr. Wallace will cut in on us because he can say we have given lip service to these things by having produced very little in the last few years.

Very cordially yours,

———————

January 19, 1948

Dear Mrs. Roosevelt:

Replying to yours of the sixteenth in regard to Mrs. Anna Rosenberg, of course, I'd be glad to use Mrs. Rosenberg any time and anywhere— she is a very able person.

I've been making a real fight for all the social things I've advocated ever since I've been here. You will remember, if I hadn't made the fight

Henry never would have gotten through the Senate on his last adventure into the Cabinet.

We are faced with a very serious situation in the Congress now, however, because we have more Democrats who are helping the Republicans than we have Republicans who are helping the Democrats in both Houses. There has only been one time and that was on an amendment to the interim Aid Program. We have at least six Senators on the Democratic side who always vote with the Republicans on any forward-looking measure and there are only three Republicans on whom we can count in the Senate.

Of course, I intend to continue to make all the fight I am capable of making, just as I always have done. With the help of yourself and forward-looking people like you, I think we can make some impression but I am not at all optimistic about the final results. . . .

I think I am as familiar with procedure in the Congress as anybody possibly can be and I use every means at my command to make use of that familiarity. We did succeed in getting an Interim Aid measure through but when it comes to social reforms those people simply are not interested in social reform—in fact they'd like to turn the clock back.

We are making progress on the European Aid Program. We have them extremely worried by our tax proposal. The people are with us on Universal Training. The people are with us on our social program too. We shall keep pounding away and I hope for the right result finally, but I fear that will take an election. I am talking to General Marshall tomorrow about your suggestion.

It was certainly a pleasure to talk with you the other day and I am sincerely sorry that I didn't have a longer period in which to discuss some of the matters that are pending before Congress.

With kindest regards and best wishes, I am

Sincerely yours,

Anna Rosenberg (1902–1983), who was among the great public officials of her time, served during World War II as director of the War Manpower Commission for New York State, as FDR's personal representative to the European theater, and was the driving force in establishing the GI Bill of Rights. Truman appointed her in 1946 as a member of the

United Nations Educational, Scientific and Cultural Organization (UNESCO). In 1950, at the urging of General Marshall, Truman nominated her for assistant secretary of defense.

Mrs. Roosevelt worried that the Progressive Party, founded by Henry A. Wallace, could split the liberal vote and help Republicans capture the presidency in 1948. She had long admired Wallace but became disillusioned when he refused to criticize Soviet foreign policy, while blaming the United States for the Cold War. It also bothered Mrs. Roosevelt that her husband's former vice president accepted support from the American Communist Party, which followed the Kremlin line. "He never has been a good politician, he never has been able to gauge public opinion, and he never has picked his advisers wisely," she wrote in Democratic Digest. "All of these things might have been less important if he had been a disinterested, nonpolitical leader of liberal thought, but as a leader of a third party he will accomplish nothing. He will merely destroy the very things he wishes to achieve." Writing to her daughter, Anna, in January of 1948, Mrs. Roosevelt reiterated her concern about the Wallace threat: "He will get many votes I think & achieve none of his objectives except perhaps to defeat Truman."

January 29, 1948

Dear Mr. President:

I read Mr. Reston's article in the New York Times the other day and I feel I want to write you on the question of Palestine and the United Nations.

It seems to me that if the UN does not pull through and enforce the partition and protection of people in general in Palestine, we are now facing a very serious situation in which its position for the future is at stake.

Since we led in the acceptance of the UN majority report on Palestine, and since we feel that the existence of the UN is essential to the preservation of peace, I think we should support a move on their part to create an international police force, perhaps from among the smaller nations. We should stand ready at the request of the UN to remove our embargo on arms and to provide such things as are essential to the control of

Arabs, namely, modern implements of war such as tanks, airplanes, etc.

If we do not take some stand to strengthen the UN organization at the present time, I shall not be surprised if Russia does, which will put us in a difficult position to say the least.

Great Britain's role, of course, is not only to please the Arabs, but probably to arm them because she knows very well that only the United States and Great Britain are going to buy Arab oil and she wants to be sure to hold her full share.

If the UN is going to be an instrument for peace, now is the crucial time to strengthen it.

With the deepest concern, I am,

Very sincerely yours,

February 2, 1948

Dear Mrs. Roosevelt:

I appreciated very much your letter of January twenty-ninth. General Marshall and I are attempting to work out a plan for the enforcement of the mandate of the United Nations. I discussed the matter with Franklin, Jr. the other day and I sincerely hope that we can arrive at the right solution.

Your statements on Great Britain are as correct as they can be. Britain's role in the Near East and Britain's policy with regard to Russia has not changed in a hundred years. Disraeli might just as well be Prime Minister these days.

I understand all that and I am trying to meet it as best I can.

Sincerely yours,

The United Nations General Assembly on November 29, 1947, approved the plan for the creation of Jewish and Arab states in what was then the mandate of Palestine. "The vote in the UN," Truman wrote former treasury secretary Henry Morgenthau, "is only the beginning and the Jews must now display tolerance and consideration for the other people in Palestine with whom they will necessarily have to be neighbors." The Truman administration imposed an embargo on arms shipments into the region. Mrs. Roosevelt favored a tough response by the United Nations to what she regarded as British imperialism.

James Reston (1909–1995), whose article is cited by Mrs. Roosevelt, was then chief diplomatic correspondent in the Washington bureau of the New York Times.

———

February 13, 1948

Dear Mr. President:

Judge Florence Allen tells me that Judge Marion Harron is up for reappointment to the Tax Court of the United States.

I have known Judge Harron for a long time and I hope that it will be possible to reappoint her. I know that she is known not only as a good Democrat, but also her record for good work and judicial integrity is fine, and I also understand that she has never been reversed by the Supreme Court. In sending you this letter of recommendation, therefore, I feel I am only emphasizing what other people tell you.

Very sincerely yours,

———

February 18, 1948

Dear Mrs. Roosevelt:

Thanks for yours of the thirteenth (written on Mrs. Truman's birthday). I had expected all along to reappoint Mrs. Harron to the Tax Court but I am more than happy that you found it necessary to ask me to do it.

Judge Florence Allen came to see me and I had a most pleasant visit and conversation with her. I told her that I had expected all along to reappoint Mrs. Harron.

I hope everything is going well with you? What do you think of the Bronx and Ed Flynn's control now?

Sincerely yours,

There was thunder on the left when a third-party candidate supported by Henry A. Wallace won a special congressional election in the Bronx on February 18, 1948. New York's twenty-fourth congressional district, *whose residents were predominantly Jewish and low-income, was the home base of former Democratic national chairman Edward J. Flynn. At his request, Mrs. Roosevelt campaigned for regular Democratic nominee Karl Propper. But her prestige wasn't enough. American Labor Party candidate Leo Isacson, who campaigned with Wallace, won by twenty-five percentage points. Wallace asserted that the Bronx vote was a repudiation of Truman's foreign policy. At least for the moment, Wallace appeared to be a political force. Democratic National Chairman J. Howard McGrath made a public appeal for Wallace to come back to the party. The former vice president declined. Isacson's tenure would be brief. Nine months later, the Democrats easily recaptured the congressional seat.*

Mrs. Roosevelt's concept of an international police force was similar to Truman's. In June of 1950 he would refer to his intervention in Korea as a "police action."

New York
February 20, 1948

Dear Mr. President:

I was interested in your comment on the defeat of Ed. Flynn's candidate in Bronx County. I think Ed. Flynn has proved the point which he has been trying to make for a long time, namely, that in large urban areas there are great groups of people who are extremely radical and very much opposed to what they feel is military and Wall Street domination in our present administration.

These people in the Bronx followed my husband because they felt he understood their needs and they were getting, domestically, protection which they had never had before. There has always been a strong element of communism in this section of the Bronx. I can remember it specifically among the youth groups back in 1933 and 1934. I noticed the night I spoke that every time Mr. Wallace's name was mentioned, it was cheered.

I was not very much surprised by the results of the vote because in the big, urban centers, even those who are Democrats just do not come out to vote because they are still radical enough to be unhappy about what they feel are certain tendencies they observe in our administration.

Ed. Flynn has told you this, I think, on a number of occasions. It is important because if the Democrats are going to win in a state like New York, they have to carry by the great majority the big urban centers. I am sure you are well aware of this, but I feel it my duty to reenforce what already has been said, disagreeable as it is.

I never thought this district was a good one to hail as a pilot light of what would happen in the national election, but naturally it would be one which Mr. Wallace and the American Labor Party would pick to make much of, since they were almost sure of success.

Ed. Flynn, I think, felt that his organization would do much better than it did, but he did not count on the fact that even Democrats in areas such as this are unenthusiastic at the moment.

I wrote in my column the other day, as a result of the indications I find in my mail, that the two things bothering the average man most at present are inflation and the fear of another war. Congress is doing all it can to help us, I think, because certainly they are showing a complete disregard for the high cost of living as it affects the average human being, but you never know how many people realize this.

I know that in order to obtain what we need in the way of military strength for defense, it would seem almost essential to whip up fear of communism and to do certain things which hurt us with the very element which we need in the election. How we can be firm and strong and yet friendly in our attitude toward Russia, and obtain from Congress what we need to keep us strong, is one of our most difficult problems. I have often thought if you could explain the whole situation over the radio in a series of talks to the people of our country, it might clear up some of our difficulties, because I find great confusion in the minds of the average citizens.

Very sincerely yours,

P.S. James told me of Mr. Forrestal's feeling that no American should be allowed to volunteer in an international police force. I think Mr. Forrestal is entirely wrong. I was shocked at the suggestion that any American volunteering to fight in Palestine would lose his citizenship, and I could not understand why that was not invoked when Americans went to Canada and enlisted in the Canadian forces before we were in the war. It seems to me that if the UN calls for an international police force it might very well say that the quotas should be equal from all nations, big and little, and then we should call for volunteers within our nation. To say that just because Russia might have some soldiers in Palestine on an equal basis with us and all the other nations involved, we would have to mobilize fifty percent for war, seems to me complete nonsense and I think it would seem so to most of the people of the United States.

————————

Key West
February 27, 1948

Dear Mrs. Roosevelt:

I appreciated very much your letter of February 20 in regard to the Bronx election. Naturally, all sorts of conjectures are given as to the reason for that return. It is my honest opinion that people everywhere are in an unsettled frame of mind, that revolt in 1946 is not yet finished, and that you must also take into consideration the fact that the leaders in the Democratic Party are tired, with the long grind through which we have been, due to the terrible depression and World War II. I have to do things my own way, but I was a member of the resolutions committee that had a great deal to do with writing the Democratic platform of 1944, and I have been trying religiously to carry it out. We haven't had a Congress since 1944 that had any idea of abiding by that platform.

I can't bring myself to line up with the crackpots who are trying to sell us out to the Russian government, nor can I see anything good in the Harry Byrds and Eugene Coxes. That is the situation with which we are confronted now. I shall continue to do the best I can to meet the problems with which we are faced. The result is probably in the lap of the gods, although sometimes a little help and a little energy will get results in spite of that situation.

I hope you have a most pleasant visit in Great Britain, and that I will have a chance to talk with you when you return as to conditions over there, which you no doubt will observe carefully.

I had a most pleasant visit with Jimmie the other day, and the secretary of defense has been informed as to my views on the international police force. Of course, if the United Nations international police force is organized, the citizenship of the members of that force in their native countries should not be disturbed.

Sincerely yours,

New York
March 4, 1948

Dear Mr. President:

I was very much interested in your letter of February 27th, and I am glad you are not going to line up with those who want to sell us out to the Russian government, or with the Byrds and the Eugene Coxes!

These Southern statesmen seem to be very shortsighted and you are right when you say that the leadership in the Democratic Party is tired. Perhaps the people are too. Unfortunately, this is a bad time to be tired.

Thank you for your good wishes on my trip to Europe. I shall try to observe conditions and I shall try to find out from the secretary of state before I go whether he has any particular points that he wishes stressed and any he wishes me to avoid in any speeches which I may make. I am going to London as you know, and to Brussels and to Holland. If you have any suggestions I shall be grateful to you if you will send them to me.

I hope your trip to Florida was enjoyable and of great benefit.

Very cordially yours,

Mrs. Roosevelt, while agreeing with Truman that their party's leadership is tired, implies that it may be time for a fresh face.

March 8, 1948

Dear Mrs. Roosevelt:

I certainly appreciated yours of the fourth and I sincerely hope that your trip to Europe will be a happy one. I should like very much to talk with you when you come back.

The Florida trip was very restful and accomplished the purposes for which it was made—a few days rest.

Sincerely yours,

Hyde Park
March 13, 1948

Dear Mr. President:

I am enclosing to you this copy of a letter which I have just sent to the secretary of state.

I do not think I have been an alarmist before but I have become very worried and since we always have to sit down together when war comes to an end, I think before we have a third World War we should sit down together.

You and the secretary must feel the rest of us are a nuisance. Nevertheless, as a citizen I would not have a clear conscience if I did not tell you how I feel at the present time.

Very cordially yours,

March 16, 1948

Dear Mrs. Roosevelt:

I appreciated mostly highly your letter of the thirteenth enclosing copy of the one which you had written to the secretary of state. I think all of us are in practically the same frame of mind and I, of course, am glad to have your ideas and viewpoint.

I think if you will go over the history of the relationship between Russia and us you will find that every effort was made by President Roosevelt and by me to get along with them. Certain agreements were entered into at Tehran and Yalta and so far as our part of those agreements is concerned we carried them out to the letter.

When I arrived at Potsdam for that conference I found the Poles at the suggestion of Russia had moved into eastern Germany and that Russia had taken over a section of eastern Poland. The agreement at Yalta provided for free and untrammeled elections in Rumania, Bulgaria, Yugoslavia and Poland. I found a totalitarian Soviet government set up in Poland, in Rumania, in Yugoslavia and in Bulgaria. Members of our commissions in Bulgaria and Rumania were treated as if they were stableboys by the Russians in control in those two countries. Russia has not kept faith with us.

I myself discussed the Polish situation with the Polish government in Potsdam and got no satisfaction whatever from them—yet we made certain agreements in regard to the government of Germany which we have religiously tried to carry out. We have been blocked at every point by the Russians and to some extent by the French. The Russians have not carried out the agreements entered into at Potsdam.

The Russians are of the opinion that Henry Wallace and a depression are facing this country—they honestly believe that Wallace is going to be the next president. Of course, we all know that is absurd—we are much more likely to have the worst reactionary in the country for president than we are to have Wallace.

I shall go to the Congress tomorrow and state the facts. Beginning with my message to the Congress on September sixth, 1945, I have constantly informed the Congress and the country of our needs in order to make the United Nations work and to arrive at a peace for the welfare and benefit of every country in the world.

The first decision I had to make after being sworn in at 7:09 p.m. April 12, 1945 was whether to have the United Nations Conference at San Francisco on April 25, 1945. The Charter of the United Nations is a document under which we could work and have peace if we could get Russian cooperation. Twenty-two vetoes have been exercised in the last two and one-half years by the Russian government. As you know, I had to send Harry Hopkins to see Stalin in order to get Molotov to agree to the fundamental principles of the United Nations Charter.

I am still hopeful and still working with everything I have to make the United Nations work.

Our European Recovery Program and the proper strengthening of our military setup is the only hope we now have for peace in the world. That I am asking from the Congress.

If the people who know the facts and who understand the situation are willing to say that we've done wrong in this matter I don't see how we can expect to come out at all in its solution. It is the most serious situation we have faced since 1939. I shall face it with everything I have.

Of course, I am always glad to hear from you and I appreciate your frankness in writing me as you did.

Sincerely yours,

Only three years earlier the Soviet Union and United States were allies in crushing Nazi Germany. By March of 1948, they had become global rivals. Though Stalin had agreed at Potsdam that a four-power Allied council would govern occupied Berlin, the Soviets began imposing restrictions on access to western sectors. The communists were gaining wide popular support in French and Italian elections. But the Kremlin preferred to use force. A Soviet coup in February brought an abrupt end to democracy in Czechoslovakia. On March 10, Czech foreign minister Jan Masaryk, a friend of Mrs. Roosevelt's, was tortured and then either jumped or was pushed to his death from the window of his bedroom in the Czernin Palace, Prague. Mrs. Roosevelt suggested in her March 13 letter to Marshall that a face-to-face meeting of Western and Soviet leaders might ease tensions. She still favored reducing Germany to a pastoral and agricultural state and told Marshall that Stalin had legitimate concerns about the Western effort to revive Germany's industrial capacity. "I am sure they believe we are trying to build up Germany again into an industrial state," she wrote the secretary of state. "I sometimes wonder if behind our backs, that isn't one of the things that our big business people would like to see happen in spite of two world wars started by Germany."

––––––––––

Hyde Park
March 22, 1948

Dear Mr. President:

The events of the last few days since my last letter to you have been so increasingly disquieting that I feel I must write you a very frank and unpleasant letter.

I feel that even though the secretary of state takes the responsibility for the administration's attitude on Palestine, you cannot escape the results of that attitude. I have written the secretary a letter, a copy of which I enclose, which will explain my feelings on this particular subject.

On Trieste I feel we have also let the UN down. We are evidently discarding the UN and acting unilaterally, or setting up a balance of power by backing the European democracies and preparing for an ultimate war between the two political philosophies. I am opposed to this attitude because I feel that it would be possible, with force and friendliness, to make some arrangements with the Russians, using our economic power as a bribe to obstruct their political advance.

I cannot believe that war is the best solution. No one won the last war, and no one will win the next war. While I am in accord that we need force and I am in accord that we need this force to preserve the peace, I do not think that complete preparation for war is the proper approach as yet.

Politically, I know you have acted as you thought was right, regardless of political consequences. Unfortunately, it seems to me that one has to keep one's objectives in view and use timing and circumstances wisely to achieve those objectives.

I am afraid that the Democratic Party is, for the moment, in a very weak position, with the Southern revolt and the big cities and many liberals appalled by our latest moves. The combination of Wall Street objectives and military fears seem so intertwined in our present policies that it is difficult to quite understand what we are really trying to do.

I realize that I am an entirely unimportant cog in the wheel of our work with the United Nations, but I have offered my resignation to the secretary since I can quite understand the difficulty of having someone so far down the line openly criticize the administration's policies.

I deeply regret that I must write this letter.

Very sincerely yours,

March 25, 1948

My dear Mrs. Roosevelt:

I have read with deep concern and not without anxiety your letter of March twenty-second together with the copy of your letter to the secretary of state of the same date.

It would be impossible for me to minimize the importance of support of the United Nations with every resource at our command. It is the world's best if not sole hope for peace. If the United Nations fails all is chaos in a world already beset with suspicion, divisions, enmities, and jealousies.

Since you were good enough to let me see the text of your letter to General Marshall I asked him for a copy of his reply, which is before me as I write. I hope sincerely that the conversations which you are scheduled to have with Mr. Bohlen tomorrow will dispel at least some of your doubts and misgivings and that there may be further clarification if you are able to see Dean Rusk.

I should deplore as calamitous your withdrawal from the work of the United Nations at this critical time. Such a step is unthinkable. The United Nations, our own nation, indeed the world, needs the counsel and leadership which you can bring to its deliberations.

The United Nations' trusteeship proposed to the Security Council is intended only as a temporary measure, not as a substitute for the partition plan—merely an effort to fill the vacuum which termination of the mandate will create in the middle of May.

I sought to clarify our position in a statement issued today. Although I am sure you have read it, or heard it, I enclose a copy for your convenient reference.

May I appeal to you with the utmost sincerity to abandon any thought of relinquishing the post which you hold and for which you have unique qualifications. There is no one who could, at this time, exercise the influence which you can exert on the side of peace. And peace and the avoidance of further bloodshed in the Holy Land are our sole objectives.

May God bless you and protect you as you set out to fulfill so honored a mission to London.

Very sincerely yours,

In the midst of what would be a most difficult run for reelection, Truman did not want to lose Mrs. Roosevelt from his administration. Her biographer and close friend Joseph Lash wrote that Truman's reply "moved her deeply," though she would continue to question policies she did not agree with.

Like Mrs. Roosevelt, Truman was exasperated with the Mideast situ-

ation. On March 18, he pledged to Chaim Weizmann, president of the
Jewish Agency for Palestine and the World Zionist Organization, that the
United States would recognize the new Jewish state even if the United
Nations failed to establish a temporary trusteeship. A day later, the
U.S. ambassador to the United Nations, Warren Austin, asked the Security Council to drop its efforts to implement the partition plan. "This
morning I find that the State Department has reversed my Palestine policy," Truman wrote in his diary. "The first I know about it is what I see in
the papers! Isn't that hell? I'm now in the position of a liar and a double-
crosser. I've never felt so in my life."

Truman made known his displeasure to the State Department and
reiterated his commitment to Weizmann. "I think the proper thing to do
and the thing I have been doing is to do what I think is right and let
them all go to hell," the president wrote his brother Vivian on March 22.

The problem of Trieste dated back to World War I and the creation of
Yugoslavia from the old Serbia together with parts of then Austria-
Hungary. Italy had long wanted Trieste, a city with a magnificent har-
bor on the northern end of the Adriatic Sea. Following World War I,
Italy gained control of the city. When Marshal Tito took power in
Yugoslavia at the end of World War II, he sought to regain control of
Trieste. In 1946 the United Nations established the Free Territory of Tri-
este, splitting 293 square miles into two zones. The Americans and
British occupied the city and areas to the north. Yugoslavia occupied an
area south of the city. Though Tito made several threats to take the city
by force, he acted with more restraint after breaking with the Soviet
Union.

On March 17, Truman went before Congress, warning that U.S.
national security was threatened by the Soviet Union's expansionist
ambitions. He sought to restore the military draft and called for universal military training. Mrs. Roosevelt thought Truman had overstated
his case and that he was misguided in bringing back the draft.

Her comments about "Wall Street objectives" were disingenuous.
She was referring to Secretary of Defense James V. Forrestal, Under
Secretary of State Robert A. Lovett, and foreign policy adviser W.
Averell Harriman, who had similar backgrounds as Wall Street finan-

ciers and favored a hard line against the Soviet Union. All three were veterans of the Roosevelt administration.

———

New York
March 26, 1948

Dear Mr. President:

Your letter has reached me on the eve of my departure. It is a very fine letter and I am grateful to you.

I had a talk with Mr. Bohlen this afternoon and though I haven't heard from the secretary he brought me some messages from him. I must say that talking with Mr. Bohlen did not give me a feeling of any great decisions on various questions, though he did make me feel that there was deep concern, and I understand some of the difficulties and intentions better than I did before.

However, I can not say that even now the temporary measures that we have suggested for Palestine really make anything simpler or safer than it was before, but perhaps it will prove to be a solution and I certainly pray it will.

At the end of his visit Mr. Bohlen asked me about a statement which Franklin, Junior had made and I want to tell you that while Franklin told me he intended to make this statement, he did not ask me for my opinion.

There is without any question among the younger Democrats a feeling that the party as at present constituted is going down to serious defeat and may not be able to survive as the liberal party. Whether they are right or wrong, I do not know. I made up my mind long ago that working in the United Nations meant, as far as possible, putting aside partisan political activity and I would not presume to dictate to my children or to anyone else what their actions should be. I have not and I do not intend to have any part in pre-convention activities.

Very sincerely yours,

Three of Mrs. Roosevelt's four sons (James, Franklin Jr., and Elliott) played prominent roles in the movement to dump Truman and draft General Eisenhower as the 1948 Democratic presidential candidate. Her close friend Joseph Lash was also involved in this effort. While assuring Truman that she was neutral, evidence indicates otherwise. The young Hubert H. Humphrey, who was then mayor of Minneapolis and would be elected later that year to the U.S. Senate, disclosed in his memoirs that Mrs. Roosevelt called him several times in behalf of the Draft Ike campaign. She shared her sons' disappointment when Eisenhower chose not to run. After the GOP nominated Thomas E. Dewey for the presidency with Earl Warren as his running mate, Eleanor lamented to a friend, "The Republican ticket is a strong one and I feel Eisenhower will not be drafted and I don't think Truman can win against it."

London
April 14, 1948

Dear Mr. President:

I am enclosing these programs of the ceremonies at Grosvenor Square on the morning of the 12th, and of the Pilgrims' dinner in the evening. I thought you would be interested to see them.

There is so much heartfelt gratitude here for what the United States was able to do to help the British people, I wondered whether you would have or would like copies of the speeches which were made on that day. I have them for the library at Hyde Park, and when I get home I will be glad to have them copied and sent to you.

I have been deeply touched by all of the expressions of affection for my husband and by the regard for our country.

Very cordially yours,

The program, "Order of Ceremony at the Unveiling of the Memorial to President Roosevelt by Mrs. Roosevelt in Grosvenor Square, London, Monday, April 12th, 1948," is in Truman's papers. "The pure in heart are free from suspicion," Mrs. Roosevelt said in her dedication speech. "The great and humble cannot be humiliated. Pray God we join together and invite all others to join us in creating a world where justice, truth, and good faith rule."

April 27, 1948

Dear Mrs. Roosevelt:

I appreciated most highly your note of the fourteenth from London, enclosing me a copy of the program of the Unveiling of the Memorial of President Roosevelt on April twelfth, and a copy of the program of the Pilgrims Dinner at the Savoy Hotel that evening.

I am very happy that everything went over satisfactorily and that you are pleased with the ceremony. I wish I could have seen it.

I'd certainly like to have copies of the speeches that were made on that day if it isn't too much trouble to send them to me.

I hope to see you sometime soon.

Sincerely yours,

May 11, 1948

Dear Mr. President:

I have just sent a letter to the Secretary of State, a copy of which I enclose for your information.

As I have said, I have no idea what the attitude of the Administration on the recognition of the Jewish State is going to be. If we are going to recognize it, I think it would be a mistake to lag behind Russia. If we are not going to recognize it, I think we should make our position known as quickly as possible and the reasons for whatever position we take.

This action, as far as I am concerned, is interesting to me only from ethical and humanitarian points of view, but of course, it has political considerations which I am sure your advisers will take into consideration. I am quite hopeful that whatever our policy is, it will be clear and consistent for I am more convinced every day that had the Arabs been convinced of what we really meant to do, they might have accepted the UN decision and not put us in the rather difficult position which the Security Council, minus any force, finds itself in today. I have heard it said that we were afraid of a UN force which included the Russians because of the difficulties we have had with them in Germany and Korea. Some day or other we have to be willing, if we are going to work out some peaceful solutions, to serve in some kind of joint force and to agree we will all leave whatever country we may be in when the UN tells us to leave.

I was much encouraged by the report of the conversations between Ambassador Smith and Mr. Molotov as it came over the radio this morning. I think that kind of straightforward statement to fact is helpful and leaves the way open for peaceful negotiations in the future.

With my warm regards to Mrs. Truman and Margaret, I am,

Very cordially yours

In a handwritten postscript, Mrs. Roosevelt added, "I personally believe in the Jewish State."

May 11, 1948

Dear Mr. Secretary:

Thank you for sending me Ambassador Douglas's letter. I am very happy that he told you what I said and that he felt the visit to Great Britain was helpful and created good feeling. I hope the visits to Holland [and] Belgium did the same.

I have just heard from some of the Jewish organizations that they have heard that Russia will recognize the Jewish State as soon as it is declared which will be midnight on Friday, I imagine. The people who spoke to me are afraid that we will lag behind and again follow instead of lead.

I have no idea what the policy of the Administration and the State Department is going to be on this, and I am only just telling you what you probably already know about the Russian position. I have no feeling that they have any principles or convictions in what they are doing, but wherever they can put us in a hole they certainly are going to do it.

The attitude of the International Law Committee of the Association of the Bar of the City of New York on the draft of the declaration of Human Rights and the Convention, of course, is going to coincide with the British Government's attitude as expressed by Lord Jowitt in Parliament the other day. Neither country, apparently, is anxious to do anything at the present time. I feel that the Human Rights Commission has an obligation to present the best draft it can to the Economic and Social Council, but if they wish to recommend to the General Assembly that the Assembly consider the present documents and then refer them to governments for further comment, that is up to the Economic and Social Council or even to the Assembly itself.

It would please the Russians to begin all over again as they have suggested in this meeting, and try to find points on which we can all agree and base a Declaration on such points. I doubt very much if they at any time would consider a Convention.

I doubt very much also if the very restricted Convention suggested by the Bar Association will satisfy the European countries or the smaller countries on the Human Rights Commission, but I think we may have to state quite openly that we want a document which the larger number of governments can adhere to, that we hope there will be future conventions and that perhaps even we, ourselves, in view of the fact that Congress would have to ratify such treaties, can not agree to wording which goes beyond our own Constitution. It is an acknowledgement, of course, of the fact that we have discrimination within our own country. As that is well known, I do not see what we should not acknowledge it and bring out the fact that the Supreme Court has just taken a step forward and we feel we are moving forward, but that in international documents it would be a deception to agree to go beyond what we could obtain ratification for in Congress.

I am sorry I did not see you when I was in Washington and I shall be delighted to have a chance to talk with you whenever it is possible. Just now my presence at the UN daily seems to be the most important thing to me.

Very cordially yours,

P.S. I failed to say that personally I feel there is right back of the establishment of a Jewish State.

———————

New York
May 17, 1948

Dear Mr. President:

I am enclosing a copy of a letter which I just sent to the Secretary of State.

You will begin to find me such a nuisance you will wish I would go home and stay there! However this question of having the foreign policy integrated with the work of the United Nations seems to me of paramount importance.

Very sincerely yours,

May 16, 1948

Dear Mr. Secretary:

Having written you before what I had heard on the subject of the recognition of Palestine, I feel I should write you again.

The way in which the recognition of Palestine came about has created complete consternation in the United Nations.

As you know, I never wanted us to change our original stand. When I wrote to the President and to you the other day what I had heard, I thought, of course, that you would weigh it against the reports which you were getting from the United Nations. Much as I wanted the Palestine State recognized, I would not have wanted it done without the knowledge of our representatives in the United Nations who had been fighting for our changed position. I would have felt that they had to know the reason and I would also have felt that there had to be a very clear understanding beforehand with such nations as we expected would follow our lead.

Several of the representatives of other governments have been to talk to me since then, and have stated quite frankly that they do not see how they could ever follow the United States' lead because the United States changed so often without any consultation. There seems to be no sense of interlocking information between the United States delegate and the State Department on the policy making level. This is serious because our acts which should strengthen the United Nations only result in weakening our influence within the United Nations and in weakening the United Nations itself.

More and more the other delegates seem to believe that our whole policy is based on antagonism to Russia and that we think in terms of going it alone rather than in terms of building up a leadership within the United Nations.

This seems to me a very serious defect and I do not see how we can expect to have any real leadership if,

1—We do not consult our people in the United Nations on what we are going to do, and

2—If we do not line up our following before we do the things, rather than trusting them to influence them afterwards.

I can not imagine that major considerations on policies such as this are taken at such short notice that there is not time to think through every consequence and inform all those who should be informed.

I have seldom seen a more bitter, puzzled, discouraged group of people than some of those whom I saw on Saturday. Some of them I know are favorable to the rights of the Jews in Palestine, but they are just non-plussed by the way in which we do things.

I thought I had to tell you this because I had written you before and as you know, I believe that it is the Administration's desire to strengthen the United Nations, but we do not always achieve it because, apparently, there is a lack of contact on the higher levels.

With deep concern, I am,

Very sincerely yours,

May 20, 1948

Dear Mrs. Roosevelt:

Thanks very much for yours of the seventeenth enclosing me a copy of a letter you had written to General Marshall about the recognition of Palestine.

I am sorry, of course, that you were disturbed by the procedure but, under the circumstances, there was not much else to be done. Since there was a vacuum in Palestine and since the Russians were anxious to be the first to do the recognizing General Marshall, Secretary Lovett, Dr. Rusk and myself worked the matter out and decided the proper thing to do was to recognize the Jewish Government promptly. Senator Austin was notified of what was taking place but he didn't have a chance to talk with the other members of the delegation until afterward. I am sorry that it caused any disturbance.

Sincerely yours,

At 6:11 p.m., eastern standard time, on Friday, May 14, Truman recognized the state of Israel just eleven minutes after it became a nation. The White House issued this statement: "This government has been informed that a Jewish state has been proclaimed in Palestine and recognition has been requested by the provisional government thereof. The United States recognizes the provisional government as the de facto authority of the State of Israel."

Mrs. Roosevelt, though pleased that Truman had recognized the Jewish state, was insulted that the administration had failed to alert the U.S. delegation to the United Nations. Marshall was concerned that the entire U.S. delegation might quit in protest.

New York
May 13, 1948

Dear Mr. President:

A group of people came to see me the other day about conscientious objection as related to human rights. At the same time they spoke to me about the conscientious objectors of the last war.

The following is an excerpt from their statement to me: "The second matter has to do with the amnesty or pardon, for conscientious objectors in the United States in World War II. As you undoubtedly know, the commission headed by former Justice Roberts reported to the President in December and on December 23, 1947, the President issued pardons to the persons listed by the Roberts Commission.

"However, only about 1500 of the 15,000 Selective Service violators were included in the pardon. Of the approximately 1100 recognized as conscientious objectors by the Department of Justice only about 150 received pardons. Of the 3,000 or more Jehovah's Witnesses only a couple of hundred were included.

"In a very real sense those who were not included in the Commission's recommendation are now worse off than they were before, since the Department of Justice is taking the position that these persons have all been considered and is therefore declining to consider applications for individual pardons. . . .

"Another extremely serious aspect of the matter is that the Roberts

Commission applied a very narrow conception of 'religious belief' in determining which conscientious objectors were entitled to pardon. This appears to open the way for retrogression in dealing with conscientious objectors under any future military training or service act.

"The American Friends Service Committee, the Federal Council of Churches, and the American Civil Liberties Union, as well as the Committee for Amnesty, which is composed mainly of non-pacifist sponsors, have protested and urged a full amnesty, that is restoration of civil rights, for all conscientious objectors and Jehovah's Witnesses. However, at present there appears to be no progress."

I am sending this to you to ask if now full pardon should not be given?

Very cordially yours,

May 17, 1948

[Unsent]

Dear Mrs. Roosevelt:

I read your letter of [May] thirteenth with a great deal of interest. I have thoroughly looked into the conscientious objectors case and, I think, all the honest conscientious objectors have been released.

I'll admit that it is rather difficult for me to look on a conscientious objector with patience while your four sons and my three nephews were risking their lives to save our government, and the things for which we stand, these people were virtually shooting them in the back.

I ran across one conscientious objector that I really believe is all man—he was a young Naval Pharmacist Mate who served on Okinawa carrying wounded sailors and marines from the battlefield. I decorated him with a Congressional Medal of Honor. I asked him how it came about that he as a conscientious objector was willing to go into the things of the battlefield and he said to me that he could serve the Lord and save lives there as well as anywhere else in the world. He didn't weigh over 140 pounds and he was about five feet six inches tall. I shall never forget him.

My experience in the first world war with conscientious objectors was not a happy one—the majority of those with whom I came in contact were just plain cowards and shirkers—that is the reason I asked Justice Roberts to make a complete survey of the situation and to release all those that he felt were honestly conscientious objectors and that has been done. My sympathies with the rest of them are not very strong, as you can see.

On October 12, 1945, Truman presented a Medal of Honor to Private Desmond T. Doss of Lynchburg, Virginia, a conscientious objector whose acts of valor on Okinawa earned him the nation's highest military honor. As a combat veteran, Truman had strong views about conscientious objectors. In this letter, which he did not send, he may also have been expressing his bitterness toward the Roosevelt family for their efforts to deny him renomination. The president often wrote letters when he was angry and then, instead of sending the angry message, would keep it in his files. On May 22, Truman dictated a second letter, which he also did not send.

May 25, 1948

Dear Mrs. Roosevelt:

I read your letter in regard to the pardon for conscientious objects with a great deal of interest and I had the Attorney General prepare me a memorandum on the subject.

The memorandum is enclosed for your information—it covers the situation completely.

Sincerely yours,

Attorney General Tom Clark's memorandum defended the administration's rejection of appeals for amnesty. Clark noted that approximately a thousand persons convicted of Selective Service violations "claimed to be conscientious objectors." The president's Amnesty Board recommended pardons for only 150. "The Board declined to recommend amnesty in those cases where the individual's claim was recognized and he was classified as being opposed to both combatant and non-combatant military service, and was ordered to report for work of national importance in lieu thereof and

either failed to so report or violated some phase of the Act while in a civil-
ian public service camp. It appears that the Board adopted the viewpoint
that these persons were accorded classification as they had requested but
simply set themselves up as being greater than the law." Clark said that
the majority of convictions involving conscientious objectors were for
refusing to transfer to another civilian service camp or for deserting.

———————

As for cases involving Jehovah's Witnesses, Clark said that these indi-
viduals rarely claimed to be conscientious objectors but sought exemp-
tions from the draft as ministers. "The fact that all members of this sect
claim to be ministers is indicative that none is a minister in the sense
that Congress used the term in the Selective Service Act. Where the
facts supported claims to be a minister, Jehovah's Witnesses were gener-
ally accorded ministerial classifications by local boards."

In addition to conscientious objectors and Jehovah's Witnesses, Clark
reported that ten thousand were designated as "willful violators or draft
dodgers." Truman agreed with that classification.

———————

June 27, 1948

Dear Mr. President:

I am enclosing another letter on the subject of conscientious objectors
for your consideration. I wrote Mr. Muste that he could not publicize the
former correspondence.

With kindest regards, I am

Very cordially yours,

In a June 21 letter, Muste wrote Mrs. Roosevelt that the Justice Depart-
ment memorandum "bears out the contention of the Committee for
Amnesty that the Roberts Board did not propose and the President did
not grant amnesty at all." Muste sought her permission to make public
her correspondence with Truman.

———————

August 10, 1948

Dear Mrs. Roosevelt:

After reading your letter of August sixth, I can fully appreciate all that you have to do before your departure for Paris for the third Session of the General Assembly of the United Nations. Of course, I had hoped that it would be possible for you to accept appointment as one of the Special Ambassadors to represent the United States at the Golden Jubilee of Queen Wilhemina of The Netherlands and the Coronation of Princess Juliana, but I quite understand why you feel that you must decline.

I am more grateful than I can say for your thoughtfulness in sending me a copy of the full account of the Ceremonies in London at the unveiling of the Memorial to President Roosevelt. This particular copy will take its place among my treasured papers.

Very sincerely yours,

Hyde Park
August 19, 1948

Dear Mr. President:

I want to thank you for your kindness in seeing me yesterday and to tell you that I appreciate the difficulties under which you have labored. I wish you could have had better assistants.

Above everything else, I hope that the national committee will ask of the state committees that they make an aggressive campaign, picking every mistake made by the other side, such as this Italian situation and pointing out again and again that they know what you stand for, and therefore, it is essential that they give you the kind of men in Congress who will make it possible for you to carry through a program for the benefit of the average man.

I do not feel that the national committee is getting the maximum out of the state committees and while I am a great believer in the necessity for appealing to the independent voter, I also realize that our own machinery must function as well as possible.

I hope your holiday will be a very pleasant one.

Very cordially yours,

Mrs. Roosevelt is referring to GOP criticism of the administration's military and economic aid to Italy's moderate government headed by Premier Alcide de Gasperi, a Christian Democrat. In the bitterly fought 1948 Italian elections, the communists and their allies won a third of the vote. With an assist from Truman, de Gasperi retained power. Italian-Americans returned the favor in the '48 election.

September 17, 1948

Dear Mrs. Roosevelt:

I am indeed grateful for your letter of September twelfth mailed on the eve of your departure for the conference in Paris.

You have done yeoman service for the Democratic Party in your column and I know those you left behind to cover the day while you are en route will serve a like purpose.

It is not surprising that the Russians are making friendly advances to the State of Israel. I do not however believe in view of Russia's ruthless betrayal of every nation that trusted her and her default in practically all of her commitments that she will fool so canny a people as those in Israel. You may be sure that I will give careful consideration to the angle of where Israel is going to turn as we shape a policy on recognition and the lifting of the embargo and the granting of the loan. We must make the new state our friend otherwise we shall, as you observe, lose a strategic position in the Near East. The problem which Russia presents cannot be minimized. I am glad you are totally opposed to appeasement. That situation must be faced squarely. It is among the imponderables.

I have a feeling that you and the other members of the delegation will come into close accord as the discussions progress. It is characteristic of you to write thus frankly as you did and you know I have the highest respect for your opinions and your observations.

I write in great haste on the day of my departure for a campaign trip. Take care of yourself and conserve your energy. Your country needs you.

Always sincerely,

Paris
October 4, 1948

Dear Mr. President:

I understand that there is some comment in the newspapers in the United States that I have not come out for you as the Democratic candidate and prefer the election of the Republican candidate. I am unqualifiedly for you as the Democratic candidate for the presidency.

This year I hope every Democrat and independent voter is concentrating on the election of as many liberal Democrats to Congress as possible. I hope for this particularly from the labor and farm groups who have perhaps the greatest stake in the preservation of liberal leadership.

Liberal policies during these next few years are of vast importance on domestic issues. A Democratic administration, backed by a liberal Democratic Congress, could really achieve the policies for which you have stood.

As delegate to the United Nations I have become very much aware of the fact that stability in our own government and in its policies is essential to help the Western democracies on their road to rehabilitation.

With every good wish I am,

Very cordially yours,

Frances Perkins had telephoned Mrs. Roosevelt in Paris and alerted her that the syndicated political columnist Drew Pearson was reporting that she favored Dewey. "I haven't actually endorsed Mr. Truman," Eleanor wrote Perkins, "because he has been such a weak and vacillating person and made such poor appointments in his Cabinet and entourage, such as Snyder and Vaughan, that unless we are successful in electing a very strong group of liberals in Congress, in spite of my feelings about the Republican Party and Governor Dewey, I cannot have much enthusiasm for Mr. Truman. Though there are many people in government that I would hate to feel would not be allowed to continue their work, I still find it very difficult to give any good reasons for being for Mr. Truman."

Because of her lukewarm endorsement, Mrs. Roosevelt was uncertain whether the sentence in her letter to Truman would be made public.

"If it ever sees the light of day," she wrote Lash, "I hope you will approve."

October 17, 1948

Dear Mrs. Roosevelt:

I am deeply grateful to you for your generous letter of October fourth. Have I your permission to release it for publication?

Very sincerely yours,

Paris
October 21, 1948

Glad have you use letter any way you wish.

Regards,
Eleanor Roosevelt

Truman recalled years later that many prominent Democrats were reluctant to endorse him. "They all thought I didn't have a chance to win," he said. "Even Mrs. Roosevelt had a terrible time making a statement in support of me."

On election eve, at Flynn's urging, she made a brief radio talk in behalf of Truman's reelection. After the president's upset victory, she wrote privately, "I didn't think Truman could be re-elected & now that he is I have a terrible sense of responsibility. He made so many promises which can only be carried out if he gets good people around him & that he hasn't done successfully yet!"

November 20, 1948

Dear Mr. President:

I thought you would be interested to see this letter.

With best wishes, I am

Very sincerely yours,

Charles G. Hamilton, chairman of the Young Democrats of Mississippi, had written Mrs. Roosevelt on November 8 that Truman had been cheated out of thousands of votes in his state by the old-guard segregationist political establishment, which had supported the third-party candidacy of South Carolina governor J. Strom Thurmond. The States' Rights ticket carried South Carolina, Alabama, Mississippi, and Louisiana.

December 13, 1948

Dear Mrs. Roosevelt:

I appreciated your note of the twentieth with the enclosed letter from Mr. Hamilton, chairman of the Young Democrats of Mississippi.

It is a most interesting piece of information and sometime or other we will get the situation worked out I am sure. At least the Democratic Party is no longer in the position of the dog whose tail wags him. We are not only rid of the fringes on the left end but we are free of the so-called solid South and I hope to see a Democratic Party from now on that will really be a Democratic Party and represent all the people.

The Republican Party should represent the special privilege boys—as it always has.

Sincerely yours,

New York
December 16, 1948

Dear Mr. President:

I quite understand your not wanting to be bothered just now with reports from your delegates but I am going to Washington on the 11th of January and I would be able to go and see you on the 13th, providing you are willing, any time in the morning or afternoon.

I will send you in the course of the next week or so a memorandum on thoughts which have occurred to me as a result of this last contact with Europe.

With best wishes to you, Mrs. Truman and Margaret for a happy holiday season,

Very cordially yours,

December 21, 1948

Dear Mrs. Roosevelt:

I shall be delighted to see you on Thursday, January thirteenth, at twelve o'clock noon and shall look forward with keen anticipation to receiving from you a firsthand account of the deliberations in Paris in which you bore so important a part.

I sincerely hope that you have not overtaxed your strength during the long succession of busy days. I have marveled at the poise and patience that you and the other members of our delegation have maintained in the face of the maddening technique of the Russians. Not only have they been deliberately non-cooperative but they have conducted themselves with a boorishness worthy of stable boys. I have observed with great satisfaction that you have put them in their place more than once.

Always sincerely,

The Universal Declaration of Human Rights, Mrs. Roosevelt's most enduring accomplishment, was approved by the United Nations General Assembly on December 10, 1948. Truman was her staunchest ally in this great endeavor. "We have played a leading role in this undertaking, designed to create a world order of law and justice fully protective of the rights and the dignity of the individual," he noted in his 1948 civil rights message. (See appendix for complete document.)

December 29, 1948

Dear Mr. President:

I am sending you this lengthy report which I hope you may have time to read and I look forward to seeing you on the 13th of January.

With every good wish for the New Year to you and Mrs. Truman and Margaret, I am,

Very cordially yours,

December 28, 1948

Memo for the President:

First of all I want to tell you, Mr. President that when the news of your election reached Europe, there was general rejoicing. It gave to many statesmen and even to the people on the street who felt that there might have been a change in our foreign policy, a sense of security that that which is now being done would be continued.

Next, I think I should say that generally there is a feeling that Mr. Harriman has done a very good job and a devoted one. As you know, I have not always felt that he had a broad enough point of view and grasp of the world situation, but he struck me as having greatly broadened and having been capable of growing with the opportunity which you have given him, which after all, is the greatest thing that one can ask of any one. He has chosen a good staff and everywhere I heard good things said of these people. People wrote me about the representatives they considered particularly good in a number of cases. I heard also that Mr. Harriman had handled labor very well.

France, as he undoubtedly told you, is the greatest headache still. I think he understands what some of the greatest difficulties are. Many of the young men who fought in the resistance movement, or who were taken to [forced labor] camps out of the country returned or finished their period of the war, depleted physically and mentally. The food has not been sufficient in energy giving qualities. You can not, for instance even today, unless you are willing and able to buy in the black market get butter and sugar and only small children can get milk. Until one comes back physically, one can not come back mentally and spiritually. Also the constant change of governments, due in large part to a very complicated situation which I will be glad to explain if you are interested, has made life for the working people in the cities very difficult and creates a lack of confidence in the government.

The hardships are real and the Soviets through their communist party in France have offered both rural and city people certain benefits which they could not well resist. The French are not naturally communists but they find it hard to be staunch in the sense that the British are and so they have accepted many communist things. This does not frighten me for the future but it creates great difficulties for the present.

This question of economic well-being is exploited by the USSR in all nations and they promise much until they gain complete control, then people are worse off than they were before but up to that time they have hopes of being better off and this is what creates one of the dangers for us. Since we are really fighting ideas as well as economic conditions the Russians do a better propaganda job because it is easier to say that your government is a government of workers for the benefit of workers than it is to say that a democratic government which is capitalistic benefits the workers more in the end. The only way to prove that to them, I think, is gradually to have more of them see conditions in our country, under supervision of course, and with every arrangement made for them to return to their own country, but the USSR is as loathe to let them come over as we have been to allow them to enter which makes this solution very difficult.

Great Britain is going to pull through because it has stood up under incredible drabness of living and I think will know how to use the aid coming to good account. Our relations with the British must, I think, be put on a different basis. We are without question the leading democracy in the world today, but so far Great Britain still takes the attitude that she makes the policies on all world questions and we accept them. That has got to be remedied. We have got to make the policies and they have got to accept them. Mr. Bevin has been unwise in many ways but I will not put on paper what I would be willing to tell you.

I hope very much that the situation between ourselves and the USSR can change in the coming year and that we can accomplish final peace settlements. Germany can not return to any kind of normality until that is done, for at present the heap of ruins and disillusioned people in the center of Europe makes it difficult for all around to recover.

I have a feeling that your attitude on Palestine did a great deal to straighten out our own delegation and help the situation from the world point of view. The Arabs have to be handled with strength. One of the troubles has been that we have been so impressed with the feeling that we must have a united front in Europe that it has affected our stand in the Near East. I personally feel that it is more important for the French and for the British to be united with us than for us to be united with them, and therefore when we make up our minds that something has to be done, we should be the ones to do what we think is right and we should not go through so many anxieties on the subject.

There are all kinds of hidden reasons why nations and their statesmen desire certain things which are not the reasons they usually give. The most truthful of the statesmen that I talked to while in Paris was Robert Schuman of France, but it does require some knowledge of the past and much background to be always on your guard and figure out what are the reasons for certain stands that are taken.

I have great admiration for the Secretary of State and for many of the people in our State Department, but sometimes I think we are a little bit too trusting and forget the past. In giving me as an adviser Mr. Durward Sandifer, a lawyer of experience and assistant to Mr. Dean Rusk in the Department, I could not have been better served, but I still feel it is hard for the Department to accept policies, without certain individuals trying to inject their own points of view and I do not think all of them have the knowledge and experience to take a world point of view instead of a local one and by local I mean the point of view which is affected by the particular area in which they have special knowledge and experience.

I should like to say a word to you when we meet on the subject of the bi-partisan policy and the representatives of the other party.

I also learned that the Philippine representatives were very much affected by the Equal Benefits Bill which is in Congress and I think if this goes through we will have a remarkable rise in their loyalty.

The thing above all others which I would like to bring to your attention is that we are now engaged in a situation which is as complicated as fighting the war. During the war my husband had a map room and there were experts who daily briefed him on what was happening in every part of the world. It seems to me that we are engaged in the war for peace in which there enter questions of world economy, food, religion, education, health, and social conditions, as well as military and power conditions. I have a feeling that it would be helpful if you could build a small group of very eminent non-political experts in all these fields whose duty it would be to watch the world scene and keep you briefed day by day in a map room. No one man can watch this whole world picture or have the background and knowledge to cover it accurately. It must be achieved by wise choice of people in the various fields to do it well and understandingly.

I have a feeling that our situation in Europe will be solved in the next year without too much difficulty. Our real battlefield today is Asia and our real battle is the one between democracy and communism. We can not ruin America and achieve the results that have to be achieved in the world, so whatever we do must be done with the most extraordinary wisdom and foresight in the economic field. At the same time we have to prove to the world and particularly to downtrodden areas of the world which are the natural prey to the principles of communist economy that democracy really brings about happier and better conditions for the people as a whole. Never was there an era in history in which the responsibilities were greater for the United States, and never was a President called upon to meet such extraordinary responsibilities for civilization as a whole.

I think you are entitled to the best brains and the best knowledge available in the world today. Congress must understand this picture but it can not be expected to follow it in the way that it has to be followed, for the knowledge must come from a group which you set up and from you to them. You need something far greater than political advice though that is also an essential in the picture at home as well as abroad. The search should be for wise men of great knowledge and devoted to mankind, for mankind is at the crossroads. It can destroy itself or it can enter into a new era of happiness and security. It seems to me that you are the instrument chosen as a guide in this terribly serious situation and if there is anything which any of us can do to help you, you have a right to call upon us all.

CHAPTER 5

1949

Eleanor Roosevelt did much to change public attitudes about women in public office. In 1938, the Gallup Poll reported that only 22 percent of the American public approved of married women working. By 1947, a plurality of Americans said they approved of women serving as governors, senators, doctors, or lawyers. In 1949, a majority of the public supported the appointment of women as ambassadors or ministers. When the Gallup Poll first asked respondents in the fall of 1948 to name the woman, in any part of the world, whom they admired the most, Eleanor topped the list.

In May of 1949, Truman sat next to Eleanor during the annual dinner of the Women's National Press Club. As he presented her with an award, the president reminded his audience that he had recognized her diplomatic skills in nominating her to the United Nations General Assembly. If the death of her husband had made him president of the United States, Truman took great pride in making Mrs. Roosevelt "the First Lady of the World."

That same month, Truman showed that he did not hold her sons in similar esteem. Franklin D. Roosevelt Jr., who had been among the leaders of the 1948 Draft Eisenhower movement, ran as the nominee of the splinter Liberal Party in a special election to fill the New York City congressional seat of the late Sol Bloom. Democratic National Chairman J. Howard McGrath, with Truman's approval, supported Judge Benjamin Shalleck, the regular Democratic nominee. Roosevelt, who was then thirty-five years old, easily won. His mother assured Truman that he would be a good Democrat.

Three weeks after the 1948 election, the Trumans moved across Pennsylvania Avenue to Blair House while the White House underwent major renovation. They would not move back for more than three years. Mrs. Roosevelt endorsed the president's effort to save the executive mansion. "I feel very strongly that, as far as it is humanly possible, the outer shell [of the White House] should be preserved," she wrote in a column. "The repairs certainly should be made, but in such a way that the house should be reconstituted as nearly as possible as it has been since George Washington planned it. No new design or new house could possibly have the historic interest of this old one.

"The President told me that he had the woodwork, fireplaces, mirrors and chandeliers all carefully stored away and he had even had plaster casts made of the ceilings since they are among the greatest beauties of the house. There is a dignity and a simplicity about the White House that many foreigners, coming here, comment upon and which give to many of our own people who visit it a sense of pride."

Mrs. Roosevelt wrote in her column with sorrow about the riots in Peekskill, New York, that disrupted a meeting where the African-American political activist and singer Paul Robeson was scheduled to speak. "I think if we care for the preservation of our liberties," she wrote, "we must allow all people, whether we disagree with them or not, to hold meetings and express their views unmolested as long as they do not advocate the overthrow of the government."

Truman was asked for comment about this column. "I think Mrs. Roosevelt covered the situation perfectly and thoroughly," he replied.

The triumph of Mao Tse-tung's Red Army after twenty years of civil war and the founding of the People's Republic of China was regarded by many Americans as a foreign policy disaster. Truman was blamed by political opponents for the "loss" of China, though no one explained how it was his to lose. "China is too big a country, it has too many people for any other nation to be able to fully control," Mrs. Roosevelt wrote, "unless they wish to invade and control by force."

Truman had numerous foreign policy successes in 1949. The North Atlantic Treaty, which would hold the line against Soviet expansionism in Europe, was signed in April by the United States and eleven other nations. A month later, Stalin lifted his blockade of West Berlin, a concession of defeat in the first major battle of the Cold War.

This I Remember, Mrs. Roosevelt's memoir of her White House years, was published by Harper & Brothers. "It is almost shockingly delightful to read a book which could have been written by absolutely no one else in the world than the great and important figure whose name is signed to it," Elizabeth Janeway wrote in the *New York Times Book Review.* "More than readable, this is a delightful book . . . tragic and noble and very human."

January 3, 1949

Dear Mrs. Roosevelt:

I appreciated most highly yours of December twenty-ninth, enclosing me a memorandum on your recent visit to Europe. It is a most interesting document and I appreciate your sending it to me.

I am looking forward to seeing you on the thirteenth of January.

I hope you had a pleasant Christmas and I also hope that the New Year will be entirely good to you. Mrs. Truman and Margaret join me in these good wishes.

Sincerely yours,

———————

Hyde Park
January 16, 1949

Dear Mr. President:

This letter seemed to me very well written and therefore I am drawing it to your attention.

Very cordially yours,

———————

January 25, 1949

My dear Mrs. Roosevelt:

Thanks very much for sending me a copy of the Herbert Bayard Swope, Jr. letter on the foreign policy.

I wonder if he still acts as a brain trust for Mr. Baruch. He was in to see me the other day with the Civil Rights Committee and I had a very pleasant conversation with him.

Thanks again for calling attention to the letter.

Sincerely yours,

Hyde Park
January 29, 1949

Dear Mr. President:

The letter I sent to you was from the son of Mr. Swope who is, I imagine, paid by Mr. Baruch. They are two entirely different people.

When I read about the inauguration I thought you and Mrs. Truman and Margaret would be exhausted, but the papers reassured me.

With every good wish, I am,

Very cordially yours,

The letter, from Herbert Bayard Swope Jr., had appeared in the New York Times *and called for the United States to exert world leadership through a foreign policy of peace through strength. Truman did not know the author of the letter. But he disliked the elder Swope (1882–1958), former executive editor of the* New York World, *who had been closely associated with the New York financier Bernard Baruch for more than thirty years. In August of 1948, Truman asked Baruch to become his finance chairman. But the old man turned him down. "A great many honors have passed your way," Truman wrote back, "and it seems when the going is rough it is a one-way street. I am sorry that this is so." Baruch, no shrinking violet, denounced HST as a "rude, uncouth, and ignorant man." It was at the urging of the elder Swope that Baruch publicly repudiated Truman.*

January 16, 1949

Dear Mr. President:

I am sending this note hoping you will feel perfectly free to consider it as my resignation as delegate to the adjourned session of the General Assembly of the United Nations.

HST, who nominated Eleanor as a member of the U.S. delegation to the United Nations, said that she was the "First Lady of the World." *(Truman Library)*

On the first anniversary of FDR's death, Eleanor and Harry stand at
the late president's grave. *(U.S. Information Agency)*

Every Memorial Day, Eleanor invited Truman to Hyde Park. But
he would never make it back during Eleanor's lifetime. This picture
was taken on April 12, 1946. *(Abbie Rowe, National Park Service/
Truman Library)*

HST dedicates Franklin D. Roosevelt's home at Hyde Park as a national shrine. Speaking from the front portico, Truman was flanked by Eleanor on the left and on the right, next to a pillar, Franklin D. Roosevelt Jr. The noted contralto Marian Anderson is seated at the left. *(Abbie Rowe, National Park Service/Truman Library)*

On October 27, 1945, Truman spoke at the commissioning of the USS *Franklin D. Roosevelt* from a platform on the carrier. The ceremony took place at the New York Navy Yard. *(U.S. Navy photograph/Courtesy Truman Library)*

Arriving at the Lincoln Memorial for the closing session of the 1947 NAACP convention, Eleanor and Harry were accompanied by Walter F. White, executive secretary of the civil rights organization. On this occasion, Truman became the first American president to address the NAACP. *(Abbie Rowe, National Park Service/ Truman Library)*

In the summer of 1948, there was speculation that Truman might choose Mrs. Roosevelt as his running mate. After Truman commented on this possibility at a press conference, the Associated Press moved this photograph with the caption: "Mrs. Roosevelt on the Democratic ticket?" She replied from Hyde Park that she had no intention of running for any office. *(Wide World)*

At the 1952 Democratic convention, Eleanor received a prolonged ovation from the faithful. Addressing delegates for the first time in a dozen years, she explained the importance of the United Nations. Truman persuaded her to make this talk. (Chicago Sun-Times)

Eleanor, who had early doubts about her husband's successor, came to regard him as one of America's better presidents. "I felt that he had to make more than his share of big decisions," she wrote, "and that he made very few mistakes in times of crisis."
(Truman Library)

Eleanor and Harry were on opposite sides in the 1956 Democratic presidential race. She backed Adlai E. Stevenson *(center)*, while Truman favored New York governor W. Averell Harriman. *(Truman Library)*

In January of 1957, Eleanor and Harry became co-chairmen of the Democratic Advisory Council at the invitation of Democratic National Chairman Paul Butler (center).
*(*New York Herald Tribune/*Truman Library)*

Eleanor, who served on the committee that raised funds for the construction of Truman's presidential library, received the grand tour when she visited Independence in 1960. *(Truman Library)*

Eleanor was buried next to her husband in the Rose Garden at Hyde Park in November of 1962. From left, Franklin D. Roosevelt Jr., Jacqueline Kennedy, President John F. Kennedy, Vice President Lyndon B. Johnson, former president Harry S. Truman, Bess Wallace Truman, and former president Dwight D. Eisenhower. *(Eisenhower Library)*

It has been an honor and a privilege to serve as a delegate, as well as an educational experience for me. I realize, however, that you may decide that it is wise to appoint some one in my place, and if so I shall understand. I shall, of course, always stand ready to help in any way I can.

With my deep appreciation of my past opportunities, I am,

Very sincerely yours,

February 21, 1949

My dear Mrs. Roosevelt:

This makes belated acknowledgement of your letter of January sixteenth. For your sake I wish I could release you from further service as Representative to the adjourned session of the General Assembly of the United Nations.

You have earned a respite from your continued and arduous labors with that body. But frankly, I think you have rendered a service to your country in a difficult time which could not have been performed by any other citizen. Nor can I think of anyone who could carry on in your place.

Your country needs you—indeed, this troubled world needs you and the counsel which you can bring to the UN, out of your rich experience and deep sympathy with the needs of humanity.

I have, therefore, no recourse but to send your nomination to the Senate today along with the names of the other Representatives and Alternates previously appointed during the recess of that body.

God speed you in your noble mission.

Very sincerely yours,

February 22, 1949

Dear Mr. President:

I am deeply honored to be renominated as delegate to the adjourned session of the General Assembly of the United Nations and I shall be glad to serve if I can be useful.

With many thanks, I am

Very cordially yours,

April 7, 1949

Dear Mrs. Roosevelt:

My thoughts go back to the April day three years ago when I stood with you at Hyde Park beside the white marble memorial just put up at the grave of the leader whose passing bereft a nation on April 12, 1945.

Flowers will be placed on that grave in the rose garden next Tuesday in token of the love and gratitude of all sorts and conditions of men. I wish I could be with you and with his old neighbors and friends to join in tribute to this great American. His place in the hearts of his countrymen is reflected in the steady flow of pilgrims to his last resting place. While half a million make this reverent pilgrimage every twelve months, we know that his memory lives in the hearts of grateful people all over the world.

Ours is the task to hold aloft the torch which his falling hands released.

Very sincerely yours,

June 21, 1949

Dear Mr. President:

I want first to thank you for the opportunities you have given me to work on the Human Rights Commission. The session closed last night.

Realizing that you probably do not want to be bothered by a personal report at the present time, I am writing this, though, of course, if you want me to come to Washington I shall do so.

The result of our work is only the first draft of the Covenant. We discussed only political and civil rights. The document which will go to the governments, however, will be accompanied by different plans for ways of enforcing the rights that are to be accepted in the final Covenant.

Our only plan is a joint plan with the United Kingdom and it will go forward with the others. This is the only thing on which we were able to agree with the United Kingdom. I have never known them to be so uncooperative as they were in this session. That may be due to the fact that the young Foreign Office adviser on the delegation staff accepted all the directions that came from the Foreign Office as being final and therefore was not able to negotiate on any changes of any kind in words. It was unfortunate especially because in previous sessions we have been able to get together with the United Kingdom on many situations.

Needless to say we practically never agreed with the USSR, and they felt that the document was a very poor one because the economic and social rights were not really discussed and are going to governments simply as additional articles for comment by governments.

One of the things we shall have to decide before the next meeting is whether in this Covenant we shall include any of these rights. Many of our people in this country lean toward the belief that civil and political rights without some measure of economic and social rights, have comparatively little value but these are new rights to many governments and must be approached gradually. Whether we wish to deal with economic and social rights in a second Covenant to follow the first one, or whether we wish to include them in separate protocols which nations can ratify one by one as they find the atmosphere of their countries favorable, are the questions before us. These must be decided as far as our attitude is concerned before the next meeting.

The State Department will be working on these questions. I have written to Secretary Acheson and I will, of course, come down at any time if he wishes to see me

I shall be in Hyde Park all summer and I am looking forward to rest and leisure which, however, will be conditioned on the behavior of a large number of children who are going to be on the place! I hope you and Mrs. Truman and Margaret will have a pleasant and happy summer and that Congress will give you some of the things that you want so that you may have the satisfaction of feeling that your hard work has achieved good results. Franklin, Junior, enjoyed having an opportunity to see you. I hope he will be a good Democratic Congressman.

With many thanks again and my best wishes, I am

Very cordially yours,

June 25, 1949

Dear Mrs. Roosevelt:

After reading your thoughtful letter of June twenty-first I can appreciate your feeling of disappointment that more was not accomplished at the session of the Human Rights Commission. That is through no fault of yours. Your labors in this instance, as in all of your activities as your country's representative to the General Assembly of the United Nations, have been prodigious and as I have previously said, magnificent.

When necessary you have without fear faced the Russian Bear with an admirable defense of democratic institutions and objectives. Who can tell—you may ultimately break down Soviet resistance. It is deplorable, indeed incomprehensible, that the United Kingdom should have been so uncooperative. Let us hope that Britain sends a more mature adviser next time. That was no place for a boy.

Anyway, it is no fault of yours if the first draft of the Covenant to be submitted to the governments is less than we could hope for. Your report indicates that the State Department has much to do before the next meeting.

I am glad you are to be in Hyde Park for the summer and feel that you will achieve a degree of rest and quiet no matter how many children are there. On this account I would not intrude upon your well-earned leisure to ask you to come to Washington for the sole purpose of reporting to me in person. If, as would seem probable, you do come down to confer with the Secretary of State, I hope you will advise me well in advance so I can arrange to see you.

Margaret joins me in reciprocating your good wishes. Mrs. Truman is at present in Missouri.

Gratefully and Sincerely,

Hyde Park
July 31, 1949

Dear Mr. President:

I have heard unofficially that my name is on the state department list to be presented to you for the next General Assembly of the United Nations.

Because of this strange campaign that Cardinal Spellman has started against Mr. Lehman and against me in public fashion, I am wondering if it will not embarrass you to send my name to the Senate. I want you to know that if your decision should be to leave me off I will quite understand and will not be in any way upset.

With every good wish, I am,

Very cordially yours,

Francis Cardinal Spellman became involved in a dispute with Mrs. Roosevelt over the question of federal aid to education. A House bill sponsored by North Carolina Democrat Graham A. Barden sought to provide funding only to public schools. Spellman, the nation's most influential Catholic leader, denounced this legislation as "a craven crusade of religious prejudice against Catholic children." The New York archbishop wanted federal aid for nonreligious textbooks, bus transportation, and health services for 2.5 million Catholic parochial-school students.

In three columns, Mrs. Roosevelt opposed the use of taxpayer funds for private or parochial schools. "The separation of Church and State is extremely important to any of us who hold to the original traditions of our nation," she wrote on June 23, 1949. "To change these traditions by changing our traditional attitude toward public education would be harmful, I think to our whole attitude of tolerance in the religious area."

Firing back in a public letter, the cardinal wrote on July 21, "Even though you may again use your columns to attack me and again accuse me of starting a controversy, I shall not again publicly acknowledge you. For whatever you may say in the future, your record of anti-Catholicism stands for all to see—a record which you yourself wrote on the pages of history which cannot be recalled—documents of discrimination unworthy of an American mother."

Mrs. Roosevelt answered, "I have no bias against the Roman Catholic Church and I have supported Governor Smith as governor and worked for him as a candidate for the office of President of the United States. I have supported for public office many other Roman Catholic candidates." She added, "I assure you I have no senses of being an

*'unworthy American mother.' The final judgment, my dear Cardinal
Spellman, of the worthiness of all human beings is in the hands of
God."*

———————

August 2, 1949

Dear Mrs. Roosevelt:

Yours of July 31 just came to my desk. I want you to go back to the
United Nations General Assembly. It is more necessary now than ever.

My sympathies are all with you in the controversy over the Aid to
Education Bill. You are right and the Cardinal is wrong!

Will write you more fully at a later date.

Sincerely,

———————

Hyde Park:
August 5, 1949

Dear Mr. President:

You were very good to take the time to write me. I deeply appreciate
your confidence in me.

I do hope the excitement over the recent controversy will die down. It
was most unfortunate.

Very cordially yours,

*During a press conference, Truman had declined comment when asked
about the Spellman controversy. Mrs. Roosevelt was most grateful for
the president's handwritten note.*

———————

August 24, 1949

Dear Mrs. Roosevelt:

It gives me great pleasure to invite you to serve as a member of the
National Committee for the Midcentury White House Conference on
Children and Youth.

This will be the fifth in a series of conferences on children held every
ten years on the call of the President of the United States. Each of the

earlier conferences made notable contributions to national understanding of the needs of children and youth and to the development of principles and programs to advance their well-being.

I know of no greater challenge facing the world today than how it can help its children to be secure in themselves, in their families and in their communities. It is through secure and happy children and families that we make an important contribution toward that kind of national and international well-being that makes for world peace.

The Midcentury White House Conference on Children and Youth has, I believe, a rare opportunity to turn its searchlight on the great advances made in the last decade in health, welfare and education. Part of the responsibility of the Conference will be to bring together our best knowledge about children and to ascertain ways of applying this knowledge in homes, schools, churches and the entire community. Through the cooperation of State and local groups throughout the Nation, I am asking that study be undertaken of significant, unsolved problems in child life in this country. Through the joint efforts of citizen groups everywhere, and of competent experts, I look for solutions to some of the unanswered questions about child life in this country, for guides to parents and to all who work with children.

Groundwork has been well laid for the Conference by the National Commission on Children and Youth, the Federal Interdepartmental Committee on Children and Youth, and many cooperating national organizations and State committees, as well as individuals having broad concern for children and their needs. The Congress has made possible the work that has been done to inaugurate this project by appropriating funds to the Children's Bureau.

I see in the Midcentury White House Conference on Children and Youth an opportunity for a stock-taking and a pointing to the future. I believe it can be a conference focused on sound planning and vigorous follow-up action.

The members I am asking to serve on the National Committee will give general direction to the whole undertaking, including the completion of the prepatory work and the arrangements for and program of the Conference itself. It will also be responsible for developing plans for post-Conference follow-up activities.

The first meeting of the National Committee will be held in the East Wing of the White House on September 8 and 9, 1949. I hope that you will accept membership on the Committee, attend this first meeting, and by your continuing interest and participation help give leadership to this important activity in our national life.

Very sincerely yours,

Eleanor replied that she would "be glad to serve but I fear I can not give enough time." She could not attend the panel's first meetings because of a prior commitment to speak in Atlanta, "which I can not break at this late date." Truman understood the demands on her time and welcomed her participation at future sessions.

New York
September 20, 1949

Dear Mr. President:

I know that everybody has been importuning you about coming on to lay the cornerstone on United Nations Day. Of course, they will make whatever day you decide to come "your day." This is simply to tell you that they are simply breathless waiting to hear from you, and to add my word that I hope you will be able to do it on October 24.

Very cordially yours,

Truman, who replied that he would come if he could, laid the granite cornerstone for the thirty-nine-story UN Secretariat Building that would also include the domed General Assembly Hall. "These buildings are not a monument to the unanimous agreement of nations on all things," he declared. "But they signify that the peoples of the world are of one mind in their determination to solve common problems by working together." After New York was chosen in 1946 as the permanent headquarters for the U.N., John D. Rockefeller Jr. donated seventeen acres overlooking the East River in midtown Manhattan. His son Nelson served as an assistant secretary of state in the Roosevelt and Truman administrations.

October 5, 1949

Dear Mrs. Roosevelt:

We fought a good fight in behalf of Leland Olds even though we lost—for the time being. I do want you to know how deeply I appreciate the magnificent way in which you came to his defense. I read your column on the subject with great satisfaction. No one has stated the issue more clearly or forcibly than you did. My heartfelt thanks are yours.

Very sincerely yours,

Leland Olds (1890–1960), a staunch defender of the public interest, served on the Federal Power Commission from 1939 until 1949. When Truman renominated Olds in 1949, the special interests launched a campaign to block his confirmation. The oil-and-gas lobby and their stooges viciously portrayed him as a Communist or fellow traveler. Mrs. Roosevelt, in her column, said that Olds was under attack because he had been vigilant in his opposition to price gouging. After the Senate rejected Olds by 53 to 15 votes, Truman wrote Mrs. Roosevelt: "I think we can safely leave the Olds case now before the bar of public opinion made up of those who pay gas and electric rates."

New York
October 6, 1949

Dear Mr. President:

From what I hear I am getting rather anxious about the way the campaign is going here for both Governor Lehman and Mayor O'Dwyer.

It is quite evident that the Catholic Church is showing no great backing for Governor Lehman and with Mr. Dubinsky anxious to stress the Liberal Party and not anxious to stress the mayor, I feel that perhaps it would be very advisable if you could combine a big meeting, sponsored by other labor groups, in Madison Square Garden, for both the governor and the mayor.

My chief concern is the good of the party in the future. If in this state it is evident that there has been defection in the Catholic vote where Governor Lehman is concerned, I am afraid it will mean a desertion from the Democratic Party by a great many of the Jews, some Protestants and some liberals—all of whom will join the Liberal Party which will weaken the Democratic Party.

This kind of thing is bad for our democratic system which should if possible primarily remain a two-party system.

I feel a little responsible for the situation here because undoubtedly Governor Lehman's statement against the Cardinal's letter to me is one of the things influencing the Catholic hierarchy and there are always some Catholics who can be influenced by a word passed down to the priests.

I do not know whether you are being urged to make other speeches here for the two candidates or not, but I do not feel the campaign is going any too well and upstate the Republicans are making a vigorous senatorial fight, which will help the Fusion candidate in New York City. Apparently the Republicans by their "holy crusade" against the communists are making a direct appeal for the Catholic vote and will be so recognized by them. It has nothing of course to do with the actual issues of the campaign or the value of either candidate, but like so many campaign tricks it may succeed in swinging the votes.

You will know better than I do whether politically any of this is important enough for you to think about, but I felt I should tell you what my feelings are at the present moment.

Very cordially yours,

October 12, 1949

Dear Mrs. Roosevelt:

I read your thoughtful letter of the sixth with a great deal of interest. You have, I believe, stated with great clarity the factors which enter into a political situation which must be handled with the utmost tact and discretion. I want to do everything within my power to help, particularly in supporting the candidacy of Governor Lehman.

I have been in conference with both Paul Fitzpatrick and Ed Flynn on the subject. I am coming to New York on October twenty-fourth to lay the cornerstone of the United Nations Building and I understand that I am to have luncheon with Mayor O'Dwyer at Gracie Mansion and that both you and Governor Lehman will be present. It may be possible for us to have a little conversation which will be helpful.

Paul Fitzpatrick indicated, wisely I thought, that he did not want me to come into the state of New York in a manner that indicated Governor Lehman was in distress and needed help. Of course, if the Democratic organization finally decides that my presence will be helpful, I shall be standing by to aid in any manner that can be of real help. What I must avoid under all circumstances is any act or gesture which could be construed as unwarranted interference by an outsider. I certainly want to see Governor Lehman win and am ready and anxious to make whatever contribution I can to achieve that happy result.

I was in Charlottesville over the last week end and paid a call on Mrs. Watson. I greatly admired a picture of you and the president—an informal one taken at the table and autographed by both of you. Very generously she gave it to me. I shall always treasure it. I think it is far and away the best picture I have ever seen of you and the president together.

With every good wish,

Very sincerely yours,

New York's Governor Dewey had appointed veteran diplomat John Foster Dulles to the Senate seat left vacant by the resignation of Robert F. Wagner. In a special election, he was in a dead heat with Lehman, a popular former New York governor. On election eve, Truman endorsed Lehman in a radio address from the White House. Mrs. Roosevelt introduced him. Partly because of Truman's intervention, Lehman narrowly won. Dulles made it close because of Catholic defections as the result of Lehman's public support for Mrs. Roosevelt during her feud with Cardinal Spellman.

CHAPTER 6

1950

In June of 1950, Truman faced what he called the most difficult decision of his presidency. After North Korean forces invaded South Korea, the president committed American troops without seeking congressional approval. Truman said that he took this action to save the United Nations. But in making this commitment, he bypassed the 1945 United Nations Participation Act, which authorized the use of military forces in UN missions only with congressional approval.

Mrs. Roosevelt, who believed that nothing but military force would impress the Soviet Union, supported Truman's intervention in Korea. "When the attack occurred, we had two choices," she said. "We could meet it or let aggression triumph by default, and thereby invite further piecemeal conquests all over the globe. This inevitably would have led to World War III, just as the appeasement of Munich and the seizure of Czechoslovakia led to World War II." In the wake of the North Korean attack, she felt that Truman had upheld the credibility of the United Nations. She had long favored the use of an international police force to thwart aggression.

Closer to home, she got so annoyed with Truman during the 1950 midterm campaign that she came close to resigning from the United Nations delegation. Her eldest son, James, leader of the dump-Truman forces at the 1948 Democratic National Convention, won his party's nomination in 1950 for the California governorship. Late in the campaign, Truman came out for California Democrat Helen Gahagan Douglas for the U.S. Senate over Republican congressman Richard M. Nixon. But he made no reference to Roosevelt's gubernatorial bid. "Mrs. R. suddenly stated with very great feeling that she had almost resigned from the UN a couple of days ago because of Truman's endorsement of Helen without an accompanying endorsement of Jimmy," Joseph Lash wrote in his diary. "I was considerably shaken. Mrs. R. does not separate her feelings for her children and her role as a public servant."

Republican incumbent Earl Warren, who had been the 1948 Republican nominee for vice president, won reelection to a third gubernatorial term with nearly two-thirds of the vote. "You had tremendous odds against you & Truman didn't help," Mrs. Roosevelt wrote her son following this defeat.

Mrs. Roosevelt, whose husband narrowly escaped an assassination attempt in 1933, wrote with compassion and understanding when two Puerto Rican nationalists opened fire on Blair House on November 1 and tried to kill the president. A White House guard was slain and two others were wounded in the attack. One of the assailants was killed. "The only thing you have to worry about is bad luck," Truman said afterward. "I never had bad luck."

"Any President of the United States, or any ruler of any country, or any public official who holds a position of great responsibility and power," Mrs. Roosevelt wrote, "must face the fact that they run this type of risk. . . . I used to think when my husband was President whenever we went anywhere that there was nothing in the world that could prevent a bullet from finding its target."

On numerous occasions, she faced death threats. Yet she refused to be intimidated. "I think I am pretty much a fatalist," she once told the journalist Edward R. Murrow. "You have to accept whatever comes and the only important thing is that you meet it with courage and with the best that you have to give."

February 11, 1950

Dear Mrs. Roosevelt:

I read the letter of Mr. Henry Toombs which you sent me on February eighth with a great deal of interest. I'll immediately get busy on it and see if something can't be done about it.

Our difficulty in the southern situation is due to the fact that the people we have working for these agencies of course, are people who are steeped in violent prejudices affecting the negroes of the South. It is just as difficult as it can be to find people who have an idea of fair treatment for the descendants of the former slaves. I am doing everything I can educationally and otherwise to overcome that feeling. I believe we are making some progress particularly in North Carolina, Tennessee, Arkansas, and Texas. The most difficult situation is in Georgia, Alabama, Mississippi and Louisiana. We are particularly handicapped in Georgia on account of the Governor but we are going to keep hammering at that thing and eventually we will get results.

I appreciate most highly your interest.

Sincerely yours,

Mrs. Roosevelt noted that Southern conservatives were obstructing Truman's civil rights program. In this letter, Truman is referring to Governor Herman Talmadge, who had introduced a voter-registration system with the intent of disenfranchising 80 percent of Georgia's African-American residents. Talmadge, who served as governor until 1955, represented Georgia in the U.S. Senate from 1957 until 1981, where he persisted in his opposition to civil rights until blacks began voting in larger numbers.

––––––––

New York
March 21, 1950

Dear Mr. President:

My breakfast was enhanced yesterday when I read in the *New York Times* about your indulgence in poetry. The *Home Book of Verse* has been a joy to me for many years. Do you happen to know "The Calf Path"? It is in that volume and it might be worth reading to some of the Senators.

I hope your vacation is affording you a real rest.

Very cordially yours,

The poem goes:

> *For men are prone to go it blind*
> *Along the calf-paths of the mind,*

And work away from sun to sun
To do what other men have done . . .
But how wise old wood-gods laugh,
Who saw the first primeval calf . . .
For thus such reverence is lent
To well-established precedent.
　　　—Sam Walter Foss

———————

Key West, Florida
March 25, 1950

Dear Mrs. Roosevelt:

Your letter of March twenty-first is a happy reminder that we all love the old songs and the old poems best. "The Calf Path" to which you call my attention is an old favorite. I have read it again since receiving your letter.

There is merit in your suggestion that it might be worthwhile to read Sam Walter Foss's lines to some of the Senators. I fear, however, that they have for too long been,

"Prone to go it blind
Along the calf-paths of the mind."

Thanks for your letter which brightened my day.

Always sincerely,

Sam Walter Foss (1858–1911), a New England poet and librarian, celebrated the common man in his verse and enjoyed great popularity in his time. "The Calf-path" is a satirical gem about the legend that the streets of Boston were laid out by a calf, which Foss used to gently mock the willingness of people to follow established tradition. His best-known poem is "The House by the Side of the Road."

Where the race of men go by—
They are good, they are bad, they are weak, they are strong,
Wise, foolish—so am I . . .
Let me live in my house by the side of the road . . .

———————

New York
April 17, 1950

Dear Mr. President:

I want to send you my congratulations on the vetoing of the Kerr Bill. I know it took a lot of courage.

With best wishes, I am,

Very cordially yours,

April 24, 1950

Dear Mrs. Roosevelt:

Thanks a lot for your note of the seventeenth. There was only one answer to the Gas Bill and, I think, it was stated in the veto message.

Sincerely yours,

Robert S. Kerr (1896–1963), a self-made oil millionaire, represented Oklahoma in the U.S. Senate from 1949 until his death. This legislation would have deregulated the oil and natural gas industry. Harry McPherson, assistant counsel for the Senate Democratic Policy Committee in the 1950s, wrote of Kerr: "He seemed to be saying, 'If I can be so open in defending those interests, they can't be wrong; and even if they were, none of you has the guts to challenge me.' " Truman did what he thought was right. Though he liked Kerr personally, the president also regarded him as a tool of the special interests.

June 13, 1950

Dear Mr. President:

I am enclosing to you a copy of a letter which I have sent to Mr. Hickerson to give to the Secretary if he thinks it worthwhile. I am sending you this copy simply because when I spoke to you about this trip you said you would be interested in my impressions. I realize quite well that you have so much information this may be completely valueless.

While over here I have spoken a good deal about you and your administration and the ideals for which you stand. I would like you to be in close touch with what I do as I hope that you will feel it is a support to your policies.

With warm good wishes and the hope that you will get some holiday time this summer, and with my kind regards to Mrs. Truman and Margaret, I am

Very cordially yours,

———————

Helsinki
June 13, 1950

Dear Mr. Secretary:

Now that I have reached Finland I want to send you just a line because I feel in the first place, I want to thank the people in the Department who so kindly spoke to all our representatives over here and I also want to tell you how extremely kind Mr. and Mrs. Bay, Mr. and Mrs. Cummin and Mr. Cabot have been, as well as their staffs.

I am not writing this letter, however, just to say thank you. I feel you might be interested in the impressions gathered by an unofficial observer.

In these countries I feel that everywhere there is fear but at the same time, a desperate kind of courage. They do not talk of war and they go about their daily business and they build and they do try to improve the life of the people. In fact they put a tremendous amount of vigor into the effort they are making to improve life for the people as a whole and yet you feel there is a constant shadow not very far away.

In Norway the heads of government talked guardedly and having joined the Atlantic Pact they, of course, are anxious to be reassured about our attitude. They must count on us if trouble comes, but they are going to do everything possible to carry their full share.

I was particularly interested in some talks with members of the Parliament and government officials in Sweden. I have been very careful neither to ask questions nor to offer any views of my own on public questions, but they went out of their way to tell me about their differences of opinion on the Atlantic Pact. As you know, only four members of the Swedish Parliament voted to join but they told me that this did not indicate they were not anxious to do their full share in preparation for defense. The party in power, socialists and farmers, want to preserve the traditional Swedish neutrality, but there is a group which is a large one, that would like to join unofficially in having a joint defense program with Norway and Sweden. This is a little difficult since they are unable to join the Atlantic Pact openly, but they are not comfortable about that and I felt there was an apologetic attitude.

On the whole, I think all of them are grateful to the United States and recognize that the things they believe in and live by are really the things represented by the United States. On the whole most of the responsible people do not seem to be taken in by Soviet propaganda.

I hope that in my speeches and press conferences and talks in general, I have done some good. I am sure that all of our Ambassadors must be very anxious when strangers who are not familiar with the situations come and talk during these very touchy times but I do not think I have said anything which is not in complete harmony with the foreign policy as stated by you and the President.

Now I just report something that troubles me, namely, some of our industrialists and some of the members of Congress seem to have left the impression that we are not averse to going to war on the theory that we will have to go to war in the end and we might as well do it while the balance of power is on our side. I do not know that they have actually said it but that is the impression they left and it frightens most of the people very much indeed. It is hard for them to realize that this attitude does not represent the attitude of the administration or of the majority of our people. In addition, some of our senators, belonging to both parties, seem to have said things over here which they could say easily at home and which would be understood as a reflection of partisan or personal views, but over here it seems to be disloyalty to the present administration and results in complete confusion on the part of those to whom they talk. I do not know how this could be prevented unless it were possible to say to each individual coming over that they have a responsibility to prove that our country is a unified one on its foreign policy and above everything else we mean to support the United Nations and work for world peace.

Some of these people seem to have left the impression that they consider the UN a complete failure and not really worth paying any attention to, which of course, takes away one of the things that these people pray will be a bulwark for peace.

I am sure you get much more real information from your own people over here but they are official and while my impressions are gathered on the run, and of course not to be trusted against more reliable sources of information, I thought even such unofficial conversations might be of some interest to you and the Department.

With renewed thanks for all of the courtesies that the Department has extended to me, I am

Very sincerely yours,

June 21, 1950

Dear Mrs. Roosevelt:

I certainly did appreciate most highly your good letter, enclosing me a copy of one which you sent to the Secretary of State. The information contained in your letter is highly appreciated both by me and the Secretary.

You must have had a wonderful trip. I noticed this morning where you have been entertained by the Roosevelts of Holland. That must have been an interesting experience.

I hope to see you when you return and have a long conversation with you on what you saw and the impression you got as to the situation in Europe generally.

Sincerely yours,

On her trip, Mrs. Roosevelt visited all the Scandinavian and Benelux countries. She dedicated a monument to her husband in Oslo, watched a performance of Hamlet *at the Castle of Elsinore, and conferred with government officials at each stop. Most of this region was occupied by Nazi Germany during World War II, and at this stage of the Cold War, its people felt vulnerable to the Soviet Union.*

Hyde Park
July 11, 1950

Dear Mr. President:

I read your speech at the laying of the cornerstone of the new United States Court Building with great interest.

Now that I am home I would like to see you sometime at your convenience to tell you of some of my conversations with various people in Europe.

With every good wish, I am

Very cordially yours,

July 15, 1950

Dear Mrs. Roosevelt:

I appreciated very much your letter of July eleventh. I am glad you liked my cornerstone speech for the United States Courts Building.

Of course, I'll be most happy to see you any time that is convenient to you. If sometime in the month of August will suit your convenience just tell Matt Connelly when you are coming and arrangements will be made for you to come in promptly.

Sincerely yours,

On June 26, Truman laid the cornerstone for the new U.S. Courts Building for the District of Columbia. In his remarks, he talked about the principle of equal justice under the law and expressed the hope that the Universal Declaration of Human Rights would be adopted as international law.

August 9, 1950

Dear Mr. President:

You will forgive me, I hope, if I send you this personal letter.

The story written by Homer Bigart in the *Herald Tribune* yesterday morning is, from my point of view, if true a very shocking one and I am afraid it will have a very bad effect on the morale of mothers and wives in this country.

For a rich country like ours to be sacrificing its boys with imperfect equipment when they have to face the latest and newest USSR equipment is going to bring not only attacks from the Republicans but violent feeling on the part of the women of the country. To send the Marines from Hawaii with trucks which were old and rebuilt and which promptly broke down, is really a crime.

I cannot tell you how the feeling against Secretary Johnson is building up because people feel that for political reasons he tried to go even beyond what was asked for in the way of economy and is therefore responsible for our poor showing in the way of equipment. It may be completely unfair but the fact remains that is what a great many people are beginning to feel.

I do hope we can open the United Nations General Assembly with a very strong speech, giving our plans for peace and not leave the initiative to the USSR. They will certainly present theirs and somehow ours should be a better one and presented first.

I am deeply concerned and regret that I felt I had to write you this.

Very cordially yours,

August 22, 1950

Dear Mrs. Roosevelt:

I share all of the apprehension expressed in your recent letter about Korea and particularly the bad effect of much of the news during the earlier weeks on the morale of mothers and wives in this country.

I read very carefully Homer Bigart's story in the *New York Herald Tribune* to which you called attention. I checked the Bigart story with no less an authority than General Bradley himself. He told me Bigart's assertion that our men were called upon to fight with old and defective equipment was untrue. That had been my understanding and I was glad to have General Bradley's confirmation.

What is more reassuring is that adequate forces and supplies are now being built up which will enable the situation to be stabilized in Korea. This should prevent serious recurrences of other events as reported by Mr. Bigart and other correspondents and I know the news from Korea will be increasingly acceptable from now onwards. Nevertheless I fervently wish that some of my top men would learn the old, old lesson about the golden quality of silence.

I share wholeheartedly your view that we must open the United Nations Assembly with a strong pronouncement on our plans for peace. We must not leave the initiative to Moscow. I am grateful to you for writing as you did. I hope you will profit from your stay in Campobello.

Faithfully yours,

At the beginning of the Korean War, American forces were ill-equipped. Homer Bigart (1907–1991), a legendary war correspondent, won Pulitzer prizes in World War II and Korea. Based on the early setbacks in Korea, Truman knew that Bigart's devastating report was accurate. "We were, in short, in a state of shameful unreadiness," said General Matthew Ridgway, then serving as deputy chief of staff.

Defense Secretary Louis Johnson (1891–1956) was perhaps the worst appointment of Truman's presidency. In his zeal to cut spending, Johnson undermined the nation's military strength. Mrs. Roosevelt's opinion of Johnson was shared by Generals Bradley and Eisenhower. Truman wrote in his diary that Johnson had "almost wrecked" the armed services. In June of 1950, "I made up my mind that he had to go." Truman fired Johnson in September and replaced him with General George C. Marshall.

As Mrs. Roosevelt suggested, Truman went before the United Nations General Assembly. In an October 24 address that was carried on a nationwide radio broadcast, Truman declared: "The invasion of the Republic of Korea was a direct challenge to the principles of the United Nations. . . . The people of almost every member country supported the decision of the Security Council to meet this aggression with force. . . . In uniting to crush the aggressors in Korea, these member nations have done no more than the charter calls for."

Hyde Park
August 15, 1950

Dear Mr. President:

Mr. Joseph D. Lohman of the National Committee on Segregation in the Nation's Capital has just written me of the success they have had in St. Louis in keeping their swimming pools unsegregated.

He tells me that the courageous attitude shown by the administration in supporting democratic principles in the Washington situation has helped the situation all over the country. You and Secretary Chapman have shown great courage in bringing this about. It is these step-by-step achievements which will in the end bring us real equal rights in our own nation.

Very cordially yours,

––––––––––

August 22, 1950

Dear Mrs. Roosevelt:

I certainly appreciated your letter of the fifteenth regarding the operation of the swimming pools in St. Louis and Washington. I think the secretary of the interior has done an excellent public relations job in these two instances.

Sincerely yours,

Truman, on the recommendation of his Committee on Civil Rights, integrated parks and recreation areas in Washington, D.C., where White and Colored signs had been displayed for more than a half century. These racial barriers also began falling in local hotels and restaurants. In 1950, the House approved legislation granting voting rights and home rule to residents of the nation's capital. But in the Senate, Southern Democrats blocked these measures through filibusters.

Joseph D. Lohman (1910–1968), a lecturer in the department of sociology at the University of Chicago, was recruited by the Interior Department to help promote the integration of swimming pools in the nation's capital. Lohman, who served as a member of the National War Labor Board during World War II, was elected Illinois state treasurer in 1958 and ran unsuccessfully for governor in 1960.

September 2, 1950

Dear Mrs. Roosevelt:

I was happy to read a tribute to you in the August 1950 *Reader's Digest*. Belatedly, I send congratulations not only on this appreciation by Frances Whiting but because the *Digest* consented to include it at all. That was surprising in a reactionary publication which looks backward with nostalgia to the good old days when the law of tooth and claw ruled.

Very sincerely yours,

The Reader's Digest, *founded by DeWitt Wallace in 1922, had a reader-ship of more than 8 million in the Truman years. As Truman noted, the magazine stood for traditional values and had a conservative outlook. The article about Mrs. Roosevelt reflected her popularity. In 1950, Wallace launched the hugely successful* Reader's Digest Condensed Book Club.

New York
December 14, 1950

Dear Mr. President:

The General Assembly has come to an end for all intents and purposes, though I understand it will probably only recess and that the delegates may be on call.

In any case, I want to thank you for giving me the opportunity of serving in this General Assembly and to tell you that I have been somewhat disturbed by the atmosphere which I found prevalent toward the United States.

Committee No. 3, not being a political committee as you know, the members of the various delegations act with a good deal of freedom and less direction from the top than they would in a political committee where the results of their actions would have more immediate political repercussions. Therefore I think one sees what might be called honest-to-goodness trends of feeling.

It certainly is a trend of dislike of the domination of big nations and a feeling that small nations should have more to say.

The race question has become a very vital one since much of the feel-

ing is that of the colored races against the white race. We are classed with
the colonial powers as having exploited them because our businessmen
in the past have exploited them, so we have no better standing than the
United Kingdom or any other colonial power. I think we have to reckon
with this in our whole world outlook because we will need friends badly
and it is surprising how few we have in spite of all we have done for
other people in the past.

I realize I sound like Cassandra, but I think this situation should be
bending every effort to correcting it as soon as possible.

Very sincerely yours,

December 20, 1950

Dear Mrs. Roosevelt:

I have read very carefully the thoughtful observations on the sessions
of the General Assembly embodied in your letter of December fourteenth.

I attach the greatest importance to everything you say, particularly
the trends of discussions in Committee No. 3. It is indeed regrettable
that those trends indicate dissatisfaction and a feeling that the big
nations dominate and that the small nations think they are not having
an opportunity to express themselves adequately. After all, this indicates
some of the many pitfalls which await us as we strive through the
United Nations to reach the ideal in international relations.

Far from your offering thanks to me for an opportunity of serving in
this General Assembly, I feel that it is for me to express to you the gratitude of the nation for the great public service you are giving your country and indeed the cause of civilization.

Very sincerely yours,

*In 1950, only fifty-five nations were members of the United Nations
General Assembly. With the breakup of colonial empires, the collapse of
the Soviet Union, and the creation of scores of new countries since 1950,
the membership of the UN has tripled. Mrs. Roosevelt hoped that the
emerging nations of the third world and Western democracies could
find common ground. But the Assembly has become more polarized.*

CHAPTER 7

1951

General Douglas MacArthur (1880–1964), who commanded United Nations forces in Korea, repeatedly tested President Truman's authority. During World War II, the Far East general had frequently differed with Franklin D. Roosevelt, yet the two men appeared to have had considerable respect for each other. Roosevelt chose MacArthur as supreme commander of all forces in the Pacific, promoted him to five-star rank, and decorated him with the Congressional Medal of Honor. Truman, who regarded the general as a prima donna, did what Roosevelt would have done in appointing him as supreme commander of Allied occupation forces in Japan and later as commander of United Nations forces in Korea.

MacArthur turned the tide of the Korean War with the landing of UN troops at Inchon in the fall of 1950. Following this triumph, he held his first and only meeting with Truman at Wake Island. As the Americans advanced into North Korea toward the Yalu River, Chinese forces entered the conflict and drove MacArthur's troops beneath the thirty-eighth parallel. By early 1951, MacArthur favored withdrawal from Korea because it was a war that could not be won. In looking for a scapegoat, MacArthur blamed Truman for not allowing him to bomb Chinese bases in Manchuria.

When MacArthur went public with his dissenting views, Mrs. Roosevelt thought he was on dangerous ground. "I cannot feel," she wrote in her column, "that a commanding general in the field, particularly when he commands for a group of nations, should take it upon himself to announce the policy that in his opinion should be followed in the area of the world where he commands troops."

Truman, who detested MacArthur, would not tolerate any commander who showed disrespect to the office of the presidency of the United States. Two days after Mrs. Roosevelt's column, he fired MacArthur for insubordination. "The President did the only thing he could do," Eleanor wrote her daughter Anna. ". . . but it is going to be stormy for a while."

Truman's popularity dropped to 23 percent in the wake of MacArthur's dismissal. Though Eleanor had backed the president in most conflicts and crises of his administration, her support was particularly welcome in April of 1951.

That same month, Mrs. Roosevelt relinquished her chairmanship of the Human Relations Commission while remaining a member of the panel. She reported to Truman about the growing tensions at the United Nations between the countries of the third world and the major Western democracies; her hope for establishing a future relationship with the People's Republic of China; and a European perspective on the Korean War.

During a visit to Chicago, Mrs. Roosevelt was asked by reporters about the president's occasional displays of anger. In early December 1950, Truman had penned an angry letter to *Washington Post* music critic Paul Hume, who had written a negative review of Margaret Truman's Washington, D.C., concert. Mrs. Roosevelt said that Truman's flare-ups were unfortunate, but that "we should be more careful in our criticism" because the president "carries the greatest load any man in history has carried." She was then asked if Truman faced greater problems than any of his predecessors, including FDR. "Definitely I do," she replied.

February 28, 1951

Dear Mr. President:

I am sending you the enclosed because it seems to me very well thought out and typical of a number of letters that have come to me though it is far better expressed.

On the whole I agree with what the gentleman says and I am troubled at several trends today.

I hope that before I go to Geneva, if the Human Rights Commission has to meet there in April, that I may have an opportunity to see you for a few minutes to tell you of our position so you will be acquainted with the situation. I was not very happy over some of the trends in the last General Assembly but I wrote you a report on that.

Now I feel we are badly in need of a speech from you in the simplest possible terms, simplifying and clarifying for the people the whole present situation in the field of foreign and domestic affairs.

Very cordially yours,

―――――

March 7, 1951

Dear Mrs. Roosevelt:

I am always glad to have your thoughtful letters, and appreciate now, as in the past, your conscientious approach to all of the problems which come before you in your arduous labors with the Human Rights Commission.

Of course, I am always glad to talk over these problems with you, for I always find your reports not only interesting, but stimulating. I shall be most happy to see you before you go to Geneva.

I have read very carefully the letter from your correspondent which you enclosed. I would not dismiss his apprehensions lightly. The temptation, however, is strong to observe that from the vantage point of second sight he oversimplifies our foreign relations. After all, both China and Spain present imponderables.

But I am gratified that you have sent me the letter, and I am very glad also to have the benefit of your correspondent's observations.

Very sincerely yours,

Truman and Mrs. Roosevelt shared a mutual dislike of the Spanish dictator Francisco Franco (1892–1975). But as the Cold War developed, Truman, in December 1950, resumed diplomatic relations with Spain because of its strategic importance. Eleanor passed along a letter from a Robert Hamlisch of Washington, D.C., who objected to a U.S.-Spanish alliance but wanted the administration to open relations with the People's Republic of China. In February 1951, at Truman's urging, the UN General Assembly passed a resolution denouncing China for entering the Korean War. Mrs. Roosevelt, who supported Truman in Korea, also favored U.S. recognition of the Chinese government.

March 30, 1951

My dear Mrs. Roosevelt:

I am distressed beyond measure by the unqualified falsity of statements in an article in the current issue of *Cosmopolitan* regarding my sentiments toward you and all the members of the Roosevelt family, not omitting even calumnious statements concerning my attitude toward my lamented predecessor.

In the face of all this false witness, this perjured evidence, I cannot restrain the impulse to write you this assurance that the entire article is a tissue of lies, a willful distortion of truth and fact. In my heart I feel that this disclaimer in toto on my part is unnecessary but I shall feel better for having written you.

With highest esteem and respect,

Faithfully,

Hyde Park
March 31, 1951

Dear Mr. President:

I have not read the article in *Cosmopolitan* but I assure you that I would not be in the least disturbed about it. There have been many things printed that I know to be untrue and I ceased long ago worrying about them.

With my good wishes, I am

Very cordially yours,

William Bradford Huie (1910–1986), a journalist and novelist, excelled as an investigative reporter and did his best work in the fields of military reform and race relations in the South. "The Terrible-Tempered Mr. Truman," in the April 1951 Cosmopolitan, *was closer to the mark than the president would acknowledge. Huie documented his subject's differences with the Roosevelts. But the author overstated his case in claiming that Truman was more of an Eleanor-and-Franklin hater than was the right-wing columnist Westbrook Pegler. Truman's private criticism of the Roosevelts was hardly comparable to Pegler's very public rants.*

New York
April 9, 1951

Dear Mr. President:

I am sorry to leave for Geneva without having gone to Washington again but I will come down soon after I return the end of May to report to you whatever is accomplished at the meeting of the Human Rights Commission.

Our position seems to me constructive and wise and I hope we can get it through. I do not think any of us want to take up your time unless it is essential, and as the state department did not feel it was necessary for me to come at this time, I think it will be much wiser for me to come when I will be able to report the results of this meeting.

I had the pleasure of telling the author of that disagreeable article in *Cosmopolitan* in a radio interview the other day that as far as I was concerned, and of course I can only speak for myself, I had never found you anything but kind and considerate in every way which was a great satisfaction to me.

Very cordially yours,

April 12, 1951

Dear Mrs. Roosevelt:

I certainly did appreciate yours of the ninth and, of course, I am sorry that conditions were such that I didn't get a chance to see you before you left but I'll be most happy to talk with you when you come back.

I think our position is the correct one with regard to Human Rights and with regard to the world foreign policy, which covers the whole globe and not just one location.

I am glad you got a chance to tell that *Cosmopolitan* author some of the facts. That is one of the most vicious articles that has ever been written with regard to my relations with you and President Roosevelt. Putting it mildly there just wasn't one word of truth in it. You, of course, know that to be a fact.

I hope you will have a most successful meeting and that I will have the pleasure of talking with you about it when you return.

Sincerely yours,

In April of 1951, Mrs. Roosevelt ended her five-year tenure as chairman of the UN's Human Rights Commission. The East-West and North-South tensions in the Assembly were a factor in her decision. "As representative of the United States, one of the great powers," she wrote in her column, "I did not feel I should continue to hold the chairmanship of this important commission." She would stay on as a member of the commission and U.S. delegate to the General Assembly.

April 11, 1951

To the President:

My congratulations on your courage. It seems to me you have done the right thing.

Eleanor Roosevelt

April 13, 1951

Dear Mrs. Roosevelt:

I highly appreciate your kind message of commendation and approval of the course I took. It certainly was with the deepest personal regret that I found myself compelled to replace General MacArthur, but the cause of world peace is of major importance and there must be no doubt or confusion as to our policy in the Far East.

My thanks and good wishes,

Very sincerely yours,

General MacArthur publicly differed with the administration's Korean War strategy. MacArthur favored bombing Chinese bases in Manchuria, a blockade on the Chinese coast, and accepting Chiang Kai-shek's offer of Nationalist troops. The general shared these views in a letter to House Minority Leader Joseph W. Martin. On April 11, 1951, the president removed MacArthur from his command for insubordination. Though Mrs. Roosevelt supported Truman's decision, two-thirds of the American people had a different view.

May 1, 1951

Dear Mrs. Roosevelt:

It is always good to hear from you and I am especially grateful for your thoughtful letter of April twenty-fourth. It is particularly gratifying to have your assurance that my action in the MacArthur case has brought new hope into the international situation.

Mine was a stern and unpleasant duty to perform but it was and is my settled conviction that there was no alternative action in the interest of peace and security.

I have been going over with great interest your memorandum of the conversation with Colonel Arthur Murray as well as the text of his letter to the *Times of London*. He surely writes out of a long and rich experience in Chinese and Far Eastern affairs generally and I am glad to have the benefit of his opinions.

Take good care of yourself and guard your health always. I appreciate fully the task you are engaged in is a hard one.

Always sincerely,

April 27, 1951

Dear Mr. President:

I am enclosing this copy of a letter which I wrote to General Marshall for your information. I have already sent you a copy of the report of my conversation in London.

Very cordially yours,

April 27, 1951

Dear General Marshall:

The other night at dinner, I had a talk with the head of the International Red Cross, Dr. Ruegger. He said many fine things about his devotion to you. The Consulate here has had some difficulties in getting any answers from him as regards prisoners of war in Korea. He murmured to me, when I asked him about these difficulties that there was no difficulty on top levels between the United States and the International Red Cross and you and he had always been friends. He said he had sent many inquiries but had been unable to get any answers and I imagine he was irritated at being asked when he could not get any answers, so perhaps this little difficulty will soon blow over.

I did want to tell you that I asked him about the trip from which he has just returned. He went to Peking with his wife. He says that Madame Sun Yat-sen is active in the government, that he saw some other people who were working and had a long talk with Chou En-lai. He says he does not think he is a communist, certainly not a communist in the Russian sense. Dr. Ruegger seems to think that the reforms are genuine and that they are actually trying to get a clean government, free of graft. Chou said nothing which Western Europe could resent and I thought he felt that with proper handling something might be done to straighten out the present difficulties between China and the rest of the world.

I am enclosing to you a report of a conversation which I had in London and which might give you a side light on a certain type of British thinking. My conversation with Dr. Ruegger coming on top of it seems to confirm some of the things said and make it advisable for us, by hook or by crook to find out whether a United Nations advance would get any consideration in Peking.

Dr. Ruegger said he had just had a letter from the Chinese Ambassador whom he had seen over there. He thinks that is the only link with the outside world and that link should not be broken. He also felt he was feeling his importance somewhat.

He has admiration for Nehru, but he felt Nehru has not stood on the right side very often of late and I think it is because Nehru was appalled at the thought of having China as an enemy.

I know we can not appease and I am not suggesting any action because I do not know enough but I felt these two observations might be of some help to you and to the efforts made by the United Nations if there is a chance that there may be Chinese officials who are not communists. Some of the efforts being made for peace might have a hearing.

Very sincerely yours,

Chou En-lai, who held the dual role of premier and foreign minister of the People's Republic of China, once described himself as "more Chinese than Communist." Mrs. Roosevelt's judgment would be vindicated. Two decades later, Mao's longtime ally would play a critical role in the normalization of relations between the United States and China. She admired Indian prime minister Jawaharlal Nehru (1889–1964). "He bears the burdens, which are almost overwhelming," she wrote a friend, "in a calm and courageous manner."

Geneva
May 6, 1951

Dear Mr. President:

Thank you very much for your very kind letter. I do hope you will not bother to answer my letters because I know how busy you are.

I am enclosing this report of a conversation which I had with Mr. Jean Monnet. I thought you might be interested.

I will come to Washington to see you shortly after my return.

Very cordially yours,

The following was enclosed with Mrs. Roosevelt's letter.

Mr. Jean Monnet was kind enough to invite me, with my son, Elliott and his wife, to dine on Saturday night at his country home which is about thirty-five minutes out of Paris. He retires there every night. He seemed cheerful and relaxed and ready to talk.

The Far East is, of course, on everybody's mind and I was rather interested in the things he said. He thinks France should give up Indo-China.

If they did so, the expenses for rearmament at home could be easily absorbed without making any great sacrifices in their own standard of living. He does not think that anything of the kind should be done in North Africa because France has been much longer in North Africa, and in addition, it is right at their backdoor. Of course, if the wave of nationalism succeeds, there is no assurance that it will not spread. France has been so long in North Africa and accomplished so little in raising the standard of living and in giving the people education that I do not know how long they can hope to keep their power unchallenged.

In Asia Mr. Monnet feels that all of us play into the hands of the communists. We should long ago have recognized the great movement for nationalism which is sweeping over that whole area and even though there was infiltration by the communists and nationalism was used by them, we should not be fighting against it. He also said we should have offered our help in the economic field or in any field that they desired and cheerfully have assured them that it was their business as to what kind of a government they set up. He feels that because of the fact that Russia could not supply the whole area with the things they need, like locomotives and machinery, they would undoubtedly have turned to the West and we would have had a better chance to keep them free from communist domination than we have had in fighting them in a way which the communists have been able to capitalize on by saying that we were fighting their desire for freedom. He does not think they can possibly get on without help from Western Europe and the United States, and he thinks as the hardships grow greater, the communists will play more and more on the fact that we are to blame. The bitterness which has been building up for a long time, first because they have felt themselves treated as racial inferiors and then because they have been exploited colonially and by business groups in our country, will intensify instead of growing less.

Mr. Monnet was very guarded, of course, on what we were doing but we put the question bluntly as to whether he felt the United Nations should get out of Korea since he felt that the French should get out of Indo-China. He said, no, that was quite a different situation, that the United Nations would have to stay until some solution was found, but he felt we should try to hold the line rather than go forward to conquer the whole area and that the effort to come to any agreement with the Chinese should not be given up. I gather that he thought it would have been wiser if the United Nations had never committed itself in Korea, but having done so, there was no turning back.

Mr. Monnet said he was not a pessimist in the present situation. By that I gathered that he meant that he did not think the USSR would provoke a war but he did say he felt she would continue to be as irritating as she possibly could be.

In view of Gromyko's outbursts I am wondering whether the USSR is not a little afraid that China may force her under their treaty agreement to come to China's aid and whether the USSR is loathe to do this and is trying to warn us by their statements on Korea that this may happen. If it does, it means total war.

On the other hand, Mr. Monnet seemed to feel that China would not try to draw the USSR into her own territory. Though their bonds with the USSR might be close, he did not think they trusted them enough to want their military strength actually within their borders. He said it did not make much difference to the Chinese if they have to send armies into Korea to be killed because manpower was the one thing they did not lack, and our "meat grinder" policy could be used to awaken their resentment against us and all the white peoples of the world so as to build up their own nationalist feeling.

Mr. Monnet is an able businessman and has probably saved France financially so I imagine his thinking carries some weight. He lived in China for a short time and has a good many Chinese friends. He also, as you know, spent a good many years in America and speaks excellent English. He lives simply and hates the city. Perhaps there is a peasant background. In any case, he was close to Mr. Blum and is close to President Auriol and Mr. Schuman. I speak of Blum simply because Madam Blum was there, and she has always been at President Auriol's when I have gone there "en famille." In spite of her husband's death, I think her thinking probably carries some weight with them all because of their affection for her husband. Curious for a financier, almost a financial genius to have been such a close friend of socialists.

In talking to some of the best informed Swiss people, namely, Professor Rappard, I find there is a feeling that the USSR does not want war now, and I think they are going ahead here in business in a way which indicated that they feel a certain amount of stability is to be expected for the next few years.

May 15, 1951

Dear Mrs. Roosevelt:

I can't tell you how very much I appreciate your letters of April twenty-seventh and May sixth—one enclosing me a copy of a letter which you sent to General Marshall, and the other one a memorandum of a conversation you had with the Honorable Jean Monnet. They are most interesting and helpful—furnishing me with background information. You are very kind to keep me informed on these matters.

I shall certainly be happy to see you when you return.

Sincerely yours,

Jean Monnet (1888–1979), the French economist, was highly regarded by Truman. The advocate of European unity came up with the idea of a six-nation European coal-and-steel community governed by a supra-national authority. When the initiative was announced in May 1950 by French foreign minister Robert Schuman, it became known as the Schuman Plan. Monnet cared more about getting results than taking credit. Known as the father of modern Europe, he also drafted the plan for the European Common Market and spent years promoting a United States of Europe.

In her memorandum, Mrs. Roosevelt also refers to Léon Blum (1872–1950), France's premier before and after World War II; Schuman (1886–1963); and Soviet diplomat Andrey Gromyko (1909–1989).

Geneva
May 15, 1951

Dear Mr. President:

More notes that may be of possible interest, nothing important but I send them to you for what they are worth.

Very cordially yours,

At dinner with the Yugoslavs the other night I had the most interesting conversation. He told me that great changes had come about since they had broken with the USSR; they had much more recognition of the individual's importance and they had been brought to this because they had to acknowledge that passing edicts did not accomplish anything. People had to want to do the things. For instance, there must be cooperatives on the farms because they just did not have machinery enough to make the farms more productive unless there were cooperatives, but they had to go about it simply and educate the farmers to the point of wanting to cooperate and it was far from being accomplished as yet.

He also told me that they had passed an edict that all Moslem women must take off their veils. They even got one hundred women to agree to take them off, and took them on a grand tour to see Belgrade, etc., but the Moslem women did not take off their veils.

He also told me there had been a fearful fight in the revision of their penal code or constitution, but Miss Whiteman is trying to get hold of a copy to find out definitely which it is. He said it had been just like the USSR article but when they brought it up again it was violently protested on the part of large groups among the Yugoslavs. They finally succeeded in getting it changed as now it protects the rights of the individual against the government instead of making the state superior over the individual.

He further said they were so poor it was very difficult for them to do many of the things they would like to do, but they would be more than glad to show any of us what they were trying to accomplish and they invited us all collectively to come and see Yugoslavia, and the government invited me officially.

I now have formal invitations to visit India, Pakistan, Israel and Yugoslavia. I could stay away for a year without seeing all the places I have been asked to visit. Unfortunately I do not want to stay away and I am not at all sure it is as useful to be away from home as it is to be at home.

Miss Bowie told me she talked with the little USSR man whom the Yugoslav told her was a member of the NKVD. He speaks good English and told her she would be welcome in Moscow, but too many people came there just to criticize. She said they should be able to take it, and he replied that they were still too new to stand it, which was an interesting admission.

I had quite a talk with Mr. Morosov and explained to him in detail just why we had to fight for a federal-state clause, that we might not win but we had to fight for it because without it, a treaty of this kind might not be considered constitutional and would stand very little chance of being accepted by our Senate. I explained to him that education was a state function, that things touching on the economic, cultural and social rights were many of them in state jurisdiction. I also illustrated for him the fact that on trains now, because the federal program could control interstate commerce, we had been able to do away with segregation, but we could not through federal edict do away with it in all the states. That had to come by state action and in a democracy you could not order, the people had to be persuaded to do it themselves. He is a jurist and so is his inter-preter and I think they understood very well. What they will make of it and what the next attack will contain because of it, remains to be seen.

They were very anxious to have me see some photographs (when I went to their house for a reception). Mr. Charles Malik took me into the room to show them to me and one of their young men hovered around to hear my comments. They were extraordinary photographs of pro-jected buildings and buildings under construction. The University of Moscow looks like a tremendous undertaking and should be most impressive with a large pool in front of it and some fine landscaping. They may have administration buildings and apartment houses under construction, going as high as fifty stories. They told me that was like ours, and I said: "Yes, but not the kind of house I would like to live in." The NKVD man said: "I have been to Hyde Park and know you like little houses." As I left, Mr. Morosov asked me what I thought of the buildings and I told him I thought there was an extraordinary amount of new con-struction going on in Moscow. He said it was in different parts of the city and certainly it was making a great change. Then he asked me what I thought of the architecture. I told him I could not tell from the photo-graphs what the detail was like but the building effort was certainly very impressive.

Then I remarked that if so much building was going on in a short time

Mr. Vishinsky would not be able to say that there was not enough housing in Moscow to host the General Assembly of the United Nations and so they would have to invite the Assembly to meet there. Mr. Morosov smiled, and then I said: "You know, sir, you are building so much there must not be a war because so much that you love and I love will be destroyed if there is." He said that was true, there must not be.

With that we parted with very warm handshakes all around. If they were ordinary human beings I would say that the frank conversation had been valuable but the Lord only knows what will be the result and I shall wait further exchanges with him in the Commission with curiosity.

May 25, 1951

Dear Mrs. Roosevelt:

Again I want to thank you very much for your notes on the interview with the Yugoslav people. They are most interesting and informative. I appreciate your taking the trouble to send them to me and I want to assure you that they are very helpful.

Sincerely yours,

Truman provided military and economic assistance to Yugoslavia following Marshal Tito's break with the Soviet Union in 1948. Mrs. Roosevelt, who visited Tito in 1953, regarded him as one of the few giants of the Cold War era. In her memorandum, she also refers to Lebanon's Charles Malik, who succeeded her as chairman of the Human Rights Commission.

May 27, 1951

Dear Mr. President:

I am sending you the enclosed, a copy of which I have sent to the State Department. I thought it might suggest some questions that you wanted to ask me.

I am glad I am going to have the opportunity of seeing you on Tuesday.

Very cordially yours,

I want to re-emphasize the same observations which I made after the meeting of the General Assembly last autumn and particularly my experience in Committee #3.

I think the great nations, but especially the United States, have got to understand that there is a feeling in the world of a desire to attain some kind of a better standard of living and they feel that particularly the United States has an obligation to make the plans and help them to carry them out to apply those standards.

They are a little fearful:

1. That we do not care what happens to colored populations throughout the world.

2. That our main interest is in power and gain for ourselves.

3. That we are building up so much military power that while on one hand they hope it will protect them against the military power that they know is in the hands of the USSR, on the other hand they are a little afraid of it as a weapon which may be used to gain economic advantage.

Altogether their feelings are highly mixed about us. They are afraid of the USSR but in some ways most of these nations have never known freedom and therefore it is almost easier to accept the type of totalitarian system that tells them definitely what to do than it does to accept the democratic system which seems to require so much of them.

Just to illustrate my point, Dr. Charles Malik of Lebanon, told me he felt we had missed a great opportunity when the Shah of Persia was here. We should have had a plan ready to clean up his government and help him to help his people and we should have made him accept it and we should have sent people to help him put it in operation. Dr. Malik openly told me, in confidence of course, that no government in the Near East was anything but rotten, that the King of Egypt was a fool and unless we were going to take hold, the USSR undoubtedly would. This is a very tall order because it requires an amount of organization on our part and the searching for personnel first of all to make the plans and then to help carry them out. It is almost going to require a different type of education in our colleges.

I also have a feeling that at the proper time some top level gesture will have to be made in relation with the USSR, but that is something I would like to talk over with you.

In talking with the Dutchman who heads up the World Council of Churches who had just come back from a trip in the Near East, this feeling was emphasized, that something had to be done to re-settle the refugees and to straighten out those governments. He used China as an example to show what would happen if bad government was allowed to continue in the way it had continued in China.

It is hard for us to realize but I felt it in the committee and got repercussions from the World Health Organization, that they balance the amount of money that we contribute against the results that that money can bring about in their countries. They do not realize that it means a sacrifice on our part because they do not measure the results in the standard of living against what we now have, but they measure against their own standard of living and they feel, of course, that we have lost nothing. This is ridiculous and should never be accepted but it must be understood because it is one of the reasons why they feel as they do. The reason they go all out on economic and social rights in the Human Rights Commission is because those are the rights that mean something tangible to them in their every day lives. They do not expect them to be achieved overnight but they use the word "right" in a different sense than we do legally.

How are we going to explain all this to the American Bar Association and Congress I really do not know, but somehow it has to be got across because everywhere the emphasis is going to be on how they are going to get a sense of hope of attaining even one notch on the upward path.

As I am going to see you I will make this brief but these are the fundamental things I think we have to accept and consider in making our future policies and are the things which somehow we have to get across to the Congress and to the people of the United States.

From the beginning of her service at the United Nations, Mrs. Roosevelt was disappointed by the polarization between the Western democracies and the emerging nations of the third world. She accurately reported conditions in the Mideast. King Farouk (1920–1965), a silly playboy, would be ousted in a 1952 military coup led by Gamal Abdel Nasser. Mohammad Reza Pahlavi (1919–1980), the Shah of Iran, was another playboy king who lost influence when the nationalist leader Muhammad Mosaddeq (1880–1967) became prime minister in 1951. The Shah returned to power in 1953 as the result of a coup supported by the Central Intelligence Agency.

December 21, 1951

Dear Mr. President:

I imagine as I am only going to be home from the morning of the 22nd until the afternoon of the 31st, that you will be in Independence and not anxious to see me. You know, of course, that if you want to see me I could arrange to come to Washington, Friday afternoon the 28th. I can be reached on the telephone at Hyde Park where I will be from the 23rd or early morning on the 24th until the afternoon of the 25th. Then I will be in New York until the late afternoon of the 28th. . . . Then I will be in Hyde Park until the morning of the 31st when I leave for Paris.

I am very conscious of the responsibility which has fallen on my shoulders but I can assure you it is not really very heavy, for the representatives of the State Department—Dr. Jessup, Mr. Sandifer, Ambassador Gross of the US Mission and other members of the delegation with their staffs are doing the really important work. We are deprived of Ambassador Austin's friendships with the heads of delegations here who come from the permanent groups in New York and I am sorry that I do not feel that I can make up for that constant contact which he had, but I am doing my best and I hope when the final report is in you will feel satisfied.

It is still my belief that we should do as Mr. Cohen and I suggested in trying to have General Eisenhower in civilian clothes, state the purpose of NATO but we have had no answer to the telegram so I do not know what your thought on this really is.

There is much of interest to tell you but if I go straight from Paris to Pakistan and India as the State Department asked me to do, I am afraid it will be spring before I get back to report to you. However, much of what

I have to say will keep. It is long-range stuff and the others will tell you what the thought is on the immediate subjects better than I can.

With every good wish to you and the family for Christmas and the New Year, I am

Very cordially yours,

Warren R. Austin (1877–1962), a Republican senator from Vermont, was named by Truman in 1946 as United States ambassador to the UN When Austin became ill in late 1951, the president asked Mrs. Roosevelt to chair the U.S. delegation at the sixth General Assembly, which would be held in Paris.

Mrs. Roosevelt relied on the advice of Philip C. Jessup, an ambassador-at-large and former professor of international law at Columbia University; Durward Sandifer, who had been assigned by the State Department as her aide; and Ambassador Ernest Gross, Austin's deputy.

Eisenhower, the first Supreme Allied Commander of NATO, was already maneuvering to seek the presidency in 1952. Truman would have supported him for the Democratic presidential nomination. Much to the disappointment of Eleanor and Harry, Ike declared himself a Republican.

CHAPTER 8

1952

At the end of March, Truman announced that he would not seek reelection to a third term. He would be the last chief executive eligible to run for more than two terms. Five years earlier, Republican majorities in the House and the Senate had passed a constitutional amendment that stipulated "no person shall be elected to the office of President more than twice" or more than once if a president had served for more than two years of an unexpired term. This measure was a vengeful reprisal by the GOP against Franklin D. Roosevelt, who had broken the two-term tradition started by George Washington. Forty-one states ratified the amendment within four years, and in 1951 the Twenty-second Amendment became part of the Constitution. As a sitting president, Truman was exempted from the two-term limit. Mrs. Roosevelt, who had not favored her husband's candidacy for a third term, would have supported Truman in 1952. But though he did not like the amendment, Truman believed in the two-term limit. If he had run again, it is doubtful whether he could have won. Truman sensed that the country was ready for a fresh start after twenty years of Democratic administrations.

Eleanor was touted by some of the New Deal faithful as a possible successor to Truman. "I've always wondered whether, if mother had run, she might not have won as the presidential candidate," James wrote in 1976. "It's interesting to ponder the possibility that she just might have made it as our first woman president."

Like Truman, she was disappointed when General Dwight D. Eisenhower decided to seek the presidency as a Republican. "It will be a sad day for him, & in a way for the country, if he runs for President," she wrote Joseph Lash in January. "He will win but as a hero he will be tarnished & it will get worse and worse. We need our heroes & we need him here & I doubt we need him more as President."

Truman and Mrs. Roosevelt were elated when the Democratic National Convention in Chicago nominated Illinois governor Adlai E. Stevenson as Eisenhower's opponent. The president and Eleanor, who had admired Eisenhower, were appalled when he bowed to expediency and made campaign appearances with the witch-hunting Republican senators Joseph R. McCarthy of Wisconsin and William E. Jenner of Indiana, both of whom had slandered Ike's great mentor, General Marshall. "I stand by my friends," Truman told a cheering throng in Boston.

In her gentle way, Mrs. Roosevelt reprimanded Eisenhower. "I know it must have been terrible to face yourself—to realize that you have been persuaded that you must go out and stand beside men who always said things about someone who has been your best friend, someone who had really given you the opportunity to rise to great position," she told a crowd in Harlem.

"Yet he [Eisenhower] stood by the side of Jenner, who said that General Marshall's life was a living lie.

"How General Eisenhower could do that I cannot understand. I cannot understand how he could give a mark of approval to Senator McCarthy."

Eisenhower was embarrassed when the *New York Times* reported that he had deleted a favorable reference to General Marshall from a speech that he delivered in McCarthy's presence. In his presidential memoirs, Eisenhower wrote that he would never have agreed to this deletion if he had been fully aware of the political implications. He was stung by the criticism from Truman, Mrs. Roosevelt, and others.

Neither Truman nor Mrs. Roosevelt was surprised that America liked Ike in the November 4 election. Two of her four sons, Elliott and the Republican John, supported Eisenhower. "It was my opinion," Eleanor later wrote, "that Governor Stevenson would probably make one of the best Presidents we ever had had, but I also believed that it was practically impossible for the Democrats to win the election because of the hero worship surrounding General Eisenhower."

Hotel Crillon, Paris
January 29, 1952

Dear Mr. President:

I have not written you before but I am afraid I must now break my silence about the appointment of an ambassador to the Vatican. I am getting letters on every side as I am sure you are too and I feel that perhaps I should tell you it seems to me since we are a Protestant country, we should heed the very evident feeling so many Protestants have against having an ambassador at the Vatican. I understand that an ambassador can be appointed only when you have signed the Concordat, but is it not possible for a state which is not a Catholic state to sign. Automatically, if the Vatican has an ambassador in a Catholic state he takes precedence over the entire diplomatic corps. This, in a non-Catholic state would make a very embarrassing situation. In the case of Great Britain, they have a minister at the Vatican for this very reason because then a minister sent by the Vatican has the same standing as the papal delegate and it does not bring the conflict that having an ambassador does. For the purpose of the U.S. I have always felt that a special representative of the President gave all the advantages and avoided the pitfalls which the appointment of an ambassador or minister brings about.

It is easy to understand this present objection. The recognition of any church as a temporal power puts that church in a different position from any of the other churches and while we are now only hearing from the Protestant groups, the Moslems may one day wake up to this and make an equal howl. For us who take a firm stand on the separation of church and state, the recognition of a temporal power seems inconsistent.

I write these random thoughts because I am sure someday someone is going to ask my opinion and I do not want to say that I think it is not a good idea without having expressed myself to you beforehand.

I will write you a report on this session before I leave on the 8th if all is well and finished here.

Please give my good wishes to Mrs. Truman and Margaret and believe me always

Cordially yours,

February 2, 1952

Dear Mrs. Roosevelt:

I can't tell you how very much I appreciate your letter of January twenty-ninth from the Hotel Crillon in Paris. My recollection of that great hotel is of Woodrow Wilson who walked down the front steps while I looked on as a spectator.

I also appreciate very much what you have to say about the Vatican situation and I am giving it a great deal of thought. I hope we can get it worked out without creating a religious controversy. I don't know whether we can or not but I expect to try.

I am always glad to hear from you and to have your frank statements of your opinion.

Sincerely yours,

As Wilson departed for the peace conference, Truman caught his first and only glimpse of the twenty-eighth president. From then on, he would always associate the Crillon with Wilson's great moment.

Truman favored extending formal recognition to the Vatican State but was inhibited from doing so because of Protestant opposition. Roosevelt had angered many Protestants in 1939 when he named steel executive Myron C. Taylor (1874–1959) as special representative to the Vatican. Taylor stayed on the job until 1949. After Truman's Washington, D.C., pastor used his pulpit to preach against recognition, the president never went back to Washington's First Baptist Church.

February 26, 1952

Dear Mrs. Roosevelt:

I have read with interest and appreciation your summary report concerning the last meeting of the United Nations General Assembly. You did a fine job.

I know that it must have been difficult to carry on with the staff problems you had, especially during a session where the problems up for discussion were tough to deal with. But I know that your leadership of the United States delegation was inspiring and I feel that what you did at

Paris carried all of us further along the road towards peace. I think particularly of action taken on such problems as disarmament and collective security.

As your letter makes clear, the General Assembly is invaluable in offering a forum for consultation and cooperation with other delegations. It gives us a chance to make our views widely known to other peoples, and vice virsa. I think it speaks well for United States policies, and the way they were presented at Paris, that our position was supported by the Assembly on almost all important items.

I was especially interested in what you had to say regarding Arab aspirations and the trance-like state of mind in Western Europe concerning the Soviet menace.

We must continue steadfast and show the way to greater strength and realism.

I thank you for all you have done.

Very sincerely yours,

Mrs. Roosevelt sent Truman a summary report of the sixth General Assembly, which was held in Paris. The document is not in their correspondence files.

Bangalore, India
March 7, 1952

Dear Mr. President:

I want to tell you now that I have been a short time in India what a really extraordinary job our ambassador, Mr. Bowles, seems to have done. In one way I think perhaps Providence did something for us when he was defeated in the last election so that he could be available for his present post.

India seems to need very special treatment at this time and seems to be very vital to our own interests. Everywhere, without exception, and I think I have met every government official thus far, tells me what a change there has been in the feeling toward the United States since Mr. Bowles' arrival. They feel now that we understand them, that we are more understanding of their isolationism and that we are beginning to realize that they do not want to become communistic but their problems are so great they feel they cannot take sides.

I only hope that we can do the things that seem essential to them. The problem here is much the same as that of China, though in Nehru we have a leader of infinitely higher quality than Chiang. Mr. Nehru has around him a great many good men. Gandhi has left his mark and there is an unselfish service being given among young and old which might be of help even in our own democracy.

Mr. Bowles has done everything possible for me but I am afraid I can never accomplish what the Indians want as a result of my visit.

With all good wishes,

———————

Key West
March 17, 1952

Dear Mrs. Roosevelt:

I certainly did appreciate your letter of March the seventh from Bangalore. I am more than happy that Chester Bowles has created the impression which we have been striving for all along in India. It is my feeling that a great many of our career ambassadors are not politicians and it takes a politician to understand the people of any country. Your statement about Chester Bowles more than confirms that opinion.

It has always been necessary whenever there is a difficult job to be done in any country, to have it done by someone who understands people and how to get along with people. That was the case when we sent Stanton Griffis to Poland, to Egypt, then to Argentina and then finally to Spain. Our ambassadors to Great Britain and France have always been men who understand people and how to get along with people.

I am more than happy that Chester Bowles has made good in India. I think your visit there has had a wonderful reaction also and I am very glad that you were able to go there.

Chester A. Bowles (1901–1986), one of the New Deal's bright young men, later served as governor of Connecticut and in the U.S. House. He

*did much to improve U.S. relations with India and developed a good
relationship with Prime Minister Jawaharlal Nehru. Stanton Griffis,
though warm and friendly, was a diplomatic lightweight. Bowles was a
major leaguer.*

April 11, 1952

Dear Mrs. Roosevelt:

I am sending you the memorandum which I showed you yesterday
from the State Department. I thought maybe you would like to have it
for your files. I've kept a copy of it.

Sincerely yours,

Memorandum for the President
Subject: Appointment with Mrs. Roosevelt, April 10

The following information is transmitted in connection with Mrs.
Roosevelt's appointment to see the President at 12:00 noon, April 10.

Mrs. Roosevelt's journey through the Middle East and Southeast Asia
(see attached itinerary) was entirely unofficial, all arrangements having
been made by her various hosts in each country. She was received everywhere with great cordiality except in the Arab states. On her arrival in
Pakistan, Mrs. Roosevelt commented that she had anticipated some hos-
tility in the Arab states, but found none and, while there was an absence
of cordiality, she was shown every consideration. Her trip to India and
Pakistan was a great success, and she appears to have done much to
increase understanding of United States foreign policy objectives.

Typical among the reactions of our embassies was that of Ambassador
Davis who reported that her visit to Israel had a tonic effect on public
morale and was an unqualified success from the standpoint of United
States interests and prestige. Ambassador Bowles has described her visit
to India as a tremendous success and as having made a deep impression,
particularly among students and the press.

Although it was undertaken in a purely unofficial capacity, Mrs. Roosevelt's journey has served the public interest exceedingly well.

Mrs. Roosevelt is now preparing for the next session of the United States Human Rights Commission which meets in New York on April 14 to complete the drafting of the Covenant of Human Rights. She was successful at the last session of the General Assembly in persuading the Assembly to reverse a previous decision and to instruct the Human Rights Commission to draft two separate covenants, one confined to civil and political rights and the other dealing with economic and social rights. This separation has been advocated consistently by this Government, and it is a credit to her effectiveness as a negotiator that she was able finally to persuade a majority of governments to support it.

Dean Acheson

April 21, 1952

Dear Mr. President:

You were very thoughtful to send me the memorandum and I am glad to have it for my files.

With many thanks, I am

Very sincerely yours,

Hyde Park
May 31, 1952

Dear Mr. President:

I try not to bother you too often but I am very much troubled at the moment about the McCarran-Walters Bill. I realize that I cannot possibly know much in detail about any legislation and this is a complex and technical subject.

However, I hear that this bill would generally restrict immigration and make it more difficult than it now is. It would remove the barriers to naturalization for certain Asiatics and provide a small quota for a number of Asiatic countries which do not have a quota.

Of course, the removal of racial barriers is all to the good but I understand that this legislation sets up a special classification for persons of Asiatic and Oriental ancestry and sets them completely apart from

Europeans and others in a highly restricted category. I am told that it even defines a fifty percent blood test for persons of Asiatic ancestry no matter where born.

The people of Asia are just at present oversensitive and very proud and I am afraid the enactment of such a bill with these provisions would be very unfortunate. I also think that the Russians would use it for plausible propaganda against us.

Most of us would like to see exclusionist bars go down but not in favor of new ones which would provide fresh evidence that we consider ourselves "superior" to the peoples of Asia.

This legislation may be before you any day for signature and if on mature consideration you think it is really bad, I hope you will veto it, though I realize I cannot be familiar with it from every point of view. I am only writing you what my general feeling has been.

Very cordially yours,

June 5, 1952

Dear Mrs. Roosevelt:

I certainly did appreciate your good letter of May thirty-first regarding the McCarran and Walters bills. They are both very bad bills and I think we would be better off with no legislation than the straitjacket they are endeavoring to give me with that legislation.

They are still working on the conference report but I am of the opinion that they can't get either one of those two measures in shape to make it a good law.

Of course, I can never publicly say what I expect to do until the legislation is on my desk but I'll say to you in confidence that if either one of those bills comes up here in the present form, it won't become law if I can prevent it.

We have sent messages to the Congress with a proposed bill for the future increase in immigration quotas for the displaced persons up to 300,000. I don't know how far we will get with it but I hope it will come to my desk before the Congress quits.

Sincerely yours,

Senator Patrick A. McCarran of Nevada (1876–1954), who chaired the Internal Security Subcommittee, was tougher, smarter, and more sinister than Joseph R. McCarthy. Truman vetoed the immigration bill on grounds that it discriminated against the nations of southern and eastern Europe and nonwhite peoples. By the narrowest of margins, Congress overrode Truman's veto.

––––––––––––

New York
June 18, 1952

The President
The White House

I understand you have been invited by NAACP to speak at their convention in Oklahoma and I have been asked to express my feelings that this is important both nationally and internationally. Even though I realize the many calls on your time.

Because of a prior commitment, Truman regretted that he couldn't make this date. In his reply to Mrs. Roosevelt, he also looked ahead to the 1952 presidential campaign: "There is only one way for the Democrats to win and that is to support the program which has been a successful one for industry, labor, farmers, and white collar workers."

––––––––––––

June 30, 1952

Dear Mr. President:

If you really meant that you want me to make a speech at the Democratic National Convention, will you please have some one let me know what day and what hour as soon as possible?

I can not be there during the day on the 21st as I have already made an engagement for the whole of that morning and early afternoon.

Very cordially yours,

––––––––––––

July 3, 1952

Dear Mrs. Roosevelt:

I told the chairman of the National Democratic Committee to get in touch with you about the day and hour for your speech on the United Nations to the Democratic Convention. You should hear from him in the next day or two.

I am very anxious that you should tell the people just exactly what the United Nations means to peace in the world. I don't think anybody in the party can do it any better than you.

Sincerely yours,

July 25, 1952

Dear Mr. President:

I deeply appreciate your telegram and am so glad you thought my speech went well. I was glad when it was over because I rather dreaded it.

My greetings to Mrs. Truman, best wishes to you.

Very cordially yours,

Many Americans were disappointed that the United Nations had fallen short of their grand expectations. In the summer of 1951, only 24 percent of respondents to a Gallup Poll said that the UN was doing a good job, while 36 percent said that it was doing a poor job. But when asked if the United States should drop out, 75 percent were opposed. "To achieve peace," Mrs. Roosevelt told the 1952 convention, "we must recognize the historic truth that we can no longer live apart from the rest of the world. We must also recognize the fact that peace, like freedom, is not won once and for all. It is fought for daily, in many small acts, and is the result of many individual efforts. . . . We should remember that the United Nations is not a cure-all. It is only an instrument capable of effective action when its members have a will to make it work."

September 6, 1952

Dear Mr. President:

Thank you so very much for the copy of your book. I think it will be of great value to many people who will, for the first time, understand some of the strains and stresses and burdens of the great office which you have held.

My warm regards and thanks and kind remembrances to Mrs. Truman and to Margaret. Tell Margaret I hope she enjoyed her trip to the Scandinavian countries. I thought they were most delightful.

Very cordially yours,

Truman's book, Mr. President *(Farrar, Straus and Young, 1952), edited by William Hillman, included excerpts from diaries, letters, and interviews. For a book written by a sitting president, it is surprisingly candid and readable.*

———————

Aboard President's Train
October 10, 1952

Dear Mrs. Roosevelt:

May I offer hearty congratulations and best wishes on this anniversary of your birth.

I know I am speaking not only for myself but for the millions of Americans who revere you for the wonderful work you are doing at the United Nations to promote better understanding among peoples and a greater respect for human rights. Your continued health and happiness is my wish and my prayer.

Very sincerely yours,

———————

October 12, 1952

Dear Mr. President:

How very kind of you in the midst of your extremely busy life to take time out to write me on my birthday. I do deeply appreciate your good wishes.

Very cordially yours,

New York
November 6, 1952

Dear Mr. President:

I will hope to get down to Washington some time before Christmas to report to you on my visit to Chile and on anything else that turns up in the General Assembly.

In the meantime I want to thank you for the many opportunities you have given me for service during your administration.

I know that after the great efforts you put into the campaign it must be a keen disappointment to you but I think we were against impossible odds, especially the feeling many people had that they want their boys home from Korea. I am afraid General Eisenhower will not be able to fulfill the hopes of these people, and it may be difficult for him in consequence. I like your offer of your own plane to go immediately to Korea.

With every good wish,

Very cordially yours,

Mrs. Roosevelt admired Eisenhower as a soldier but thought he had bowed to expediency in the 1952 presidential campaign. Shortly before his victory, Eisenhower pledged to go to Korea. Following the election, Truman offered him the use of the presidential aircraft, a DC-6 called the Independence. *Eisenhower, angered by Truman's hard-hitting rhetoric in the closing days of the campaign, declined the president's offer.*

November 12, 1952

Dear Mrs. Roosevelt:

I appreciated very much yours of the sixth. Of course, I put everything I could into the campaign and tried my best to get the facts before the people but evidently I didn't succeed very well.

I will be most happy to see you whenever it is convenient for you to come down. I am anxious to hear what happened in Chile while you were there.

Sincerely yours,

In the Republican landslide, Eisenhower crushed Democratic rival Adlai
E. Stevenson. For the first time in twenty-four years, the GOP won the
presidency and both houses of Congress. Though Truman put up a good
fight, he knew that the country was in the mood for change.

At Truman's request, Mrs. Roosevelt led the U.S. delegation to the
inauguration of Carlos Ibanez as president of Chile. Ibanez, who had
been critical of the United States., changed his stance in the wake of
Eleanor's visit.

November 15, 1952

Memorandum for: W. Averell Harriman
From: The President

Your memorandum regarding the Medal for Merit for Mrs. Franklin
D. Roosevelt has been under consideration for a long time but authority
for it has long ago expired.

If anybody deserves one she does but it takes a special Act of Congress
to get it. I regret it very much.

December 4, 1952

Dear Mr. President:

As you know, at the end of this General Assembly session all of the
delegates automatically resign so this is not a letter of resignation. I shall
write to General Eisenhower and resign as the US member on the
Human Rights Commission.

But before that time comes and when my work ends on this session, I
am hoping to come to Washington for a few hours. This will probably be
on December 20th or 22nd. May I come in to see you for a few minutes
around noon? I promise not to take up more than a few minutes of your
time.

I would also like to have an opportunity to say good-by to Mrs. Truman if she is not too busy to let me run in for a minute or two.

When you are a free and independent citizen, I hope you will occa-
sionally come to New York City and that I may inveigle you and Mrs.

Truman to spend a weekend at Hyde Park. It would be a great pleasure if you could, and even more pleasure if Margaret could be with you.

Very cordially yours,

I have just heard of the death of Mrs. Truman's mother and send my deep sympathy.

December 13, 1952

Dear Mrs. Roosevelt:

I'll be most happy to see you when you come to Washington at the time you suggest, which is around noon on either the twentieth or the twenty-second.

I'm sure it will be easy to make an arrangement for you to see Mrs. Truman whenever you find it convenient.

I certainly thank you for the invitation to spend a weekend at Hyde Park and hope that pleasure will be possible when I finally get out of the White House and get things straightened out.

Mrs. Truman and I both appreciate your sympathetic statement about Mrs. Wallace.

Sincerely yours,

December 16, 1952

Dear Mr. President:

I find now that I will not be coming to Washington before Christmas. I appreciate your kindness in being willing to see me. If I may, I shall let you know when I expect to be there.

With every good wish,

Very cordially yours,

CHAPTER 9

1953–1960

On leaving the presidency, Truman remained friendly with Mrs. Roosevelt. As the grand figures of their party, they campaigned across the country for younger Democratic hopefuls. Truman was his party's first active former president since Grover Cleveland. "Democrats have come to look on Truman as a character, sometimes amusing, always indomitable, certainly admirable, almost always lovable," *Time* magazine observed in a 1956 cover article.

Throughout the Eisenhower era, Eleanor led the Gallup Poll as the most admired woman in the world. Career diplomats at the State Department had hoped that Mrs. Roosevelt would be retained as a delegate to the United Nations. But Eisenhower, who disliked her, told Secretary of State John Foster Dulles that she would have no role in the new administration. It was a loss to this country and to the world when Eisenhower took this attitude.

Bernard Baruch, a mutual friend, confided to her that Eisenhower had been told by Perle Mesta, the ambassador to Luxembourg, that Mrs. Roosevelt had alleged that Mamie Doud Eisenhower, the general's wife, was an alcoholic. "Now, I haven't the faintest idea if Mrs. Eisenhower has a problem," Eleanor told the Reverend William Turner Levy. "I know I never spoke of it, and I'm shocked that he could believe I would gossip, especially when I and my family have suffered for so many years from maligning rumors! My own father and only brother died from drinking too much—it's not a matter I could react to other than with pain and deep sympathy. But I've been told he was infuriated by what Mrs. Mesta told him—and he's famous for his temper."

As Democratic partisans, Truman and Mrs. Roosevelt waged the good fight for national health insurance, affordable housing, civil rights, and the protection of public lands and forests from greedy special interests. Both stood up for decency and fair play during Senator Joseph McCarthy's witch-hunts.

On several occasions, most notably at their party's 1956 convention and at a 1959 Democratic dinner, the former president and Mrs. Roosevelt had public disagreements. He supported New York governor Averell Harriman while she backed Stevenson for the 1956 presidential nomination. "I was dismayed by the idea of publicly pitting my political judgment against his," she later wrote. "I could only reflect that sometimes one had to do things one does not like to do."

But when they were on opposite sides, it was never personal. "I hope you will understand that whatever action I take is because I think I am doing the right thing," Truman told her.

"Of course," Mrs. Roosevelt replied. "I know you will act as you believe is right and I know you will realize that I must do the same." When Stevenson won renomination, Truman promptly endorsed him and made numerous campaign appearances in his behalf.

As the 1960 Democratic convention approached, the former president and Mrs. Roosevelt were part of the movement to stop John F. Kennedy from winning the presidential nomination. In their opposition, there was an element of anti-Catholic bias, which reflected their backgrounds as Protestants born in the late nineteenth century. Once Kennedy won the nomination, both campaigned for him out of loyalty to their party and also because of their intense dislike of Republican presidential nominee Richard M. Nixon.

Both Democratic elders cheered their party's return to power.

Hyde Park
January 2, 1953

Dear Mr. President:

I had thought that because my work was finished as a delegate to the General Assembly of the United Nations, and as I was only appointed for this session, that you would not require a special resignation. I find that as there is to be an adjourned session we must all write you formal letters of resignation, so this is to resign as a delegate to the General Assembly which is still in session.

Very sincerely yours,

January 8, 1953

Dear Mr. President:

There seems to be a jinx on my getting to Washington! I have completely lost my voice and decided that the weather was not propitious for going down to Washington today.

This means I will not see you and Mrs. Truman before the twentieth, I am afraid, and so I want to send you this line to tell you how grateful I am for all you have given me in the way of opportunities for service in the UN in the last few years and to wish you relief from the burdens of state which I know have been overwhelming and an interesting and happy life from now on with many satisfactions.

Very cordially yours,

January 19, 1953

Dear Mrs. Roosevelt:

Your letter of resignation as a Delegate to the General Assembly of the United Nations has been received, and I regret that I must accept it, effective January 20, 1953.

I cannot leave the White House without thanking you for your unfaltering service to our country and your very real help to me. Since that evening in 1945 when you responded to my offer of assistance with, "What can we do for you?", you have done many things for me. In your work on the Human Rights Commission, you brought honor to all of us. Your poise and patience and good will have been valuable in sessions of the United Nations General Assembly as well. The reports you have brought to me have been stimulating and useful. You have been a good ambassador for America.

At home, I am sure that your efforts begun long ago to make people take an interest in affairs of their own communities have borne fruit in the public support of many of our advances in housing, health facilities, social security, civil rights, and conservation of natural resources. Your continued support of the Democratic party and its program has been important.

I have heard that you will continue your work for the United Nations as a volunteer in a non-governmental organization. You believe with me, I know, that our starting point toward world peace remains in the UN, and I am glad you will continue to build support of its aims.

I feel confident, too, that you agree that we have much to do at home in beating back fear, renewing our confidence in each other, and in building our moral power.

Again I thank you. Mrs. Truman joins me in wishing you the very best of everything.

Sincerely yours,

In January of 1953, former attorney general Francis Biddle nominated Truman for the Nobel Peace Prize. Mrs. Roosevelt wrote this seconding letter to the Nobel Committee.

January 29, 1953

Gentlemen:

I take pleasure in seconding the Honorable Harry S. Truman of the United States of America for the award of the Nobel Peace Prize.

Mr. Truman has performed a great service in preserving peace by a continuing and closely integrated policy of building the economic, political and spiritual strength of the Western World to meet, contain, and eventually to overcome the threat to Western independence, and to Western religion and culture, from Soviet imperialism. His record on the aggression in Trieste and in Teheran; his aid to Greece and his cooperation with the United Nations; his action on the Berlin air-lift; and his support of the Marshall Plan; his stand in regard to Korean Communist aggression are all things that need no elaboration by me.

Mr. Truman patiently and successfully directed the United States in its new foreign policy of Western unity.

I think President Truman played a great role in promoting cooperation among nations and presenting measures that lead to peace.

Sincerely yours,

Truman, who proposed General Marshall for the 1953 Peace Prize, was elated when the Nobel Committee honored the former secretary of state. "I hope you will share this distinction with me," Marshall wrote Truman, "because it was through your guidance and leadership that the European Recovery Plan was made possible."

In November 1964, two years after Eleanor's death, Truman wrote Gunnar Jahn, chairman of the Nobel Prize Committee, with another recommendation:

"I understand that there are regulations in your committee that rule out an award of the Peace Prize to Mrs. Franklin D. Roosevelt because she has passed away.

"The award without the financial prize that goes with it can be made. You should make it. If she didn't earn it, then no one else has.

"It's an award for peace in the world. I hope you'll make it."

The committee of the Norwegian Parliament, which awards the prize, declined to change the rules. The 1965 peace prize was awarded to the United Nation's Children's Fund, a choice that Mrs. Roosevelt would have endorsed with enthusiasm.

February 2, 1953

Dear Mr. Truman:

Thank you very much for your kind letter of January 19th.

I find there is a great deal of work in connection with the American Association for the UN. I expected to spend two mornings a week at the national office, and now find it is a full time job.

Please remember that it would be a great pleasure to be able to welcome you and Mrs. Truman at Hyde Park.

Very cordially yours,

February 18, 1953

Dear Mrs. Roosevelt:

I appreciated your letter of February second very, very much. Mrs. Truman and I will remember the invitation to Hyde Park.

I know you can sympathize with us because we have records, papers, furniture, clothing and what not piled up in every room in the house at home, in two storage places in Kansas City and in an office in the Federal Reserve Bank Building. I don't know whether we will ever get out of it or not.

I've had more than sixty thousand letters—ninety-nine and nine-tenths of which are just as fine as anybody would want to receive. I am trying to find some way to get them answered.

Whenever there is anything I can do that is of interest to you don't fail to call on me.

Mrs. Truman joins me in very best wishes and kindest regards to you.

Sincerely yours,

On his return to Independence, Truman settled into the white Victorian house at 219 North Delaware. In those days, former presidents did not receive a pension and were not protected by the Secret Service. Truman declined to commercialize on his fame by going on corporate boards and enjoyed his new role as "Mr. Citizen."

May 7, 1953

Dear Mrs. Roosevelt:

I appreciated very much your note of the first enclosing the letter from Bilimora. I read it with a lot of interest.

Mrs. Truman and I were certainly sorry to hear of Mrs. Thompson's death. We didn't learn of her death in time to write you when it happened. You must miss her very very much.

I hope everything is going well with you and that you will let me hear from you once in awhile. I think the people are just now beginning to understand how important it was for you to be a member of the United Nations Organization.

Sincerely yours,

May 11, 1953

Dear Mr. Truman:

It was good of you to write me about Miss Thompson. She was a devoted and loyal friend as well as a great help to me in my work and I miss her more and more every day.

At the moment I am very busy preparing for my departure on May 19th. When I return in August, I hope it will be possible for you and Mrs. Truman to visit me at Hyde Park.

My warm thanks for your thoughtfulness in writing and kindest regards to you and Mrs. Truman.

Cordially yours,

Malvina Thompson, who had been Mrs. Roosevelt's secretary for twenty-nine years, died in April 1953 after a long illness. Known to her friends as Tommy, she lived in the former first lady's cottage at Hyde Park and was her closest friend. "I am quite sure that no one ever lived a more selfless life," Mrs. Roosevelt wrote in her column on April 12. "She had a tremendous sense of responsibility about her work and a great sense of dignity. But because to her what she did was so important, whether the task was little or big or whether it was menial or intellectual made no difference whatever. She did every job to the best of her ability, and her greatest satisfaction lay in helping me to do whatever work I was doing as well as she thought it should be done. Her standards were high for me, as well as for herself, and she could be a real critic."

September 25, 1953

Dear Mrs. Roosevelt:

I have been a long time answering your good letter of September twenty-first but I have had some difficulty in getting things lined up so I would know just exactly what is facing me.

I certainly will be glad to attend the National Board Meeting of ADA on February sixth at the Waldorf. I don't know when I've had a happier meeting than the one I had in Washington with ADA a year ago.

I hope everything is going well with you. Dave Noyes has been here with me and your ears should have burned with the nice things we have been saying about you.

I appreciate very much your writing me about this meeting and I certainly want to attend.

Sincerely yours,

———————

September 30, 1953

Dear Mr. President:

Your letter accepting the invitation to speak for ADA was delayed in reaching me because it was directed to an old address. I am very happy that you are able to accept.

Many thanks for telling me about Mr. Noyes' visit. It is good to know that you both think well of me and I am deeply appreciative.

With kind regards to Mrs. Truman, Margaret and yourself.

Very sincerely yours,

Mrs. Roosevelt maintained residences at Val-Kill Cottage in Hyde Park and in Manhattan. Following her husband's death, she had apartments at 29 Washington Square West (1945–49); the Park Sheraton at 202 West Fifty-sixth Street (1949–53); and 211 East Sixty-second Street (1953–59). Truman's office apparently had difficulty keeping current with Mrs. Roosevelt's address.

———————

February 25, 1954

If I am not misinformed you are to be in New York City on the eighth of March. We are having a dedication of a room in the American Association for the United Nations Office in memory of Philip Murray and his interest in international affairs. We wonder if you could attend at four o'clock on March the ninth. The money to equip this room is given by the Philip Murray Foundation on whose advisory board I serve as do you. I hope very much that you may be able to join us and say a few words.

Eleanor Roosevelt

February 26, 1954

Dear Mrs. Roosevelt:

In reply to your telegram of the twenty-fifth I will be in New York on the seventh and it is necessary for me to go to Boston on the eighth.

I regret very much that I can't be with you for the dedication of the room in the American Association for the United Nations Office in memory of Philip Murray. I wish you would express my regret and tell the people there that I would like very much to have been present.

Sincerely yours,

Philip Murray (1886–1952), president of the Congress of Industrial Organizations from 1940 until his death, was an important labor ally of Presidents Roosevelt and Truman. Murray's political action committee provided critical organizational support to Truman in the '48 campaign. In the wake of Truman's victory, Murray expelled ten communist-led unions that had supported Henry A. Wallace's third-party candidacy. When Truman needed help the most, Murray came through. Truman never forgot it.

Independence
March 23, 1954

Dear Mrs. Roosevelt:

I have just received a note from Dave Lloyd telling me that you have made two donations to my Library Fund. I can't tell you how very much I appreciate it.

I am somewhat in a quandary now because two universities in this part of the country are bringing pressure on me to build a building on their campuses. I don't know what is the best way to handle it but I do want to be sure that my Presidential papers are safe and are in the hands of the Government just as President Roosevelt's are.

Mrs. Truman wants to be remembered to you.

Sincerely yours,

Truman had at first hoped to build his presidential library on the family farm at Grandview. The University of Missouri at Columbia and University of Kansas City both offered land for a site. Edwin W. Pauley, a major donor to UCLA, sought the Truman Library for its Westwood campus. But Truman chose his hometown of Independence, where he lived in the Victorian home at 219 Delaware. The town donated a park and adjoining residential property for the library site. Basil O'Connor, FDR's former law partner, who launched the March of Dimes campaign that provided funding for Dr. Jonas Salk's polio vaccine, began the Harry S. Truman Library Corporation, a nonprofit foundation, to raise money for construction of the library. Other members of the executive committee included Mrs. Roosevelt, former secretary of state Dean Acheson, former vice president Alben Barkley, and W. Averell Harriman. The HSTL Corporation would raise more than $1.7 million. Truman expressed his gratitude to Mrs. Roosevelt for $200 in early contributions to the fund.

Independence
September 29, 1954

Dear Mrs. Roosevelt:

I've sent a letter to Henry Morgenthau to be read at your dinner on Oct. 11. I am sorely disappointed that I can't be present. I'll have to admit that I haven't fully recovered from my hospital experience last June.

The Doctor's orders are all that prevent my being present.

This letter enclosed is for your files. May you have many more happy birthdays. Mrs. Truman and Margaret join me in that wish.

Sincerely,

September 25, 1954

Dear Mr. Morgenthau:

I am disappointed that I cannot be with you tonight to join in the tribute to Mrs. Eleanor Roosevelt on her seventieth birthday.

But for my recent illness, nothing could have kept me from being with you. My doctor insists that I not risk the trip and Mrs. Truman and Margaret support the doctor.

I had hoped to be able to express in person to Mrs. Roosevelt my thanks for the contributions she has made during this critical era to the cause of peace and better human relations.

May I ask you to tell Mrs. Roosevelt for me that her work in and for the United Nations has done much to strengthen this great organization so urgently needed to preserve the peace, freedom, and civilization of the world.

Mrs. Roosevelt has represented this nation to the world with imagination, grace, charm, good humor and realistic good sense. And from her wide travels she has brought us in closer contact with other nations, giving us a wise and compassionate insight into the thinking of those peoples.

Few have understood, as she has, America's new role of leadership and the new burdens of our responsibility.

She has been one of our most effective forces against Communist propaganda in many vulnerable spots of the world. The Communist conspirators of the Kremlin know this well. And that is why they vilify her at every opportunity. Unhappily some of our own extremists here at home parallel the Communists in bitter and venomous attacks.

In all ages, men and women who have had the courage to do things for the benefit of all the people have been attacked by those whose lives and living were devoted to character assassination. This quotation from Plutarch's "Life of Pericles" could have been written today:

"How can one wonder at any number of strange assertions from men whose whole lives were devoted to mockery, and who were ready at any time to sacrifice the reputation of their superiors to vulgar envy and spite, as to some evil genius."

Mrs. Roosevelt's untiring energy and devotion to the cause of peace and a more enlightened day for mankind have endeared her to us for all time. History will give major recognition to her services.

May I add a personal note. I shall never forget that at the moment tragic fate shifted the awesome burdens of the Presidency from the shoulders of that very great man, Franklin D. Roosevelt, to mine, she said to me, when I asked her what I could do: "Mr. President, you are the one in trouble. Is there anything we can do for you?"

"A Happy Birthday to you, Mrs. Roosevelt, and many more of them," is a wish in which Mrs. Truman and Margaret join me.

Yours sincerely,

New York
November 12, 1954

Dear Mr. President,

Thank you so much for your very thoughtful message which I received on the occasion of my seventieth birthday.

Your good wishes added greatly to the event, and I was so happy to hear from you.

With every best wish,

Very sincerely yours,

Though Truman did not attend, he was a member of the 70th Birthday Committee, along with Albert Einstein; contralto Marian Anderson; civil rights leaders A. Philip Randolph, Thurgood Marshall, and Walter White; Justices William O. Douglas and Felix Frankfurter; General Marshall; UN diplomat Ralph Bunche; labor leaders Walter Reuther and George Meany; and the actress Cornelia Otis Skinner.

New York
December 16, 1954

Dear Mr. and Mrs. Truman:

I find that I shall be in Kansas City for a meeting of the American Association of the United Nations on Wednesday, January fifth, which will be the first stop on a week-long trip for the Association.

If it is convenient for you both, I would be enchanted to know that you might be present at some part of the day's session, or that you might dine with Mr. Eichelberger and myself and a small group just before the evening meeting. It would be good to see you again.

Sincerely yours,

December 22, 1954

Dear Mrs. Roosevelt:

Replying to yours of the sixteenth, we shall certainly be happy to see you when you are in Kansas City and I am sure that we shall be delighted to have dinner with you and Mr. Eichelberger.

That was wonderful maple sugar which you sent us. I fear very much that I'll get very little of it, because Margaret is at home.

Sincerely yours,

Clark M. Eichelberger (1896–1980), executive director of the American Association for the United Nations (AAUN), had served as a consultant to the U.S. delegation at the 1945 San Francisco Conference at which the United Nations was established. In the winter of 1953, Mrs. Roosevelt had surprised Eichelberger by showing up at his office across from the United Nations and offering to do volunteer work. She began working out of a small cubicle in the AAUN offices at 345 East Forty-sixth Street and, in her extensive travels, would help establish new chapters of the organization around the country. Mrs. Roosevelt became chairman of the AAUN's Board of Governors.

January 19, 1955

Dear Mrs. Roosevelt:

We have a country editor over in Platte County, about twenty miles from Kansas City, who is a rabid Roosevelt and Truman Democrat. He wrote a little editorial while you were here and is anxious for me to forward it to you. I am doing so at his request.

Sincerely yours,

[handwritten] "The Boss" and I surely enjoyed the short visit with you very much.

New York
January 25, 1955

Dear Mr. President:

Many thanks for your letter and the enclosed clipping which I appreciate your bringing to my attention.

I very much enjoyed my visit to Kansas City and I was delighted to have a chance to see you and Mrs. Truman.

The country editor is indeed kind and I hope you will thank him for me.

With every good wish,

Cordially,

James Grover Cleveland Tibbetts, publisher of the Platte County Gazette *in Parkville, Missouri, who greeted the former president as "Sir Harry," had written a tribute to Mrs. Roosevelt and wanted her to see it.*

————————

Tel-Aviv, Israel
March 26, 1955

Dear Mr. President:

I wanted to tell you that in Israel I was shown the village which was named after you and which is now a thriving settlement, and everywhere I heard the hope expressed that you would be coming over here before long. I think you would find it an extremely interesting country with many problems.

While here I have been constantly reminded of the fact that my husband told me at one time that these Eastern countries had so many problems he would like to come here after he retired and try to help solve them. I protested at the time that we had enough problems of our own but I felt I would find myself traveling to this part of the world and spending a good deal of time here. I think Franklin would have found Israel a rather exhilarating spot.

Hoping you are feeling well and my best wishes to Mrs. Truman and Margaret.

Cordially yours,

April 6, 1955

Dear Mrs. Roosevelt:

I appreciated very much your good letter of March twenty-sixth from Tel-Aviv, Israel.

I wish I could take the trip and see Israel from one end to the other and someday I hope to be able to do it.

I feel just as the President did when he said he would like to go there and help settle their problems but I am of the same opinion that you are, that we have enough problems at home to keep us busy.

I hope you had a grand trip and that I will see you again sometime in the not too far distant future.

Sincerely yours,

Truman is greatly admired among Israelis for granting instant recognition to the Jewish state. A village and a forest were named in his honor. The Israelis also issued a postage stamp with Truman's image. In 1966, the Harry S. Truman Center for the Advancement of Peace was established in Jerusalem. "Those Israelites have placed me on a pedestal alongside of Moses," Truman once wrote. At the dedication ceremony for the HST Center, Hebrew University president Eliahu Elath said that Truman's May 14, 1948, act of recognition would be engraved "in golden letters in the four thousand years' history" of the Jewish people. If Truman had ever visited Israel, he would have been warmly received. Much to his regret, he never made it. Mrs. Roosevelt visited Israel on three occasions.

May 7, 1955

Dear Mrs. Roosevelt:

I haven't received a birthday remembrance or a library contribution that I appreciated more than yours. It was wonderful of you to remember me on this occasion.

I believe that the statements of policies which President Roosevelt and I endeavored to establish will be of great historical value to scholars of the future, and I hope that future Presidents will see to it that their papers are properly housed, not all in one place.

Again, I want to say I'm just as sorry as can be that I won't be able to be with you on May 30th.

Sincerely yours,

————————

December 9, 1955

Dear Mrs. Roosevelt:

Your appearance on Margie's program was certainly heartwarming to her mother and to her father. We both appreciated it most highly.

I have a special edition of my memoirs which I am mailing to you under separate cover. As soon as the second volume is published, I will send you that also.

Sincerely yours,

————————

December 12, 1955

Dear Mr. President:

Thank you very much for your nice note.

I ordered a copy of your book sometime ago but I will give it to one of my children and I shall be enchanted to have a copy from you.

I enjoyed being with Margaret and I think she is doing a wonderful job.

My warm good wishes to you and Mrs. Truman for Christmas and the New Year.

Cordially yours,

Year of Decisions, *the first volume of Truman's White House memoirs, chronicled the end of World War II, including his decision to drop the atomic bomb, the Potsdam conference, and the organization of the United Nations. "Mr. Truman's personal recollections and observations are the stuff of which history is made," the* New York Times *editorialized. "It is an extraordinary thing that he has done—to write down so fully and so candidly his impressions of his own Presidency so soon after he has left office. No other President has done anything quite like this before."*

January 13, 1956

Dear Mr. President:

I am sure that you feel as I do that the situation in the Near East is highly critical, largely brought about through Soviet planning and action, and if they succeed in getting rid of our bases in North Africa and getting rid of Israel which is the only democratic area in the Near East which can make a stand against them, they will have a bridge to Pakistan, India, and the rest of Asia. Because I feel this way, I have listened to the suggestion from some of my friends in the Jewish community that a significant statement by a few people would carry more weight than some of the statements which are being made today with a great many signatures attached.

The enclosed statement has been carefully worked out and I am sending it to you, to Walter Reuther and to George Meany hoping that you might all be willing to sign it if you think it is a wise move at this time. If there are any changes which you think wise, we would of course want you to make them. If you don't think it wise, you must, of course, also let me know. I have great faith in your judgment and therefore would like to feel that I was not moving without your agreement in this matter.

Very cordially yours,

January 18, 1956

Dear Mrs. Roosevelt:

I was very pleased to receive your letter of the thirteenth enclosing the suggested statement on the Near East, and I am in complete accord with your view that something must be done.

While I was President of the United States, I had a survey made of the whole Near East. Gordon Clapp went to the Valley of the Tigris and the Euphrates and came back with the report that it is perfectly feasible to restore those old canals constructed and used by the ancient Babylonians and the people of Ninevah under Sennacherib. With that irrigation the land could support from twenty to thirty million people. He said that there are 160 billion barrels of oil in sight in the Arabian desert and also that it is quite possible to run a syphon from the Mediterranean to the Dead Sea Valley which would create enough power to make Israel a completely industrial nation.

Dr. Bennett of Oklahoma A. & M., who worked with me on the Point IV program, spent the previous year in Ethiopia where he found a plateau of about 62,000 square miles at from six to eight thousand feet above sea level where the soil is as rich and black as it is in the Iowa corn belt. His estimate was that it could raise enough corn for a hundred million people.

As you know, we succeeded in getting Turkey to raise a surplus of food stuffs. The last year I was in the White House that country raised a surplus of four million tons of wheat. Before that, it had to import wheat from Russia.

That shows what proper development could do for the whole area, from the Adriatic Sea right around the Mediterranean to Libya, and Israel would be its industrial center.

The Nile River is being developed now, and eventually the Egyptians, who haven't had enough to eat since the first Pharaoh, will be able to feed another twenty million people.

I hope you will forgive me for taking up your time with this long dissertation, but I am extremely interested in that part of the world.

Whenever you are ready, send me the document, and I will be very happy to sign it.

Sincerely yours,

In the winter of 1956, Israel looked particularly vulnerable. For months, the British had been withdrawing troops from around the Suez Canal. Arab guerrillas began making hit-and-run attacks on Israel. The Israelis retaliated in Gaza. Egypt's President Nasser, turned down by the Eisenhower administration when he sought military aid, obtained arms from the Soviet Union. By the spring, UN Secretary-General Dag Hammarskjöld negotiated a cease-fire along the Israeli-Egyptian border. But the shooting soon resumed. When the United States reneged on an offer to build a $1 billion high dam on the Nile, Nasser seized the canal. When Israel attacked the Sinai, the French and British invaded the canal. Eisenhower threatened sanctions unless Israel and the Euro-

pean forces withdrew from occupied territory. The UN General Assembly supported Ike.

February 10, 1956

Dear Mr. President:

Would it be possible for you to be the speaker at the annual Convention banquet of Americans for Democratic Action in Washington on May 12th?

ADA delegates from all over the country will be gathered to lay plans for the elections. It would be wonderfully inspiring if they could hear you. You may remember that you spoke to the ADA Convention in 1952. No one who heard you then has forgotten your good advice. We need more of it now.

The other officers of the ADA join with me in extending this invitation most cordially and hope very much that you will be able to accept. We would like to make it sort of a birthday party for you.

Cordially yours,

February 15, 1956

Dear Mrs. Roosevelt:

I appreciated your note of the tenth and I only wish that I could say yes to the suggestion you make for I would very much like to do it.

Confidentially, I have been invited to Oxford University for a Degree. This invitation has been renewed for the last three years and I had just promised to go to England to accept it this spring.

I shall be leaving New York for Europe on the 11th of May. For reasons that are well known to you, I am asking all concerned that my plans to go to Europe be kept in confidence.

I don't know when we have enjoyed a luncheon as much as we did the one with you. Mrs. Truman and I still talk about it. She received the recipe the other day for that wonderful dessert and I am looking forward to tasting it again.

Sincerely yours,

On June 20, 1956, Truman received a Doctorate of Civil Law from Oxford University, its highest honorary degree. The citation noted Truman's leadership in the Berlin airlift, the North Atlantic Treaty Organization, the Marshall Plan, and his defense of South Korea against communist aggression. The public orator, noting the great upset of '48, evoked laughter when he told the former president, "The seers saw not your defeat, poor souls! Vain prayers, vain promises, vain Gallup Poll!" Truman later recalled, "It was a solemn affair and very impressive, particularly for the fellow getting the degree. I never saw such an aggregation of eggheads in my life. They admitted that Oxford was the factory for that sort of person, and it was highly satisfactory for me to be included."

April 18, 1956

Dear Mr. President:

I have a note from Sir Campbell Stuart which I am enclosing. I imagine you can't escape going to the Grosvenor Square statue, so perhaps you can manage to go there before going to dinner with the Pilgrims!

I hope you have a most wonderful time in England. In the meantime, I hope Margaret's wedding is everything you could wish. It is a little hard to see one's only daughter married but you are really adding another member to your family.

With affectionate greetings to you and Mrs. Truman.

Very cordially yours,

On June 21, 1956, Truman was the honored guest at the Pilgrims annual dinner. The organization, which promotes Anglo-American unity, attracted a record crowd for the HST tribute. Lord Halifax, Britain's former ambassador to the United States, presided over the dinner and toasted the former president. Sir Campbell Stuart, Mrs. Roosevelt's friend, was vice president of the Pilgrims.

In April of 1956, Truman played father of the bride. Margaret Truman married Clifton Daniel, then a correspondent for the New York Times, *who would later become that newspaper's Washington bureau chief and managing editor. As the senior news executive of the* Times, *Daniel was widely credited with making the newspaper more lively and* readable. *"Mr. Truman was not only a great president—but he was a great father-in-law,"* Daniel wrote in his 1984 memoir, Lords, Ladies, and Gentlemen.

———————

July 26, 1956

Dear Mr. President:

How very thoughtful of you to send me an inscribed copy of your second volume! I am delighted to have it and want to thank you warmly.

I was very happy to get the assurance of your support of the appropriation.

I hope you and Mrs. Truman are enjoying the summer and I look forward with much pleasure to seeing you both at the Convention.

Very cordially yours,

In Years of Trial and Hope, *the second volume of his presidential memoirs, Truman covered the Berlin airlift, the Marshall Plan, forging the North Atlantic Treaty Organization, the Korean War, and his dismissal of General MacArthur. Life magazine, which published excerpts from the book, invited MacArthur to respond. "It was a vengeful reprisal," the old soldier said of his firing.*

———————

August 11, 1956
Harry S. Truman press conference
Grand Ballroom
Blackstone Hotel

I have always believed in free and open political conventions, and I hope the delegates of this convention will have the fullest opportunity to express their free choice without undue haste.

I have little faith in the value of the band-wagon operation or the reliability of political polls.

I know that each delegate will exercise freely and independently the right of choice which is his under the law.

Following the election of 1952, we all hoped that by the time the 1956 convention came around there would be developed a number of Democratic national leaders for consideration at this convention. Today I am happy to see that this convention has many qualified men to choose from—each of whom would make a good President. I have at all times encouraged worthy candidates to enter the race and campaign vigorously, and I did so without in any way seeking to influence the political fortunes of any one man.

I knew all along that eventually I would have to express my own choice. In making up my mind I have talked to many people in many parts of the country and in all walks of life. I have received and read thousands of letters from my fellow citizens. Since my arrival in Chicago a steady procession of delegates, candidates, public officials, political leaders, and representatives of workers, business and various minorities have called on me to express their views as to who would make the strongest and best qualified candidate.

And now I have made up my mind.

I realize that my expression of a choice at this time will cause disappointment in some and may cause resentment in others.

But against the mounting crises in the world, I know that this convention must name a man who has the experience and the ability to act as President immediately upon assuming office without risking a period of costly and dangerous trial and error.

In the light of my knowledge of the office of President, I believe that the man best qualified to be the next President of the United States is Governor Harriman of New York.

He will make a fighting and successful candidate because he is dedicated to the principles of our party—the New Deal and the Fair Deal.

I know there are several other men who could wage successful campaigns with much credit to their party and the nation and they are men for whom I have great admiration.

But Governor Harriman has had long experience in top government positions at home. He has played an historic role in representing this country in Europe and Asia. He was a tower of strength all through the Roosevelt administration and all the years of my own.

I know him and you can depend on him.

From Chicago, Mrs. Roosevelt wrote her friend David Gurewitsch: "Truman's decision to support Harriman threw Adlai's people into gloom but I'm not sure it is all bad. He himself knows now that if he wins he is free and owes no allegiance to Truman." At a press conference, she ridiculed Truman's characterization of Harriman as a "fighting candidate," noting that he had ducked the primaries. As for Truman's suggestion that her candidate lacked experience, Mrs. Roosevelt said that Stevenson had a stronger background in foreign policy than Truman did on taking office.

Eleanor Roosevelt's address to the 1956 Democratic National Convention:

August 13, 1956

Twice before I have spoken to a national Democratic convention; once I came when you had nominated my husband to be your standard bearer and spoke with a message from him, and once I came at the invitation of President Truman to speak to you about the United Nations and what it meant to all of us.

Tonight I come at the invitation of the national chairman of the Democratic party to speak to you as a fellow Democrat.

I cannot talk to you about my choice as your standard bearer, but I do want to talk to you about our party and our duty. You here have a heavier responsibility than even I have, because you are delegates. You are going back into your communities all over the country, and you will tell your friends, your neighbors what you believe a Democratic victory should mean. I do not believe that victory in itself is enough. I want victory, and I believe we will have it in November—but I want even more, that each and every one of you, as you go back into your communities, take the message of what you want that victory to mean. We must be a united party.

It is true we have differences, but everywhere in our country we know that today our differences must somehow be resolved, because we stand before the world on trial, really, to show what democracy means, and that is a heavy responsibility, because the world today is deciding between democracy and Communism, and one means freedom and one means slavery.

You have seen a film tonight, which I think must have moved you, as it moved me, to pride in our record, to a recognition of what our party has meant to our country and to the world.

Great leaders we have had, but we could not have had great leaders unless they had a great people to follow. You cannot be a great leader unless the people are great. That is what I want to remind every one of you tonight. You must be a great people with great objectives.

I remember very well the first crisis that we met in '32, and I remember that we won out, because the people were ready to carry their share of the burden, and follow and carry through the words, "All you have to fear, the only thing you have to fear, is fear itself."

You must have the action of the people or your leadership will not be true leadership.

Now the world looks at us again, and what we do at home is going to be watched in the world. I have been around the world a number of times of late, and I know that much of the good will that was a reservoir for us in the world came from the fact that here at home we had decided that government had a real responsibility to make the pursuit of happiness an objective of government, and caring for the individual was a responsibility of government. That meant that we try to help all of our people to a better life, and it meant to the peoples of the world hope for the same kind of thing to happen to them as well.

Now they look to us again for the meaning of democracy, and we must think of that very seriously. There are new problems. They must be met in new ways. We have heard a great deal, and we were fired with enthusiasm by the tradition of our party. Thus, the new problems we face cannot be met by traditions only, but they must be met by imagination. They must be met by understanding and the feel of the people, and not only the people at home, but the people of the world. And it is a foolish thing to say that you pledge yourself to live up to the traditions of the New Deal and Fair Deal—of course, you are proud of those traditions; of course, you are proud to have the advice of the elders in our party, but our party is young and vigorous. Our party may be the oldest Democratic party, but our party must live as a young party, and it must have young leadership. It must have young people, and they must be allowed to lead. They must not lean on their tradition. They must be proud of it. They must take into account the advice of the elders, but they must have the courage to look ahead, to face new problems with new solutions, and in so doing, we will not only meet our own difficulties at home and find ways to solve them, but we will also meet some of the difficulties that in that great speech you heard from Governor Clement, are those pointed out as being the issues between ourselves as the Democratic party, and the Republican party.

We have great issues. I believe that it is absolutely imperative that the Democratic party come back to power, but they must come back with the right leader. They must come back with your considered and careful choice, and you must feel a very great individual responsibility when you choose your leader, when you have chosen your leaders, then to back them, then to go in and work.

It isn't just fight. It is work, and some of it is dull work, but you must be ready to go in and work because that is the way that parties win victories at election time.

The things that are done by each one of you and through you by each person in your community, that is what will win for you a victory on election day, and I personally hope that you will remember the things which have been said tonight, even those for which we prayed in the invocation for guidance and inspiration and courage. It will take all those things for us to remember the objectives for which we want a victory, for us to resolve difficult questions which will be hard for many of us to face.

It will take understanding and sympathy to think of the problems of the world and to realize that today the world has narrowed, and that we feel very quickly the sufferings of other areas of the world, and they add to our sufferings.

We might just have a vision, and I would like to give you the idea: You will remember that my husband said in one of his speeches that our job was not finished because we still had a third of our people who were ill-housed, ill-clothed, ill-fed. Twenty percent today is the figure they give us.

We have lessened that group in our country that are ill-housed, ill-clothed, ill-fed, but we still have a job to do.

Could we have the vision of doing away in this great country with poverty? It would be a marvelous achievement, and I think it might be done if you and I, each of us, as individuals, would really pledge ourselves and our party to think imaginatively of what can be done at home, what can make us not only the nation that has some of the richest people in the world, but the nation where there are no people that have to live at a substandard level. That would be one of the very best arguments against Communism, that we could possibly have.

And if we do it at home, it will spread through the world, and we will have again that surge of hope from other peoples, that surge which brought us before good will and trust and confidence, and which will do it again, but it requires from every one of you the imagination and willingness to make a great leader and to do the work to put your leaders across in November.

Truman, a defender of the faith, wanted his party to uphold the liberal traditions of the New Deal and Fair Deal. He regarded Stevenson as insufficiently committed to these programs. In her address to the convention, Mrs. Roosevelt urged her party to move beyond its glory days and embrace a new generation of leadership.

                                                      January 7, 1957

Dear Mr. President:

I very much enjoyed seeing you in Washington but was sorry to hear of Mrs. Truman's accident. I am sending her a little note under separate cover.

I hope you felt the meeting was worthwhile and that something constructive will come of it.

With my warm good wishes,

                                                      Cordially,

---

January 10, 1957

Dear Mrs. Roosevelt:

I was just about to dictate a note to you when your letter of the 7th arrived.

I felt that the meeting in Washington was a very satisfactory one and believe that it will do the Democratic party a lot of good.

Mrs. Truman is getting along all right. Her left foot is in a very uncomfortable cast, but she manages to hobble around on a pair of crutches. She will be extremely pleased to hear from you.

You were very kind to write me as you did, and I hope that 1957 will bring you everything you want.

Sincerely yours,

March 15, 1957

Dear Mr. President:

You know we have talked several times about your coming on Memorial Day to the ceremonies that are always held in the Rose Garden at Hyde Park. I wonder if by chance you and Mrs. Truman could come and spend that weekend with me or as much of it as you can spare, arriving before lunch on the 30th as they usually hold the ceremonies right after lunch?

I hope very much that this time we may be able to get you.

With affectionate regards to Mrs. Truman and the hope that she is improving rapidly.

Very cordially yours,

March 20, 1957

Dear Mrs. Roosevelt:

Mrs. Truman and I more than appreciated your kind letter of the 15th, and I sincerely hope that conditions will permit our being with you on Memorial Day.

We have had some difficulty getting the library completed, and instead of having it ready by May 8th, as I had hoped, the dedication date will have to be postponed until the first week in July. In the meantime, I am trying to get all my papers moved into the building, so that they may be indexed and filed just as President Roosevelt's are at Hyde Park. I will keep in touch with you, and I hope most sincerely that I can join you in spite of all the tearing around that I have to do.

I read in the paper that you are making a trip to Spain. I would give anything in the world for a confidential letter from you telling me what you think of that country. As you know, I have never trusted Franco and dislike his attitude toward this great republic of ours.

May you have a very pleasant trip, and when you come back, I should be able to tell you definitely what my situation will be during the latter part of May.

Yours very truly,

April 4, 1957

Dear Mr. President:

I am home from Morocco and delighted to hear that you will try to come to Hyde Park for the weekend of May 30th. It would be a great joy to have you and Mrs. Truman and I hope things will work out well so that I may have the pleasure of having you both.

With my warm good wishes and affectionate greetings to Mrs. Truman.

Cordially,

April 12, 1957

Dear Mrs. Roosevelt:

You do not know how very much I appreciated your kind letter of the 4th.

I am enclosing a copy of the telegram I sent you yesterday. The situation is a regrettable one, and if it is possible for us to meet in Washington at the time of the National Committee meeting, I'll tell you about my difficulties.

My schedule seems to become bulkier every day that I live. I know that you are in the same fix and that we can understand each other when things do not go as we want them to.

Sincerely yours,

April 19, 1957

Dear Mr. President:

Of course I understand your schedule. My own often gets out of hand and I find I am unable to do the things I want to do.

With appreciation for your kind letter and my good wishes to you and Mrs. Truman.

Cordially,

Hyde Park
July 1957

["My Day" column]

I journeyed out to Kansas City, Mo. a week ago to attend a reception given by Basil O'Connor, president of the Truman Library Association. Mr. O'Connor and former President and Mrs. Harry Truman stood in line while hundreds of people who had worked with Mr. Truman, besides his old friends who had known him and loved him, came to shake his hand and congratulate him on the dedication of the library in Independence.

We started bright and early last Saturday morning, when the weather was beautiful, if a little warm. Everything was remarkably well planned, everyone taken care of by his or her particular host. My hosts were Mr. and Mrs. Benjamin Sosland, whom I had known before and who were kindness itself.

Mr. Truman drove out to the library with me and Mrs. Truman greeted us on arrival. The building is modern and beautifully adapted to the use of both the public and the students who may come there to study this period of American history.

The landscaping, of course, is not done yet, but there will come a day when outside the President's study window there will be a lovely rose garden. It is so arranged that there are two entrances which will permit the President to come into his own office without going through the lobby or museum area.

The whole building is air conditioned and his office is well protected from surprise callers. On the other side of the stack rooms is the room for students. They strike me as being particularly attractive and comfortable. One nice touch is a little anteroom to Mr. Truman's office containing a grand piano so that he can sit down and play whenever he wishes. And right out of his study is a small kitchen which Mrs. Truman said he told her she would be frequently called upon to use.

The dedication ceremonies took exactly an hour and five minutes and I don't think I ever saw things move so smoothly and quickly. The speeches were short and to the point, and the Chief Justice made an excellent dedication address.

For me, at least, the two days were rewarding, and I hope that the library will prove to be all that Mr. Truman hopes it to be. It certainly should be a valuable addition to the educational opportunities of that area of our country.

Former president Herbert Hoover and Mrs. Roosevelt headed the list of distinguished guests for the library dedication. Chief Justice Earl Warren, who had been the 1948 Republican nominee for vice president, gave the dedication speech at Truman's invitation. Senate Majority Leader Lyndon B. Johnson, Minority Leader William F. Knowland, House Speaker Sam Rayburn, Minority Whip Charles A. Halleck, former secretary of state Dean Acheson, and New York's Governor W. Averell Harriman were among Truman's guests. "A highly nonpartisan affair with Knowland making a speech for Lyndon Johnson & himself as the Senator from Texas had to leave early for Washington," Mrs. Roosevelt reported to the Lashes. "Mr. Hoover was most affable but much older I thought. Mr. Truman beamed all day & we were most friendly."

———————

Independence
July 23, 1957

Dear Mrs. Roosevelt:

I have just received a copy of your article on the dedication of the library, and I wish it were possible for words to express my very deep appreciation.

Mrs. Truman and I were very happy to have you here with us, but we were disturbed by our inability to offer you the hospitality you would have had under other circumstances.

Some day in the not too distant future you must come back and pay us a real visit.

Sincerely yours,

March 8, 1958

Dear Mr. President:

It was a joy to see you in Norman and I think you were wonderful to join us.

I am so glad you enjoyed the *Post* articles and you were thoughtful to tell me so.

Your family will, I am sure, find it difficult to "harness" you. It is better that way because life would be dull for both of us, I fear, if we had to stay in one place.

I was delighted to find you looking so well and vigorous.

My warm and affectionate greetings to Mrs. Truman. Tell her I am looking forward with much pleasure to having all of you with me the weekend of May 30th.

Cordially,

April 23, 1958

Dear Mrs. Roosevelt:

Again, I am in trouble. Beginning last October, my engagements have numbered almost as many as yours. As you know, I have also turned columnist, and while my schedule is not as rigorous as yours, it bothers me every time I have to make a date or write a column.

I have been urged by family and friends to get out of the country for a while and just sit and rest a bit. The strenuous last two or three weeks have made me realize that I need rest, and I am sorry to admit it.

If plans work out, Mrs. Truman and I will leave the country on May 26th for about forty-five days. I regret this situation very much, because I have been looking forward to this Memorial Day visit with you, but I feel compelled to break loose for at least a few weeks.

Sincerely yours,

April 23, 1958

Dear President Truman:

I can quite understand your need for a rest and though I shall miss you and Mrs. Truman on Memorial Day weekend, I shall hope that your holiday will be a pleasant and refreshing one.

With many thanks for your thoughtful letter and my warm good wishes to both of you,

Very cordially yours,

May 1, 1958

Dear Mrs. Roosevelt:

You do not know how much I appreciated your very considerate note of April 23rd. While I was in New York this last time, they almost pulled me apart. Of course, I was quite willing to be pulled around by my friend, but I was unfortunate enough to pick up some kind of bug which upset me physically, and I have not yet been able to get rid of it.

During my visit there, Mrs. Charles Ulrick Bay, the widow of our former Ambassador to Norway, and our mutual friend Sam Rosenman persuaded me to get on a ship for a south Atlantic cruise. Mrs. Truman and my daughter give me the same advice you receive from your family, and that is to slow up and try to quit. The cruise starts about the 25th of this month, and I have been convinced that it is the right thing to do, particularly after this vicious little bug's attack.

I would not blame you if you never invited me again. If I remember correctly, this is the third attempt we have made to get together on a

May 30th. I hope I will have a chance soon to make a world-wide statement on President Roosevelt. That is what I had planned to do on this occasion, but if I keep the same pace at which I have been going, I won't be able to do anything. I am cancelling date in Chicago and several other places in order to get this rest program started.

I feel certain that you will understand my position, because you face the same problems.

Sincerely yours,

May 6, 1958

Dear Mr. President:

Many thanks for your kind letter of the first.

I am only sorry that I will not have the pleasure of seeing you and Mrs. Truman this month but of course I understand your need for rest. I hope you are completely recovered from the effects of the bug which plagued you in New York.

Do let me hear later that you will come for Memorial Day next year. With affectionate good wishes to you and Mrs. Truman.

Cordially,

May 13, 1958

Dear Mrs. Roosevelt:

You do not know how very much I appreciated your letter of the sixth.

You are more than kind, and if the good Lord shows me similar consideration, I will join you at Hyde Park on Memorial Day 1959.

Sincerely yours,

July 31, 1958

Dear Mrs. Roosevelt:

As I wrote you a few days ago, I received a letter from Mrs. Louis S. Gimbel, Jr., telling me that you were to be presented with the Woman of the Year Award by the American Friends of the Hebrew University in New York on November fifth.

I certainly wish it were possible for me to be present on that occasion. I know of no one more deserving of the award than you.

Sincerely yours,

———————

August 4, 1958

Dear Mr. President:

Thank you so much for your letter of July 31st.

I did not know the American Friends of the Hebrew University were making such a fuss and I am glad you don't have to put yourself out for November fifth!

With my warm good wishes,

Cordially,

———————

January 21, 1959

Dear Mr. President:

You will probably remember that last year you were unable to come to me for Memorial Day, and I wonder if this year you and Mrs. Truman would be able to come to Hyde Park and spend at least one night with me? I would be delighted if you could manage this.

The 30th of May is on a Saturday, so if you can come on Friday night or early Saturday morning I could arrange to have a car pick you up in New York and drive you down to Hyde Park if this is convenient for you and Mrs. Truman. Then I could take you down on Sunday.

I do hope I will have the pleasure this year of having you both with me.

Very cordially yours,

Mrs. Roosevelt added in a handwritten postscript that she would like the former president to speak at the Memorial Day ceremony.

———————

January 26, 1959

Dear Mrs. Roosevelt:

Your cordial invitation to visit with you on Memorial Day has just been received. Mrs. Truman and I appreciate it very, very much.

We accept it with pleasure. A little later on we'll let you know about our arrival in New York. Your suggestion about transportation from New York to Hyde Park is all right with us.

I'll be glad to speak if you want me to—and I'll do the best I can.

Most sincerely,

January 29, 1959

Dear Mr. President:

I want to thank you very much for your letter and to tell you how pleased I am that you and Mrs. Truman will spend the Memorial Day weekend with me.

With deep appreciation and my affectionate good wishes to Mrs. Truman.

Very cordially yours,

We count on you speaking.

April 24, 1959

Dear Mrs. Truman:

Your husband has very kindly promised that he would make the Memorial Day address at Hyde Park this year on May 30th, and I wrote that I would send my car for you the day before, May 29th, wherever you wished to be picked up. I think I will be going up myself that day, so perhaps I can pick you up around 3:30 or 4:00 wherever you wish?

I hope you will stay over Saturday and let me send you back to New York on Sunday after lunch. It will give me very great pleasure to have you with us at last, and I hope we can make you comfortable and give you an enjoyable time.

I believe that one of our Democratic clubs has asked Mr. Truman to speak at a dinner one of the nights he is in Hyde Park. I certainly hope he will feel able to do this.

With affectionate good wishes,

Very sincerely yours,

The ceremonies in the rose garden on the 30th are at 2 p.m.

May 16, 1959

Dear Mrs. Roosevelt:

I hope that you will forgive this tardy acknowledgement of the letter you wrote on April 24th to Mrs. Truman regarding our visit to Hyde Park on Memorial Day.

Unfortunately, I am in a state of some uncertainty at the moment. Mrs. Truman has been ill for several weeks, and I had to take her to the hospital for a complete checkup. It now looks as if she will have to have an operation. The doctor tries to assure me that it will not be a serious one and that she undoubtedly will be back home within two weeks. If that proves to be true, I expect to be with you on Friday evening, May 29th, and Saturday, May 30th.

Because of the indefiniteness of the arrangements, Mr. Harold M. Clay of the Franklin D. Roosevelt Home Club has, rather wisely I think, postponed his plans for a celebration on Saturday evening of the 30th anniversary of his club. I would have enjoyed attending it, and if I can stay over until Sunday, perhaps an informal meeting with the members can be worked out.

Just as soon as I know the results of Mrs. Truman's operation, you will hear from me again.

Sincerely yours,

May 25, 1959

Situation has developed so I cannot come east. I am truly sorry. Letter follows.

Harry S. Truman

May 25, 1959

Dear Mrs. Roosevelt:

That operation was a very severe one. While the tumor was not a malignant one, it was nearly as big as a basketball.

Mrs. T. is making progress toward recovery but I have to sit by her as much of the day as I can and every evening. She must stay in the hospital at least another ten days and I just can't leave her. She insists that I should because you have been so good to us.

Please forgive me I just must stay here.

Sincerely,

Mrs. Truman had discovered a lump in her left breast months earlier but had not consulted a doctor or told her family about it. "She seems to have decided she was going to die," Margaret Truman wrote in her biography of her mother. Mrs. Truman wanted to live for her husband's seventy-fifth birthday on May 8, 1959, and for the birth of a second grandchild that same month. When her husband noticed the tumor, he knew that she needed surgery. Their daughter agreed. Mrs. Truman returned to Independence and underwent a mastectomy on May 18. Her grandson William Wallace Daniel was born the next day. Mrs. Truman lived for another twenty-three years.

May 27, 1959

Dear Mr. President:

Thank you so much for your wire and letter of explanation.

Of course, I completely understand your wanting to stay with Mrs. Truman and I would not want you to do otherwise.

I realize that an operation such as Mrs. Truman has had is a difficult one and she needs you near her.

With my affectionate good wishes to Mrs. Truman for a speedy recovery and warm regards to you.

Cordially,

June 2, 1959

Dear Mrs. Roosevelt:

Thank you very much for your letters of May 27th and 28th. Both Mrs. Truman and I appreciate your thoughtfulness.

We are sad, however, that circumstances prevented our being with you on Memorial Day, but if you still are willing, we will keep trying, and one of these days we will make it.

Sincerely yours,

———————

July 3, 1959

Dear Mr. President:

I have just been sent an extraordinary article by Julius Epstein which was published in the *American Legion Magazine* of December 1954 and which tells the rather horrible story of Americans forcing Russian prisoners who had surrendered to them because they were fighting with the Germans against the Russians, into trucks to be returned to Russia.

I remember the long fight not to return the prisoners or any refugees in camps in Germany to their countries of origin against their will. This took place February 24, 1946 when the arguments were going on in the UN. Therefore, I cannot understand our government's allowing anything of this kind to happen, and I would like very much to know if this article is based on real facts.

The article puts us in a very bad light, and I cannot bear that such an article should stand unanswered.

I do not know how to answer Mr. Epstein's letter which demands that I acknowledge American guilt which, he says, both you and President Eisenhower are well aware of.

Very cordially yours,

———————

August 5, 1959

Dear Mrs. Roosevelt:

I was very much intrigued by your letter of July 3rd about Julius Epstein and his 1954 *American Legion Magazine* article about Russian prisoners of the Allies who had served in the Nazi German army.

As you remember, in 1950 and 1951 we prevented the forceful return of prisoners who had been in the Red Chinese and North Korean armies, because we did not want them to be stood up against a stone wall and shot. I refused to sign an armistice agreement on that account, but as soon as I left the White House, that agreement was signed.

The Russian prisoners to whom Mr. Epstein referred were those who were shooting not only at their own people but at us and all the rest of our World War II allies, and an agreement was made at Yalta for their return.

The Korean prisoners were in an entirely different category, and I never did agree to their return.

Sincerely yours,

Andrei Vlasov (1900–1946), a prominent general in the Red Army, was captured by the Germans in July 1942. He believed that Stalin had been a disaster as military commander and political leader. When the Germans invited him to organize an anti-Stalinist Russian Liberation Movement, he agreed. Vlasov was captured by the Red Army in May 1945 and hanged for treason in August 1946. Epstein's article was about four thousand of Vlasov's troops who had surrendered to Americans in the hope of gaining political asylum. Under the Yalta agreement, Soviet nationals who had fought on the German side were to be repatriated. With Truman's approval, the Americans sent back about 2 million Russians.

August 7, 1959

Dear Mrs. Roosevelt:

I found a book in our public library, and I assume it is available everywhere. It is by George Fischer and carries the title *Soviet Opposition to Stalin: A Case Study in World War II.* The book was published in 1952 by the Harvard University Press.

Mr. Fischer's statement of the situation to which you referred in your letter and about which I wrote you the other day covers the program very well. It seems that these deserters were ordered returned through the terms of the Yalta Agreement, and they were.

As I told you, I never agreed to return the prisoners from Red China to be slaughtered after the difficulty in Korea, but such a surrender agreement was made after I left office, and I do not know what ever became of those people.

I have been reading a lot of articles on the atomic bomb and why we dropped it. Mrs. Pearl S. Buck has written an article, part of which is published in the August, 1959 issue of the *Reader's Digest*. Hanson Baldwin, too, has talked on the subject, but the men who were on the ground doing their jobs share my opinion that their lives and the lives of a half million other youngsters were saved by dropping the bomb. I read an article only this morning about the man who actually dropped the bomb, and he feels as I do.

I cannot recall ever hearing these other sob-sisters remember Pearl Harbor and the murders committed there by the Japanese. I can see no reason for their double standard of morality.

Sincerely yours,

August 12, 1959

Dear Mr. President:

Thank you very much for the explanation which I shall pass on to the people who asked me.

As you know, I have always said that you had no choice but to use the atomic bomb to bring the war to an end. For a time I was disturbed at our having used it in Nagasaki but after being in Japan and seeing the defenses and talking with one of our representatives who had been a prisoner of the Japanese and who explained that unless there had been a second demonstration the Japanese would have felt they could defend themselves which would have resulted in the destruction of the whole of Japan and the loss of millions of our own men, I realized that you had this knowledge and that you could make no other decision than the one you made. I have since written this publicly a number of times. I would give a great deal, however, if we could come to an agreement for stopping the whole use of atomic energy for military purposes. I know that certain experiments have to go on in order to continue the development for non-military purposes but they should be done in such a way, if possible, as to protect the human race from fall-out. I realize the differences in opinion among scientists as to how much is harmful and unharmful, but if we are going to advance, this is an area where we should succeed in getting this knowledge used for peacetime uses successfully.

Your last paragraph touches on a point that I have thought on very often. We have such short memories that we now behave as though Germany and Japan had always been our best friends, and I sometimes wish we really remembered who was responsible for starting World War II. I have a feeling that we should have some fresh thinking on our whole peacetime situation.

If you are in these parts, I hope you will let me know. I would still love to have a long talk with you.

With kind regards to Mrs. Truman and the hope that she is feeling better.

Cordially,

December 2, 1959

Harry Truman

Would you have a free hour in New York this weekend in which to film an interview for the "UN in Action" television program? It would be very important for the AAUN if you could do this in your capacity as AAUN honorary national membership chairman. This will be the last opportunity as the series ends shortly. The interview could be based on the material in your, Lubbock, Texas UN Day speech. I would appreciate your answer by wire.

Eleanor Roosevelt

December 3, 1959

Mrs. Franklin D. Roosevelt

I will be glad to participate in United Nations broadcast. Will be at Carlyle Hotel Saturday morning.

Harry S. Truman

---

*Truman introduced Mrs. Roosevelt at a Democratic fund-raising dinner
in the Waldorf-Astoria Hotel. Most of their party's 1960 presidential
hopefuls attended this gala, which honored Eleanor's seventy-fifth
birthday. She was caught by surprise when Truman used this occasion
to attack "the self-appointed guardians of liberal thinking." Mrs. Roosevelt, who thought Stevenson deserved a third presidential nomination, sensed that Truman was attacking her candidate. Senator Stuart
Symington of Missouri was the former president's choice. Following his
exchange with Mrs. Roosevelt, Truman said that he was referring to the
New York Post in his comments. The afternoon tabloid, which was then
owned by Eleanor's friend Dorothy Schiff, had criticized Truman's call
for a resumption of underground nuclear weapons tests. When
reporters asked the former president to name the other targets of his
criticism, Truman declined. "At the dinner the Dem. Advisory Com.
gave for me," Mrs. Roosevelt wrote her daughter, "Mr. Truman & I had
'a little difference' again. I think I was gentle but the papers played
it up."*

Excerpts from Truman's remarks at the dinner:

And now I would like to say something about those self-appointed
guardians of liberal thinking who have become rather vocal lately.

I would like to ask this question of them: Where did they get their
mandate?

For it would appear that unless you go along with these hot-house
liberals and stand for everything they advocate, you are in for more
abuse than you get even from the reactionaries and the opposition party.

Many a genuine working liberal has been a victim of their intolerance.

As a matter of fact, the acrimonious attitude of these self-styled liberals has hurt liberalism and in many instances has paved the way for
reaction.

You have a newspaper in this town that does some remarkable gym-
nastics in its capriciousness and presumption as judge and jury of what
is liberal. This newspaper—not noted for its careful reading of texts, and
forgetful of some of its own past—has even tried to pin a reactionary
label on me. What do you think of that?

I would say to those snobs who think that they have solutions for all our problems if we would but follow them in their infinite wisdom, that they ought to put an end to their pretensions and their insistence on an all or nothing formula and stop trying to distort the objectives of the Democratic party.

The fact that this or that leader of the Democratic party doesn't represent some particular shade of liberal thinking or doctrine should not expose them to abuse or rejection.

We know that a vigorous and united Democratic party is the only decisive force for liberalism, and there is no other choice.

And we know that we must get a liberal into the White House in 1960 if we are to make up for the time lost during the past seven years.

Let us, therefore, choose a liberal who meets the requirements of the people who know the difference between a working liberal and a talking liberal.

Let us not be thrown off balance by a vociferous minority which can only divide us and deliver us to reaction again.

Excerpts from Mrs. Roosevelt's talk:

I welcome every kind of liberal that begins to learn by coming in to our party what it is to work on being a liberal.

. . . We cannot exist as a little island of well-being in a world where two-thirds of the people go to bed hungry every night.

There is a great wave, a desire for freedom all over the world where people have not had it. Change is coming, whether we want it or not. And how it comes will depend on how, I believe, our leadership helps the world to meet the challenge of the next few years.

. . . I hope it will be the Democratic party that will have the opportunity that this challenge offers. But I think that we have to prove to our own people that we are cognizant of the qualities that it will require to meet the future years. The courage, the vision, the imagination, the honesty. We will make mistakes. But if we make them and are willing to acknowledge them and to change, that will mean that we will, in the end, succeed.

I know we need a united party, but it cannot be a united party that gives up its principles. It must be a party where the majority rules, and where the principles are the basis of the party.

I want unity, but above everything else, I want a party that will fight for the things that we know to be right at home and abroad.

November 16, 1960

Dear Mrs. Truman:

This is just to say again what a joy it was to see you and President Truman and how much I appreciated all your kindness during my visit to Independence. It was delightful to have an opportunity to chat with both of you and to find you looking so well.

I loved the flowers and enjoyed them during my brief stay at the Muehlebach.

With affectionate greetings to you both.

Affectionately,

After lecturing in Boston, Mrs. Roosevelt's flight to Kansas City was canceled because of bad weather. She took an overnight train to New York and arrived just in time to make her connection to Kansas City. When Mrs. Roosevelt addressed the Independence Business & Professional Women's Club on November 14, Truman introduced her as "the First Lady of the World." During this visit, Truman gave her a tour of his presidential library. She had not been back since the dedication more than three years earlier.

December 5, 1960

Dear Mrs. Roosevelt:

I am enclosing you pictures of your visit here at the Library.

You don't know how very much Mrs. Truman and I appreciated your willingness to come to Independence. It has been the talk of the town ever since you were here.

Sincerely yours,

December 10, 1960

Dear Mr. President:

How thoughtful you were to send me the pictures taken during my visit to the Library! I am delighted to have them and want you to know of my deep appreciation.

With warm thanks and my affectionate greetings to you and Mrs. Truman.

Cordially,

A Brief Epilogue

Their relationship was unique in the history of the American presidency. She was enormously grateful that President Truman had given her the opportunity to shape an international bill of rights, which would come to be regarded as one of the great accomplishments of the twentieth century. From Hiroshima to the dismissal of General MacArthur, he would never forget that Eleanor Roosevelt provided him with public support when he needed it most. Even when the old friends disagreed, they took issue with respect and genuine affection. "I did not know him very well before," she recalled in a 1957 interview with Mike Wallace. "I would say of Mr. Truman that he rose to the responsibilities thrust upon him in a manner which was very remarkable, really, and that his big decisions are going to mean that he will go down in history as one of our very good presidents."

Because of Mrs. Roosevelt, Truman made several friendly gestures to her sons. He made taped comments for a dinner in Los Angeles chaired by her son James. When Franklin Jr. lost badly in a race for attorney general of New York, Truman wrote him a compassionate note. While being interviewed for a book of political remembrances, Truman was urged by both of his collaborators to make negative comments about Jimmy Roosevelt. The former president said that he would rather not because the "young man's mother" was one of the greatest people who had ever lived.

Until the end of their lives, Truman and Mrs. Roosevelt represented different political traditions. He remained the organization man while she was always the reformer. When Truman came to New York in his seventy-sixth year, he was honored at a reception chaired by Tammany Hall leader Carmine DeSapio. Mrs. Roosevelt and former senator Herbert Lehman led a reform movement that ousted DeSapio.

Mrs. Roosevelt supported the Montgomery bus boycott, the lunch-counter sit-ins, and the Freedom Rides of the civil rights movement.

Truman, who had done so much to launch the struggle for racial equality, disliked demonstrations and civil disobedience. Joseph Lash wrote in
his diary in the spring of 1960 that Truman sent word to Mrs. Roosevelt
that he appreciated that she had not publicly rebuked him for his comment that the sit-ins were communist-inspired. "She explained," Lash
wrote, "that Truman came from the south-inclined part of Missouri, so
he had grown up in an environment where Negroes were deferential. He
never had sat down and really thought through his position. As a result
whenever he acted from anger, he did wrong things."

In her seventy-sixth year, Eleanor sensed that the Los Angeles convention would be her last. Truman announced at a nationally televised
press conference that he would not be attending. "I am truly sorry that
Mr. Truman is not going to be here," she wrote in her column, "for
somehow he belongs at a Democratic convention."

Following John F. Kennedy's election, she was reappointed as a member of the U.S. delegation to the United Nations. Her friend Adlai
Stevenson, who had been a participant at the founding of the UN,
headed the delegation. Truman welcomed Mrs. Roosevelt's return to the
world stage. By this time she was in frail health, having been diagnosed
in 1960 as suffering from aplastic anemia.

But she still maintained an active schedule and accepted Kennedy's
appointment to chair the presidential Commission on the Status of
Women. In this role she dropped her forty-year opposition to the Equal
Rights Amendment. Since the 1920s she had argued that women should
devote their efforts to removing laws from the books that discriminated
against women. Truman had publicly endorsed the ERA in 1944 and it
was included in that year's Democratic platform. Mrs. Roosevelt had not
objected when her husband had sought her advice about its inclusion.
While speaking to the Overseas Press Club in the spring of 1962, she
was asked about the ERA. "Many of us opposed the amendment because
we felt it would do away with protection in the labor field," she said.
"Now with unionization, there is no reason why you shouldn't have it if
you want it."

In the summer of 1962, her condition worsened. She was diagnosed in
late October as having bone-marrow tuberculosis. She died in her East
Side home on November 7, 1962. The Trumans, who had not been back

to Hyde Park for sixteen years, were among the mourners at her funeral. She was buried next to her husband in the rose garden of the Roosevelt estate. President John F. Kennedy and his wife, Jacqueline, former president Dwight D. Eisenhower, and Vice President Lyndon B. Johnson attended the services.

David Gurewitsch, Mrs. Roosevelt's confidant, walked up to Ike and asked, "How could it happen that you did not make use of this lady? We had no better ambassador." Eisenhower did not answer and walked away.

Truman, who witnessed this incident, told Eleanor's friend, "I made use of her. I told her she was the First Lady of the World."

Bibliographical Essay

Since their memoirs were written when both were politically active, neither Eleanor Roosevelt nor Harry S. Truman were fully candid in discussing their relationship. Roosevelt describes the changing of the guard in *This I Remember* (New York: Harper, 1949) and her career after the White House in *On My Own* (New York: Harper, 1958). Truman covers the beginning of his administration in *Year of Decisions* (Garden City, N.Y.: Doubleday, 1955) and the rest of his presidency in *Years of Trial and Hope* (Garden City, N.Y.: Doubleday, 1956).

There is an abundance of fine literature about both subjects of this volume. Their correspondence is open to scholars in the Eleanor Roosevelt collection at the Franklin D. Roosevelt Library in Hyde Park; and in the President's Secretary's Files and postpresidential files at the Harry S. Truman Library in Independence.

Mrs. Roosevelt's longtime friend Joseph P. Lash had exclusive access to her extensive correspondence during the preparation of his authoritative two-volume biography. *Eleanor and Franklin: The Story of Their Relationship Based on Eleanor Roosevelt's Private Papers* (New York: W. W. Norton, 1971) was followed by *Eleanor: The Years Alone* (New York: W. W. Norton, 1972). Lash provided fresh insights into the Roosevelt marriage, their political alliance, and her lifetime of waging the good fight. For anyone interested in learning about Mrs. Roosevelt's dealings with her husband's successor, Lash's second volume is essential reading. Lash also edited *Love, Eleanor: Eleanor Roosevelt and Her Friends* (Garden City, N.Y.: Doubleday, 1982) and *A World of Love: Eleanor Roosevelt and Her Friends, 1943–62* (Garden City, N.Y.: Doubleday, 1984), which does much to explain Mrs. Roosevelt's mixed views about Truman. Bernard Asbell's *Mother & Daughter: The Letters of Eleanor and Anna Roosevelt* (New York: Coward, McCann & Geohegan, 1982) also includes Eleanor's private comments about Truman.

Blanche Wiesen Cook, a professor of history and women's studies at John Jay College and the Graduate Center, City University of New York, is writing a multivolume study of Mrs. Roosevelt that must be considered the definitive work. *Eleanor Roosevelt, Volume 1, 1884–1933* (New York: Viking Penguin, 1992) and *Volume 2, The Defining Years* (New York: Viking Penguin, 1999) are richly detailed and highly readable. Cook is particularly good at explaining Mrs. Roosevelt's political education and her growth and development into a major public figure.

Alidda M. Black has written a solid political biography, *Casting Her Own Shadow: Eleanor Roosevelt and the Shaping of Postwar Liberalism* (New York: Columbia University Press, 1995), and edited two invaluable collections of Mrs. Roosevelt's essays: *What I Hope to Leave Behind* (Brooklyn: Carlson Publishing, 1995) and *Courage in a Dangerous World: The Political Writings of Eleanor Roosevelt* (New York: Columbia University Press, 1999).

Doris Kearns Goodwin's *No Ordinary Time: Franklin and Eleanor Roosevelt: The Home Front in World War II* (New York: Simon & Schuster, 1994) provides an excellent account of Mrs. Roosevelt's emergence as a major force in Democratic politics, her role as an advocate for civil rights and social justice, and her disappointment at FDR's decision to dump Henry A. Wallace and replace him with Truman.

William Leuchtenburg's *In the Shadow of FDR: From Harry Truman to Ronald Reagan* (Ithaca: Cornell University Press, 1983) includes a candid and evenhanded assessment of Truman's uneasy relationship with all of the Roosevelts. Mary Ann Glendon's *A World Made New: Eleanor Roosevelt and the Universal Declaration of Human Rights* (New York: Random House, 2001) is a first-rate study of Mrs. Roosevelt's service as a delegate to the United Nations during the Truman years and chronicles her authorship of a document that may have been her most important achievement.

Margaret Truman's *Harry S. Truman* (New York: Morrow, 1972) and *Bess W. Truman* (New York: Macmillan, 1986) are a daughter's affectionate yet surprisingly revealing portraits. Like Lash, Miss Truman had the advantage of a unique relationship with her subjects and exclusive access to their private correspondence.

By the middle 1970s, most of Truman's private papers were opened to scholars, and the man from Independence became a popular subject among historians and journalists. Robert J. Donovan, former White House correspondent for the *New York Herald Tribune*, wrote a splendid two-volume history of the Truman era: *Conflict and Crisis: The Presidency of Harry S. Truman, 1945–1948* (New York: W. W. Norton, 1977) and *Tumultuous Years: The Presidency of Harry S. Truman, 1949–1953* (New York: W. W. Norton, 1982). Donovan is fair and accurate in his characterization of the relationship between Truman and Mrs. Roosevelt.

Of the many Truman biographies three are indispensable: David McCullough's *Truman* (New York: Simon & Schuster, 1992); Robert H. Ferrell's *Harry S. Truman: A Life* (Columbia: University of Missouri Press, 1994); and Alonzo L. Hamby's *Man of the People: A Life of Harry S. Truman* (New York: Oxford University Press, 1995). Each of these studies is vividly written and solidly researched.

Ferrell, Distinguished Professor of History at Indiana University, is the editor of *Off the Record: The Private Papers of Harry S. Truman* (New York: Harper & Row, 1980); *The Autobiography of Harry S. Truman* (Boulder: Colorado Associated University Press, 1980); *Dear Bess: The Letters from Harry to Bess Truman, 1910–1959* (New York: W. W. Norton, 1983); and *Truman in the White House: The Diary of Eben A. Ayers* (Columbia: University of Missouri Press, 1991). He has also written *Harry S. Truman and the Modern American Presidency* (Boston: Little, Brown, 1983); *Truman: A Centenary Portrait* (New York: Viking, 1984); *Choosing Truman: The Democratic Convention of 1944* (Columbia: University of Missouri Press, 1994); and *Truman & Pendergast* (Columbia: University of Missouri Press, 1999).

Hamby explores the relationship between Truman and Mrs. Roosevelt and the Democratic left in *Beyond the New Deal: Harry S. Truman and American Liberalism* (New York: Columbia University Press, 1973).

A selection of Mrs. Roosevelt's newspaper columns has been published in three volumes: *My Day, Volume I, The White House Years, 1936–1945* (New York: Pharos Books, 1990); *Volume II, The Post-War Years, 1945–1952* (New York: Pharos Books, 1990); and *Volume III, First Lady of the World, 1953–1962* (New York: Pharos Books, 1991). In her column she frequently commented about Truman and, though always polite, would not hesitate to disagree with her husband's successor.

Lois Scharf's essay about Mrs. Roosevelt in *The Harry S. Truman Encyclopedia* (Boston: G. K. Hall, 1989) is a thoughtful analysis of Truman's relationship with FDR's widow. George H. Gallup's *The Gallup Poll: Public Opinion Index, 1935–1971*, in three volumes (New York: Random House, 1972), effectively documents how the subjects of this volume influenced the American public.

Appendix

The Universal Declaration of Human Rights

Whereas recognition of the dignity and of the equal and inalienable rights of all members of the human family is the foundation of freedom, justice and peace in the world.

Whereas disregard and contempt for human rights have resulted in barbarous acts which have outraged the conscience of mankind, and the advent of a world in which human beings shall enjoy freedom of speech and belief and freedom from fear and want has been proclaimed as the highest aspiration of the common people.

Whereas it is essential, if man is not to be compelled to have recourse, as a last resort, to rebellion against tyranny and oppressions, that human rights should be protected by the rule of law.

Whereas it is essential to promote the development of friendly relations between nations.

Furthermore, no distinction shall be made on the basis of the political, jurisdictional or international status of the country or territory to which a person belongs, whether it be independent, trust, non-self-governing or under any other limitation of sovereignty.

Article 1. All human beings are born free and equal in dignity and rights. They are endowed with reason and conscience and should act towards one another in a spirit of brotherhood.

Article 2. Everyone is entitled to all the rights and freedoms set forth in this Declaration, without distinction of any kind, such as race, color, sex, language, religion, political or other opinion, national or social origin, property, birth or other status. Furthermore, no distinction shall be made on the basis of the political, jurisdictional, or international status of the country or territory to which a person belongs, whether it be independent, trust, non-self-governing or under any other limitation of sovereignty.

Article 3. Everyone has the right to life, liberty, and security of person.

Article 4. No one shall be held in slavery or servitude; slavery and the slave trade shall be prohibited in all their forms.

Article 5. No one shall be subjected to torture or to cruel, inhuman or degrading treatment or punishment.

Article 6. Everyone has the right to recognition everywhere as a person before the law.

Article 7. All are equal before the law and are entitled without any discrimination to equal protection of the law. All are entitled to equal protection against any discrimination in violation of this Declaration and against any incitement to such discrimination.

Article 8. Everyone has a right to an effective remedy by the competent national tribunals for acts violating the fundamental rights granted him by the constitution or by law.

Article 9. No one shall be subjected to arbitrary arrest, detention, or exile.

Article 10. Everyone is entitled in full equality to a fair and public hearing by an independent and impartial tribunal, in the determination of his rights and obligations and of any criminal charge against him.

Article 11. (1) Everyone charged with a penal offense has the right to be presumed innocent until proven guilty according to law in a public trial at which he has had all the guarantees necessary for his defense.

(2) No one shall be held guilty of any penal offense or of any act or omission which did not constitute a penal offense, under national or international law, at the time when it was committed. Nor shall a heavier penalty be imposed than the one that was applicable at the time when the penal offense was committed.

Article 12. No one shall be subject to arbitrary interference with his privacy, family, home or correspondence, nor to attacks upon his honor and reputation. Everyone has the right to the protection of the law against such interference or attacks.

Article 13. (1) Everyone has the right to freedom of movement and residence within the borders of each state.

(2) Everyone has the right to leave any country, including his own, and to return to his country.

Article 14. (1) Everyone has the right to seek and to enjoy in other countries asylum from persecution.

(2) This right may not be invoked in the case of prosecutions genuinely arising from non-political crimes or from acts contrary to the purposes and principles of the United Nations.

Article 15. (1) Everyone has the right to a nationality.

(2) No one shall be arbitrarily deprived of his nationality nor denied the right to change his nationality.

Article 16. (1) Men and women of full age, without any limitation due to race, nationality or religion, have the right to marry and to found a family. They are entitled to equal rights as to marriage, during marriage, and at its dissolution.

(2) Marriage shall be entered into only with the free and full consent of the intending spouses.

(3) The family is the natural and fundamental group unit of society and is entitled to protection by society and the state.

Article 17. (1) Everyone has the right to own property alone as well as in association with others.

(2) No one shall be arbitrarily deprived of his property.

Article 18. Everyone has the right to freedom of thought, conscience and religion; this right includes freedom to change his religion or belief, and freedom, either alone or in community with others and in public or private, to manifest his religion or belief in teaching, practice, worship and observance.

Article 19. Everyone has the right to freedom of opinion and expression; this right includes freedom to hold opinions without interference and to seek, receive and impart information and ideas through any media and regardless of frontiers.

Article 20. (1) Everyone has the right to freedom of peaceful assembly and association.

(2) No one may be compelled to belong to an association.

Article 21. (1) Everyone has the right to take part in the government of his country, directly or through freely chosen representatives.

(2) Everyone has the right of equal access to public service in his country.

(3) The will of the people shall be the basis of the authority of govern-

ment; this will shall be expressed in periodic and genuine elections which shall be by universal and equal suffrage and shall be held by secret vote or by equivalent free voting procedures.

Article 22. Everyone, as a member of society, has the right to social security and is entitled to realization, through national effort and international co-operation and in accordance with the organization and resources of each state, of the economic, social and cultural rights indispensable for his dignity and the free development of his personality.

Article 23. (1) Everyone has the right to work, to free choice of employment, to just and favorable conditions of work and to protection against unemployment.

(2) Everyone, without any discrimination, has the right to equal pay for equal work.

(3) Everyone who works has the right to just and favorable remuneration ensuring for himself and his family an existence worthy of human dignity and supplemented, if necessary, by other means of social protection.

(4) Everyone has the right to form and to join trade unions for protection of his interests.

Article 24. Everyone has the right to rest and leisure, including reasonable limitation of working hours and periodic holidays with pay.

Article 25. (1) Everyone has the right to a standard of living adequate for the health and well-being of himself and his family, including food, clothing, housing and medical care and necessary social services, and the right to security in the event of unemployment, sickness, disability, widowhood, old age or other lack of livelihood in circumstances beyond his control.

(2) Motherhood and childhood are entitled to special care and assistance. All children, whether born in or out of wedlock, shall enjoy the same social protection.

Article 26. (1) Everyone has the right to education. Education shall be free, at least in the elementary and fundamental states. Elementary education shall be compulsory. Technical and professional education shall be made generally available and higher education shall be equally accessible to all on the basis of merit.

(2) Education shall be directed to the full development of the human

personality and to the strengthening of respect for human rights and fundamental freedoms. It shall promote understanding, tolerance and friendship among all nations, racial or religious groups, and shall further the activities of the United Nations for the maintenance of peace.

(3) Parents shall have a prior right to choose the kind of education that shall be given to their children.

Article 27. (1) Everyone has the right freely to participate in the cultural life of the community, to enjoy the arts and to share in scientific advancement and its benefits.

(2) Everyone has the right to the protection of the moral and material interests resulting from any scientific, literary or artistic production of which he is the author.

Article 28. Everyone is entitled to a social and international order in which the rights and freedoms set forth in this Declaration can be fully realized.

Article 29. (1) Everyone has duties to the community in which alone the free and full development of his personality is possible.

(2) In the exercise of his rights and freedoms, everyone shall be subject only to such limitations as are determined by law solely for the purposes of securing due recognition and respect for the rights and freedoms of others and of meeting the just requirements of morality, public order and the general welfare in a democratic society.

(3) These rights and freedoms may in no case be exercised contrary to the purposes and principles of the United Nations.

Article 30. Nothing in this Declaration may be interpreted as implying for any state, group or person any right to engage in any activity or to perform any act aimed at the destruction of any of the rights and freedoms set forth herein.

Index